REDISCOVER THE JOYS AND BEAUTY OF NATURE WITH TOM BROWN, JR.

THE TRACKER

Tom Brown's classic true story—the most powerful and magical high spiritual adventure since *The Teachings of Don Juan*

THE SEARCH

The continuing story of *The Tracker*, exploring the ancient art of the new survival

THE VISION

Tom Brown's profound,  mystical experience, the V

THE

The acclaimed outdoorsman save our planet

AND HIS UNIQUE, BESTSELLING WILDERNESS SERIES:

TOM BROWN'S FIELD GUIDE TO NATURE AND SURVIVAL FOR CHILDREN
TOM BROWN'S FIELD GUIDE TO THE FORGOTTEN WILDERNESS
TOM BROWN'S FIELD GUIDE TO CITY AND SUBURBAN SURVIVAL
TOM BROWN'S FIELD GUIDE TO NATURE OBSERVATION AND TRACKING
TOM BROWN'S GUIDE TO WILD EDIBLE AND MEDICINAL PLANTS
TOM BROWN'S FIELD GUIDE TO WILDERNESS SURVIVAL
TOM BROWN'S FIELD GUIDE TO LIVING WITH THE EARTH

Berkley Books by Tom Brown, Jr.

THE JOURNEY

TOM BROWN, JR.

BERKLEY BOOKS, NEW YORK

THE JOURNEY

A Berkley Book / published by arrangement with
the author

PRINTING HISTORY
Berkley trade paperback edition / August 1992

ISBN: 0-425-13364-8

A BERKLEY BOOK® TM 757,375
Berkley Books are published by The Berkley Publishing Group,
200 Madison Avenue, New York, New York 10016.
The name "Berkley" and the "B" logo
are trademarks belonging to Berkley Publishing Corporation.

PRINTED IN THE UNITED STATES OF AMERICA

10 9 8 7 6 5 4 3 2 1

Introduction

Grandfather came from the Southwest, calling no place home for very long. He was a wanderer, a pilgrim of wilderness, a seeker and teacher of truth. He knew the physical skills of survival, tracking, and deep awareness very well, for he lived them on a daily basis. He had no home but the wilderness and these skills set him free, free from any tribe or society, allowing him to wander through the realms of flesh and spirit without restriction. Grandfather's life was one long and constant search for truth, the common reality that binds all philosophies and religions together. He searched for pure man, free of customs, traditions, ceremonies, doctrines, or dogmas that distorted or polluted the truth. The wilderness was his temple and his teacher, where there is no ruler but the Creator and the heart. In this purity of wilderness, where he learned and tested all things, he found the truth. Here, too, he found simplicity, and it was this simplicity, together with truth, that he taught.

He was raised by a people who to this day know no boundaries, or imprisoned and restricted life. His people fled into the upper Mexican mountains and deserts when he was but

1

a child. It was here he learned to survive, to track, to be aware of life on not only a physical level, but on a deeper spiritual level. Grandfather first became a scout for his people, surviving easily where others would only perish. His skills kept his people safe and free from hunger, and his abilities became legendary. His skills in tracking and awareness were unparalleled, even before he reached his twentieth winter. Yet, through the early years of his intense training, he knew his destiny lay in the realm of the spirit.

Grandfather had many visions when he was young, but none so powerful as the Vision of Spirit Warrior and the White Coyote. The vision first directed him to master all the physical skills of survival, tracking, and awareness so he could live in balance and harmony with Creation. He became a scout for his people. It was also made known in the Vision that he had to learn and master all the old ways, so they could be passed down to the grandchildren, and never be lost. It is through the physical skills that one can truly know the freedom that will allow the searcher to enter the worlds of spirit, unrestricted by society. The vision also dictated that he must learn to live in the temples of Creation without struggle or distraction.

So, too, was there a sad part of his vision. Grandfather was commanded to leave his people and search for spiritual truth for over sixty winters. His vision foretold of a search for simplicity in the wisdom of the spirit, and he had to search for that simplicity. He had to find the common truth in all religions, beliefs, philosophies, and doctrines, tearing away the customs and ceremonies of man to find the basic truth, the pure truth, that binds all things together. His was a lifelong struggle to find that truth, that purity, a struggle he gave up his life for. He made a commitment to the vision and to the Creator that he would dedicate himself completely to the task, and give up all of the things that people cling selfishly to, even himself. So he traveled for over sixty years, throughout this country, Canada, and into the depths of South America, searching for the truth: looking beyond man's facade to find the basic purity.

Grandfather believed that man had to transcend all religion, all philosophy, all doctrine and dogma, and walk a pure path without the pollutions, distortions, and distractions of man. Only when one no longer needed the religious toys could he be free to find the purity of spiritual life. All else were useless crutches, baggage, and shackles that limited one's spiritual growth. Grandfather said, "The customs and rituals of ancient man are but guidelines for future generations. They show where man has gone, and where he is going. They are a teacher, never to be a crutch, and never to enslave. The problem is that we become slaves to the ritual. People begin to worship the ceremony and believe in the shaman rather than the Great Spirit. The ancient rituals and ceremonies should then be viewed as signposts, and learned, modified, passed down, then abandoned. Rituals are more for the weak of spirit, who need something to cling to, something that makes them feel worthy and holy. For the spiritually pure, there is no need to approach the Creator carrying these things of flesh, mind, and emotion, but to seek the Creator purely without these crutches."

Grandfather also said, "Remember that all things of power, especially those things of a ceremony—words, songs, and chants—have greater power as long as they come from the heart and are delivered with pure faith. Once you begin to walk the spiritual path, the power of the ceremony will teach and guide you, as does the Vision Quest. However, once the ceremony shows you the way, and you no longer need the crutches, abandon the ceremony. Then, the only time a ceremony becomes necessary for you is when those that surround you need to see it sacredly." Grandfather didn't show any disrespect for ceremony or religious items, for he thought they could teach the way to truth. But once the way was clear, these things had to be abandoned, or they would become self-limiting crutches of the flesh. So, too, did he believe that the true temples were that of wilderness. For the wilderness was made by the Creator and obeyed every command.

Grandfather came to me in his later years, or I came to him, I do not know which. All I know is that he said our meeting fulfilled his Vision of the White Coyote. I was a willing student and he a willing teacher. Both of us struggled through the ten years we were together. He struggled with the teaching of the truths which could not be explained in words, and I struggled to learn those truths. I wanted desperately to know those truths, and he wanted desperately to pass them down, before he passed from flesh to spirit. It was easy for him to teach me the wisdom of survival, tracking, and awareness, but at the same time it was very difficult to teach the wisdom of the spirit.

Though I was very young, we came from two different worlds, two different cultures, and at first could hardly communicate in any language. The truths of the spirit were not easily understood by me at first, but as my belief system began to grow and my old values and misbeliefs began to erode away, the truth became easier for me to understand. As I look back to our first meeting, I could clearly see, even though I was only seven years old, I was already polluted by society's belief systems and ideas. It wasn't until I began to live in the wilderness and think with a wilderness mind that I could finally shed those old beliefs. Yet, at times, there was something at odds within me, because as society taught me one thing, Grandfather taught me another, often the direct opposite. It wasn't long before that conflict ended, for the customs and dogmas of society were but lies; only the wilderness is pure truth.

Even with all I have learned from Grandfather about tracking, survival, awareness, and in living with the Earth, it was only a very small part of his overall teaching. The skills became a doorway to greater things. Most of what Grandfather taught were the things of the spirit. Grandfather believed that the greater part of man's existence was in the spiritual realms and flesh was only a small part of man's life. He believed in the duality of all things, where at once we walked in flesh and at the same time in spirit. He also believed in the oneness of all things where at once we were part of Creation, and Creation was part of us, where our lives flowed through the life of the planet, Earth Mother, and Earth flowed through us. This "life force" he called the spirit-that-moves-through-all-things. Thus, there was no inner or outer dimension, just the blessed oneness, where there was no separation of self.

His teachings of the things of the spirit were very simple, so simple most people could not believe or accept them. He had said, "Modern man cannot know the worlds, these universes, beyond his own ego. The logical mind will never allow man to expand beyond the ego or the flesh, for that is where the logical mind feels safe. Modern thought is the prison of the soul and stands between man and his spiritual mind. The logical mind cannot know absolute faith, nor can it know pure thought, for the logic feeds upon logic and does not accept things that cannot be known and proven by the flesh. Thus man has created a prison for himself and for his spirit, because he lacks belief and purity of thought. Faith needs no proof nor logic, yet man needs proof before he can have faith. Man then has created a cycle which cannot be broken, for where proof is needed, there can be no faith."

For ten years I stayed with Grandfather, learning whatever he was willing to teach. For ten more years I wandered in and out of wilderness, trying to find more of the simple truths. The more I searched, the more I lived in wilderness, the more power I found in what Grandfather had taught. Now, journeying from wilderness and into the realms of society, I found these teachings have become even more real. I see a society which is crumbling, a society that lives mostly in the flesh, and knows little of the spirit. I see a people lost and searching for themselves, not knowing which way to turn to find a spiritual path in life. And I see a world that is quickly entering its final winter, where life on this planet as we now know it to exist will quickly come to an end. All I know is physical change is not enough. The global society must have a complete change, which includes a shift in consciousness to that of the spirit. Man must come back to the Earth and understand he cannot live above the laws of Creation, for now we are on borrowed time.

Many religions and philosophies today are too cluttered in custom and ceremony, shackled by dogma, and no longer work because of all the spiritual pollution and distortion. For a society that is so lost, these imprisoning dogmas afford nothing but confusion, nothing that seems real. Thus we see a shift to seek out other, nontraditional religions, bouncing between one and another, hoping to find one which is true for us. So, too, do we see society grasping for a part of one religion and combining it with another and another, hoping the end result will give some hope, set forth some answers, and produce results. Unfortunately the combinations produce complications and distortions that are worse then the originals. As far as I, and Grandfather, are concerned, the end result of any philosophy is simplicity, rapture, and reproducible results for everyone.

Grandfather so often told me I should take all things to the temples of Creation to test them out. If they are real, if they are true for everyone, if they are simple, then they are a universal truth. If these things are tested in Creation and do not work, then they should be abandoned, because they then are the workings of man's overactive imagination. It is man that complicates and distorts the simple truth. It is man's lust for complication that has caused the demise of so many religions. Today, scarcely two religions can agree with each other, doctrine is argued and the gaping chasm widens even more. So, too, does this chasm widen between the follower and the religion. Simply: the religions do not meet the needs of society, they do not seem real or viable. They, in essence, have failed, and they refuse to give up their complications to rectify their failures and become workable.

Thus it was Grandfather's quest to strip away these complications and distortions, and to get at the simple workable truth—the common thread of reality and truth that runs through all philosophies and religions of the world. To say Grandfather passed down to me only the Native American customs, traditions, and ceremonies would be a lie. Yes, he used these things, but only as a doorway, a doorway to lead to higher paths of truth. So my search continues even today, even as I teach these simple truths to many of my classes. I have picked up where Grandfather has left off in his search, but I realize Grandfather did not leave off, for he found the final truth and his search was ended. The basic truth is that the Earth must be healed, society has to be healed. Mankind must reach a balance with nature and live in harmony where the quest for the spirit is more important then the gods of the flesh. Unless we can change, and change quickly on both a physical and spiritual level, we all soon must face the Final Winter.

1

The Visionary

From almost the first moment that Rick and I met Grandfather, we knew he had mystical abilities. We knew he could do more than most people would even dream of doing. It was not just his ability to survive and track, though that was amazing enough. It was first revealed in his awareness. It was this uncanny awareness that gave us our first hint something miraculous was going on with him. It was not just his ability to know what was going on in the immediate landscape, but to know what was happening great distances away. His ability, we could plainly see, transcended the normal scope of human senses, going beyond even the most keenly aware animals. It was not only his awareness that we marveled at, but something more, something we could not identify. In our young minds, we knew beyond a doubt that he seemed to embody all that was wilderness, all that was mystical, and all that we wanted to know.

The first time we realized Grandfather knew of things beyond what most people could know was on the second day we were together. Both Rick and I were like young and eager puppies following Grandfather around a small swamp near my house.

We spent most of the morning exploring the marvels of nature, having one adventure after another. Grandfather seemed to know everything about everything. He told us about the plants and animals we came across, taking us into their secret lives, and even showing us how to get close to things we had never gotten near before. Grandfather would point to a particular plant and tell us that it was used as an arrow shaft, or the tree was used to make bows. These lessons and adventures were intermixed with stories about ancient Native Americans that used to live in the area.

We were captivated most of all by the stories of Indians. Grandfather seemed to bring them to life, holding us spellbound with the tales of their way of life. As we sat talking to Grandfather, he pulled a silver of rock from his pocket and, using an antler, began to carve chips off the rock's surface. In what seemed like no time he handed over a beautifully flaked arrowhead, telling us that this was the exact design the Native Americans of the area used. We were amazed, spellbound, because we had never seen anything so magical in our lives. We didn't realize that anyone could make arrowheads anymore and we begged Grandfather to show us how it was done. All he said was that we had many other things to learn first, but he would teach us someday, if we were still interested in learning.

Pressing further, we asked him how he knew that the Native Americans who lived around here used the same kind of arrowheads. As far as we knew, the Native Americans had moved from this area long ago. Grandfather smiled at both of us, a sly smile that goaded us on, and said, "I have asked the spirits of those past, and they told me." Rick and I laughed, knowing, and hoping, Grandfather was kidding. We told him there were no such things as spirits, and, we hoped, ghosts. He looked at us blankly and said in a matter-of-fact voice, "The spirits have just told me where to find an old arrowhead right now. If you like, you can have it for yourselves." Again we thought he was kidding, expecting him to reach in his pocket and pull out another arrowhead that he had made.

In a mocking way, I said I would love an arrowhead made by the spirits. Grandfather pointed to a smooth bank of sand near an old tree stump, to a place we had not yet explored. He said, "Just a few inches from the tree stump, on the side that faces us, you will find your arrowhead. It does not lie on the surface, so you must dig down to the depth of your fingers." There was no way, I thought, he could know that the arrowhead was there, and I didn't hesitate to tell him so. He just smiled and said, "Well, if you don't want the arrowhead, it is fine with me," and began to get up as if he was going to walk away. I told him to wait, that I really wanted the head, but I knew I wasn't going to find any. I figured that Grandfather was a little strange in the head and I had better humor him.

Rick and I walked over to the old tree stump and began to dig, giggling to ourselves about Grandfather's old mind. Our giggles stopped, however, when we had dug a few inches down and found an arrowhead, just as Grandfather had said. Suddenly, I became very nervous, nearly spooked, but also crazy with questions. We ran to Grandfather, holding up our prize in utter disbelief. Grandfather looked disinterested. We asked him how he knew the spirit and how he spoke to the spirit, and he answered saying, "The same way that I speak to you, Grandson." I was silenced for a moment by his answer and more so that he called me grandson. I wondered to myself how he could talk to something that no one could see. I also thought he was really having trouble with his mind, mistaking me for his grandson, though somehow I felt honored by the way he had said it. I wished that I really was his grandson.

Grandfather would not discuss the arrowhead any further; instead we just played and explored for the rest of the day. When Rick and I finally got back to his house at the end of the day, we sat and talked about the arrowhead for hours well past sunset. Grandfather, as usual, disappeared into the forest for the night. He didn't like houses or civilization at all. Even though we were just getting to know him, we knew we would be back together the next day. He had no trouble finding us or, rather, we finding him. I suspected that he arranged things so we would think that we were accidently running into him. Yet it was so uncanny that he could know what we were going to do and where we were going to go, even before we decided. I was also beginning to feel that he arranged lessons so we would have to beg him to teach us, for he would never force anything. He always kept us at the point of learning so that we needed to know something, not just wanted to know. This arrowhead was a prime example, for we thirsted for more.

It was not long into our discussion that Rick and I began to argue about who was going to keep the arrowhead. We finally decided that we would take turns with the possession. Rick would take the old arrowhead and I would take the new arrowhead for one or two days and then we would trade. The problem was that we could not decide on who would get which arrowhead first and again an argument would break out. It was during this time of argument that Rick's brother and his older friend joined us. They listened to our story and I could tell that the older boy looked upon it with a good deal of skepticism, even though he had the arrowhead in hand. He said that Grandfather, the "old man," as he called him, had probably planted the arrowhead and steered us into the conversation about it so we would think he was magical. He said that if he had really spoken to the spirit then we should ask him to talk to the spirit again tomorrow and ask for another arrowhead. That way we could both have one, or at least prove it had all been faked.

Rick's brother and the older boy finally wandered off, leaving Rick and I to discuss the possibility of what he had said. We both decided we would put Grandfather to the test and take him into an area that we hadn't been to before, an area of our choosing. Then we would ask him to find another arrowhead. If he couldn't do it then we would know that it had all been faked and that there were no spirits. If he could find an arrowhead, then there would never again be a question. I hoped silently he could do it, for I really cared for Grandfather and all that he taught us.

The next day we were playing by the river when we stumbled upon Grandfather sitting atop a small hill, apparently praying. We ran to him, excited to see him there. He didn't hesitate, but said, "The spirits have told me of your plan, and that you do not really believe me." His words shocked both of us for a moment, but Rick whispered to me that he was probably hiding near us last night and overheard the conversation. Grandfather then apparently dropped the subject and we all wandered off, heading up the river to the area we had been in the day before. It was then that Rick decided it was time we put Grandfather to the test. We wandered over to another sand area and sat down, waiting for Grandfather to do the same. Instead he pointed to the sand area and told us to look at its surface. Then he asked Rick to walk across the area and look back. Rick's feet sank deep into the sand and left large obvious tracks. Grandfather asked him if he saw any other tracks and Rick, feeling a little embarrassed and transparent, told him no.

Grandfather pointed to an area not three feet in front of Rick, near the center of the sand area, and told him to dig down just a few inches. Rick looked at the ground before him; it was clear of any tracks. Feeling embarrassed and knowing full well what was going to happen, Rick dug down and found another arrowhead. Rick and I were so elated that we both cheered out loud. Grandfather had not faked it after all. We both now had arrowheads and, best of all, the spirits were real. Or at least what they told Grandfather was real. We both felt so good, but also a little guilty for questioning what Grandfather had done. After all, he had done so many magical things right before our eyes, like making the arrowhead, or making fire with a bow drill, there should have been no question. But I suspected Grandfather was used to that kind of doubt.

Grandfather sat us both down by the little hole that had contained the arrowhead, and said, "I am not angry at you for testing me. Many things I do have been tested by many people, for that is the way this society thinks. People today cannot believe in the things of the unseen and eternal, and they only thirst for proof. Even when proof is provided, they make excuses for that proof, as you have done last night. Even now, there is still a little doubt in your mind that I have planted this arrowhead and erased my tracks. Faith is the most powerful force on Earth, and true faith needs no proof. You think that you want to talk to the spirits, but you cannot talk to them unless you believe. If you do not have faith, if you do not believe without proof, then they cannot and will not be seen. But if you believe, even if there is no proof, then the world of spirit will be opened unto you."

Within the same week that we had found the arrowheads, we were again introduced to Grandfather's magic, as we began to call it. We were at Grandfather's camp, deep in the woods behind my house, and were packing up our things to go home. Grandfather turned to Rick and said, "I am sorry about your brother's accident." Rick looked shocked and told Grandfather that his brother did not have an accident. Grandfather ignored this and went about his business. Rick and I giggled to each other again that Grandfather must be losing his mind. After all, Rick's brother was fine when we left the house a few hours before, and neither of us had spoken about Rick's brother to Grandfather. We chuckled all the way home, thinking that Grandfather was good at hearing the spirit voices but not human voices.

After a two-hour walk, we finally reached Rick's house, only to find that less than twenty minutes earlier Rick's brother had fallen off his bike and broken his ankle. We were upset, to say the least, but we were also spellbound. Grandfather had said that he had been sorry to hear of Rick's brother's accident, but that had been two and a half to three hours earlier. As we waited at Rick's house for his mother and brother to return from the hospital, we began to discuss what Grandfather had done. Could it be, we wondered, that Grandfather could not only talk to spirits, but also predict the future? A frightening thought occurred to us. What if Grandfather told his spirits to break Rick's brother's ankle? But we knew instantly that Grandfather was too kind and loving to do something like that. We realized then that we were doing the same thing we had done before: finding doubt and needing proof.

Shortly before they returned from the hospital, Grandfather walked out of the woods and began to talk about Rick's brother. He told us that the first X-ray would show a break, but upon taking the second one, they would find no break. Rick's brother would not need to wear a cast at all. He would only have a bruise. Rick told Grandfather, rather emphatically, that the first-aid men had seen the bone sticking through the skin, and that there was no way that it couldn't be broken. Grandfather smiled at us without saying a word and walked off into the woods. Just as Grandfather disappeared into the woods Rick's mother and brother drove in. As Rick and I got up to help his brother out of the car, we found to our amazement that his brother did not have a cast on. Instead his foot was only wrapped. His mother told us it was only a bruise, but she looked amazed when she said it.

No one was more amazed then Rick and I. We could not understand how Grandfather could predict the future that easily. We also did not know how he knew what the outcome of the broken ankle would be. We speculated well into the night that he might also have had something to do with the healing of the ankle, but we did not know what it was. We knew that Grandfather mixed herbs for medication, and we knew that Native American people called these people "medicine men," so we decided that day that Grandfather was probably one of these medicine people. That assumption created a real aura of mystery around Grandfather, and we both grew excited at the thought. We also began to understand why Grandfather so often visited many of the people that lived in the woods. He was their doctor, of sorts.

Rick and I again talked well into the night, formulating a mass of questions we would ask Grandfather. He hadn't been too free with the information about the spirits, so we figured we had better press the issue if we wanted to learn anything. The very next day, even without greeting Grandfather, we unleashed a barrage of questions. He only smiled and vaguely acknowledged each question, but answered nothing. He essentially told us that he just knew that Rick's brother would be all right, and that he may have had something to do with the quick healing of his ankle, but he said little of anything else. This tended only to make Rick and me even more curious as to how all this was done. So curious, in fact, that we could not do anything all day except discuss the possibilities of it all.

Weeks slid into months, yet Grandfather said nothing about the spirits, the healing, or the foretelling of future events. Yet almost every day there was a new miracle to add to our already fast-growing list of things that remained unexplained. With each passing day and with each new miracle, we began to understand Grandfather's world and his abilities. He did things that would baffle and amaze most people, but we began to take these things for granted. Our belief in the spirit world grew daily, though we had no real tangible proof. We just accepted these things without knowing why. Just when we thought we had seen it all, Grandfather would produce another miracle that would shock us even more. We did not realize it at the time, but Grandfather was trying to build our belief system a little at a time. That faith had to be part of us before we could take the first step in our spiritual journey.

It wasn't until the fall of the first year of which we had met Grandfather that we received our first lessons in spiritual training. Even though we had only known Grandfather for less than six months, we were already accomplished in many skills of tracking, survival, and awareness. We became staunch believers in the world of spirit and all of the possibilities that it held for us. What was also great was that our parents were allowing us to camp farther and farther from home, for longer periods of time. This gave us more opportunity to be with Grandfather and more time to practice our skills in the pure environment of the wilderness. Our friends would envy us because their parents would only let them camp in their backyard overnight. Yet the backyard would scare them, and most would never make it through. They didn't understand how we could be so comfortable so far away from home. I think that a big plus in our favor was that my folks instinctively trusted Grandfather to take care of us.

During one of our first weekend camp-outs, we were given our first lesson in spiritual truths. Many weeks had passed since we had asked him anything remotely concerned with spirituality, and we knew that we couldn't press Grandfather into answering a question, especially if he didn't feel we were ready. We were shocked when Grandfather came right out and told us that we were ready to take our first spiritual step. As soon as he said it, both Rick and I were at once excited and frightened. It was, to me, like going to meet a ghost. Up until this time, we both thought that spirits were like ghosts, and ghosts were very frightening, especially after hearing all the local stories about the feared and famed Jersey Devil. On one hand I couldn't wait to take that step forward, but on the other I didn't know if I would be able to handle the outcome.

Ironically, it was not that way at all, and it had nothing really to do with spirits, or at least so I thought. Grandfather first began the lesson by having us sit quietly by the side of the stream that ran through camp. After awhile he told us to fully focus on an object someplace in front of us, blocking out everything else, so that there was nothing but us and the object. At the time I couldn't see what all of this had to do with the spirit world, but without question I followed his instructions. It was quite difficult to focus all of our attention on one thing for very long, much less sitting still. Rick and I were just so full of energy we could not sit still for long, even when we were exhausted. After awhile I began to think that Grandfather was using this lesson as some form of punishment, like having to stand in the corner when one has been bad. It was almost an impossible task, and the more I struggled, the harder it became.

Finally, after about two hours of this inner struggle to stay still and focus, Grandfather said, "Let go of your struggle, stop trying, and allow it to just happen. Do as you did when you fed the birds. It was a struggle until the birds began to feed from your hands, then all struggle was gone. This is what you must do here and now." I remembered back to over a month ago when Grandfather had told Rick and me to go feed the birds.

We hadn't realized it at the time but that, in fact, was our first lesson in the way of the spirit. It had taught us to still our minds and subsequently our bodies. We had lain on the lawn for what seemed like days, holding birdseed in our hands and scattered over our bodies. It had been painful, because we had to lie absolutely still. Any time we moved, the birds would fly off and our wait would be prolonged. Finally when we lay still enough, the birds began to feed. Once they began to walk all over our bodies, the excitement was so great it drove all sense of time and discomfort away.

What Grandfather was now asking us to do was the same thing. This was more difficult, however, because the things we were trying to focus our attention on were not as exciting and all-consuming as birds walking on our arms and chests. I tried not to try, I tried not to fidget, and I tried not to be bored, but nothing worked. Then, as I focused my attention once again on the old tree stump I was using as my focal point, I just got disgusted with myself and gave up, or gave in, I do not know which. Suddenly, the things around me began to look different, I stopped fidgeting, the boredom left, and I was as caught up in this feeling as I had been caught up by the feeding birds. For a moment, but a brief moment, I held that feeling and I could sense things moving outside my physical senses. It was as if I had just been given a quick glimpse of a world I could not yet understand.

What felt like just a moment in this somehow altered state, actually turned out to be more than an hour. I was amazed when I finally returned to myself, because the sun had moved considerably. It was as if I had lost all track of time and place. Wherever I had been it felt great, though I had no idea as to where the feeling had come from. All I knew was I had touched something deeper than just the physical reality of my *now*, a strange new world, a world that I could not describe in my mind. Grandfather's voice shook me out of my reverie, saying, "Do not try to describe in your mind things that cannot be explained. The spirit world does not speak in the tongues of man, but through the language of the heart. You must learn to know without knowing. Learn to understand without words. Some things are just better left unexplained, for to explain them will only create confusion."

I thought that was easier said than done. My mind just needed some answers so that I could understand all that I had felt. Without waiting for me to ask any questions, Grandfather continued, saying, "The spirit world knows no time or place, nor does the spirit world communicate to us in language. It speaks to us through dreams, visions, signs, symbols, and feelings. That is why there are no words to describe what you have just felt. That is why an instant in the world of spirit was actually a long time in reality. What you have done, though you cannot explain how, is to touch the world of spirit. You have felt things moving outside of yourself, yet you will not accept them right now because they lack reality, proof, and a way to understand in words. Give up your need for thinking with your physical mind and you will understand the purity of the spirit mind, which needs no words or descriptions."

Grandfather continued, "I know this is all new to you and that you do not understand, but trust that your spirit fully understands. It is not your fault, for you have been taught by society, by your school, that the only way to understand is through your rational mind. What is new now to you is to understand through your spiritual mind. Remember, man is a duality, at once living in flesh and in spirit. So too is everything else found in this duality. Two bodies, two minds, all in the same person. You have learned to believe without physical evidence, so too must you believe without explanation that these spiritual realities are true. Whether you understand or not, you have been in contact with these spiritual worlds for a long time, but you do not understand their language. Those spiritual realities, those worlds outside the flesh have been trying to speak to you for a long time, you know their voices but you do not know when and how they speak."

From what I could understand of what Grandfather was telling me was that the spirit world had been trying to get in contact with me for a long time, but I did not know how to listen. I asked him how he could say that, for I never felt any attempt at communication. Grandfather smiled and said, "You know it all too well, but you just do not know how to identify it or communicate with that world." I was now very puzzled because I had no idea of what he was talking about and I guess it showed on my face. Grandfather smiled and said, "As I have told you, the spirit world does not communicate in the words of man, but through dreams, visions, signs, symbols, and feelings or emotions. You have had these things many times but you cannot identify them. You do not know what these things mean."

I was still puzzled, because I had none of these things that Grandfather spoke of. He continued, without waiting for me to ask, saying, "Have you ever had the feeling of being watched, or that something you are doing or a place you are going just does not feel right? Have you ever had the feeling that something was wrong at home, only to find out that there was something wrong? When you hear people talk about their intuition or gut feeling, that is the communication from your deeper self and the worlds beyond. That is what is called Inner Vision and it is one of the ways which our spirit, and so many other spirits, try to communicate with us. Now what must be done is to show you what your Inner Vision, the voices of spirit, feels like when it is trying to communicate with you, then I must show you how that voice can answer you. To me, it is the voice of Creation, the spirit realms, and even the Creator, and I obey its every command. After you learn what it is and how it talks to you, you must then learn to purify it, so that it is never distorted by your logical mind."

Grandfather then sat down by me and told me a story. He said that in this story, I was the one he was talking about, and that he was playing the role of my Inner Vision, which knew all things. He said, "Pretend that you are going shopping for your mother and she has told you to pick up several things. When you get to the store, you pick up all the things that you can remember, but as you go to pay for them, you get the feeling that you are forgetting something. As you wander up and down the store, the feeling haunts you, creating a tightness in your chest where something feels in conflict. You try, but you can't remember what that thing was, but you know that you have forgotten. It is a gnawing feeling, the same way you feel right now. Sometimes it appears as a feeling of overall uneasiness, sometimes just an overall sense that something is wrong, but most of the time it appears as a tightness in the gut, a knowing that something is wrong, something is forgotten."

Grandfather paused, allowing the feeling of forgetting something to manifest in my gut, then continued. He said, "Now, Grandson, you are paying for all the items that you have bought for your mother. The feeling of forgetting something still persists deep within you but you still do not know what it is. You pay for all the things that you bought, still feeling you have forgotten, and you begin to leave the store. You look up and see a box of light bulbs and you suddenly realize what you have forgotten to buy for your mother is a dozen eggs. You feel a relief sweep over you, finally remembering the eggs. Now you feel good, and you are finally at peace with yourself."

Grandfather continued, "The tension that you felt in your gut, the feeling of uneasiness, or that something that was just not right, was your Inner Vision trying to tell you what you have forgotten. Remember, the Inner Vision is not just the voice of the spirit world, but of your deeper self, which knows all things. Your Inner Vision cannot speak to you in words, but must use symbols, signs, feelings, dreams, and so many other things. Suddenly you see those light bulbs, packed neatly in a divided box. It is also the way the eggs are packaged, and finally your logical mind recognizes the symbol that your spiritual mind sets forth and you remember the eggs. As soon as you remember, the spiritual mind, your Inner Vision, is satisfied and there is no longer tension. When the tension is gone, the answer is yes. When the tension is there, the answer is no."

I was more than amazed, not only because of the clarity of what I felt, but because of the simplicity of it all. I had had that feeling so many times before, but until now I had no idea of what it was or what it meant. However, I was very confused because I could not understand what a dozen eggs had to do with the spirit world, or in communicating with spirits. Grandfather waited for me to collect my thoughts, then said, "Grandson, I want you to quiet yourself and ask that place, the same place you felt the tension of forgetting the eggs, if there are spirits." Quietly, in my mind, I asked myself, but there was no feeling of tension, nothing was in conflict. Grandfather then told me to ask the spirit world if it had anything to say to me right now. I did, and the center of tension appeared. Apparently the spirit world did not want to communicate with me at the moment. Grandfather said, "Before you can go any farther, you have much to learn. You will come back again to this quest for Inner Vision, but before that you must learn much more of what it is and where it comes from. It is far more than telling you that you have forgotten to buy eggs."

Later that night, when the lessons of the day were over, Rick and I found that we had almost the same experiences, though taught in a different way. We both wanted to know more about this Inner Vision thing, but Grandfather remained adamant that we had a lot to learn before we could approach it again. I knew that as far as I was concerned, I wanted it so bad I could feel it constantly gnawing at my mind and seeping into my every conversation that night. I didn't like the fact that I could not yet have its power. It was like a thirst, a need, but still so very far out of reach. Both Rick and I wondered about how far this Inner Vision could really go, and what wisdom it could take us to. I wanted it all. Especially now since I had the feeling it contained a lot of answers to many questions.

The next day Grandfather put us again at the riverbank and told us to focus on a single entity. He told us that our learning Inner Vision would do us no good unless we learned the purity of silence, but neither Rick nor I could understand what he was talking about. Again I went through torment, distraction, and boredom, until I gave up and gave in, and the same world was revealed to me. This time, however, there was more, for the tension in my gut began to speak to me. Yet, in a language I still could not understand. We spent most of the morning going in and out of this world. Whether real or imagined, it left a lasting impression on both of us. As I sat contemplating, I remembered Grandfather's words, "It is the end results which count. It is the end results, the reproducible results, that make it real."

At the end of the day, Rick and I sat with Grandfather and we talked of our experiences, though we still did not understand. Grandfather said, "You still struggle with the reality of it all. You wonder whether it is imagined or real, and as I have told you, it is the end results that are important, not how you got to them. If you are contacted by a spirit, and that spirit tells you of things which you could not possibly know through the flesh, what difference does it make whether you believe the encounter to be real or imagined. It is the wisdom given that matters." I still could not understand what Grandfather was speaking about, except to say that it is not important to wonder if it all exists. Though I did not understand, I could feel something shifting inside of me, something changing, though imperceptibly, still changing. I could only imagine, right now, this grand new world of spirit, and that seemed enough.

I asked Grandfather how he could know what was going to happen in the future, for I did not understand how it fit into the world of spirit. He said, "There is not just one future, but many possible futures. If there was but one future, then man would have no choice in life, but since we have choice there are many possible futures. It is easy to predict the possible futures through the spirit realities, by seeing the events that will surely come together to make the probable future." I looked at Grandfather, dumbfounded. I had no idea what he was talking about. I could not see how the future could be foretold. Grandfather smiled at me, the smile that told me he could see my thoughts, and said, "It is very easy to tell the future, if you can live the purity of the spirit mind. You yourself can easily tell the future right now."

Still dumbfounded, I told him there was no way that I could tell the future. Grandfather led Rick and me over to a distant grove of trees. One of the larger trees in the grove was dead, its bark peeling, and on one side a gaping hole was found at its base. Grandfather pushed gently on the huge tree and it easily rocked back and forth. Grandfather then said, "Foretelling the coming future in the spirit world is much like foretelling the future of this tree. You see how easily the tree moves, so too do you know that the next storm that comes from the north will blow this tree down. The dead and weak tree combined with a strong wind will make the future of the tree falling. It is the same as I do in the spirit world. Two events are seen coming together to make something happen. Two possibilities combine to make one probability."

Nothing more was ever said about the world of spirit or the futures that day. Grandfather told us we had a lot more to learn before we could ever understand the world of spirit, the voice of Inner Vision, and the foretelling of future. Each day that passed, I yearned for more of this strange world, but for a few more years nothing was said. Certainly there were many lessons in survival, tracking, and awareness, so too were there lessons in silencing and meditation. But it would not be until I could fully understand the most basic truths, that more teachings of the spirit realities would follow. Then when it did come, almost three years later, it came in an avalanche of understanding that took place in less than a month's time.

2

Quest for Inner Vision

It was in late June of the third year I had known Grandfather that I was again introduced to the powers of Inner Vision. Certainly I heard Grandfather talk of this remarkable power frequently, but there were no lessons in its use, nothing even in the way of tangible explanation of what this power was or where it came from.

For years we had watched the miracle of Inner Vision unfold time after time. Grandfather would astound us with the things that he could tell, things that would happen in the future, or communications from the world of nature or spirit. Grandfather seemed to use Inner Vision more than he used his physical senses or even his logical mind. I knew instinctively that it was the main guiding force in his life. He called Inner Vision the bridge between flesh and spirit, the vehicle in which we could communicate with worlds beyond the flesh. At times I heard him refer to this Inner Vision as the very voice of the Creator. To him, it was never wrong, even when the logical mind and flesh reality said differently, the Inner Vision was always trusted over all things of the mind and flesh.

Grandfather told us that man was a duality, part flesh and part spirit. Man had two minds, the logical mind, which was that overtrained and overbearing part of our thinking, and a spiritual mind, a mind which was more subtle but far more powerful than anything logic could offer. Grandfather said that there was always a battle between the logical and spiritual mind. The logical mind wanted to dominate and not relinquish control to the spiritual mind, which could not be fully understood or explained in modern tactile or logical terms. To Grandfather, it was the spiritual mind that should be dominant, for it was this spiritual mind that held the communications, visions, and secrets of the universe.

Long ago Grandfather had explained to us that man was an island, imprisoned by his logical mind, his ego, and his own flesh. He had said, "Man is like an island, a circle within circles. Man is separated from these outer circles by his mind, his beliefs, and the limitations put upon him by a life away from the Earth. The circle of man, that island of self, is the place of logic, the 'I,' the ego, and the physical self. The walls of this island prison are thick, made up of doubts, logic, and lack of belief. His isolation from the greater circles of self is suffocating and prevents him from seeing life clearly and purely. It is a world of ignorance, where the flesh is the only reality, the only god."

Grandfather continued, "Beyond man's island of ego, his prison, lies the world of the spirit-that-moves-in-all-things, the force that is found in all things. It is a world that communicates to all the entities of Creation and touches the Creator. It is a circle of life that houses all of man's instinct, his deepest memory, his power to control his body and mind, and a bridge that helps man transcend flesh. It is a world that expands man's universe and helps him to fuse himself to the Earth. Most of all, it is a world that brings man to his higher self and to spiritual rapture.

"There is a circle, an island, beyond the circle of the life force," Grandfather continued, "it is the world of spirit. Man lives also in this world, for his spirit walks this land of spirits.

Here man finds a duality in self, where at one moment he walks in flesh, and then again in spirit. It is a world of the unseen and eternal, where life and death, time and place, are a myth. A place where all things are possible. A place where man transcends self and fuses with all things of Earth and spirit. It is a place closest to the limitless powers of Creation. Beyond this place is the consciousness of all things, the final circle of power before the Creator."

"Man living in the island of self is living but a small part of what life is all about. Man must transcend the barriers, the prison of ego and thought, and reach to the Creator. All islands, all circles of power, must be bridged. Each world must be understood, then finally fused into an absolute and pure 'oneness.' There can be no inner or outer dimension, no separation of self, just a pure oneness, where man is at once all things of flesh and spirit. It is in this fusion of worlds that man will know all things, and live the deeper meanings of life. Man moves within all things and all things move within man. Then, and only then, can man ever hope to touch God," Grandfather said.

Grandfather continued, saying, "Modern man cannot know these worlds, these circles, that exist beyond his own ego. The logical mind will never allow man to expand beyond the ego or the flesh, for that is where the logical mind feels safe. Modern thought is the prison of the soul and stands between man and his spiritual mind. The logical mind cannot know absolute faith, nor can it know pure thought, for logic feeds upon logic and does not accept things that cannot be known and proven by the flesh. Thus man has created a prison for himself and his spirit, because he lacks belief and purity of thought. Faith needs no proof nor logic, yet man needs proof before he can have faith. Man then has created a cycle which cannot be broken, for if proof is needed, there can be no faith."

Grandfather had finished the conversation by saying, "Inner Vision is the spiritual mind, the vehicle, and the bridge which fuses man to the outer worlds, the outer circles and cycles of power. Inner Vision is that which helps man to transcend the flesh and logic, and to communicate with the worlds beyond the flesh. Inner Vision is the pure mind, the pure self, and must be purified and nurtured more than the mind of logic and flesh. It is the Inner Vision which helps us realize our duality and to live that duality. It is to me the real mind, and the only truth."

Even though his explanation had taken place more than a year before, it still lingered in my mind as fresh and exciting as the first day I had heard its truth. There was never a day that went by from that time on, I did not think about Grandfather's Inner Vision. I was reminded constantly of its truth by watching Grandfather use its power in some miraculous way every day. It was in this third year with Grandfather that I would finally begin to fully understand its power. It would become one of the most important lessons of my life.

We had been camping at the medicine cabin for nearly two days and were looking forward to several more days before we would have to return home. It was our first long camp-out of the season and we wanted to enjoy every moment to its fullest. School was now a distant memory and the expanse of summer before us seemed like the most precious and timeless gift on Earth. Though, on the beginning of the third day at camp as Rick and I were caught up in exploring the nearby swamp, my mind overflowed with many questions about Inner Vision.

We were well aware of Grandfather's ability to communicate with the worlds far beyond the flesh. After three years of watching miracles unfold, we had learned to listen to what he said, what he foretold, and take that as truth, even though there was no logical or physical explanation. We did not know how to use Inner Vision, but we learned to trust Grandfather's ability, because it was never wrong. The past night, while talking around the campfire, Grandfather had told us that we would be visited by five wild dogs by mid-morning and that we should be wary. We had learned never to question how he knew, but we knew that it would happen. As we explored the swamps, we awaited their arrival.

When Rick and I took a break from our exploration, I lay back to ponder the events of the past night. I remembered so vividly the way that Grandfather had drifted out of our conversation and begun to look off into the darkness with his typical far-off gaze. I knew at once that he was listening to things that the normal human mind would never understand. As soon as Rick and I watched him drift off to that other world, our conversation hushed, and we waited with trembling anticipation as to what he might be understanding. We knew, from watching him all these years, that there was something miraculous taking place, and we never ventured a question at these times.

As Grandfather sat in rapt silence, I remembered back to the first time I had ever witnessed him "drifting off," as we at first called this action. Rick and I had been heading to camp to meet Grandfather and spend time with him that weekend. On our way there we decided to get a jump on the duties of survival and set a few traps. Quite a few miles from camp, we had found a good transition area and set our traps. I set a deadfall and Rick set a snare. We had finished quickly and hurried to the camp area to meet Grandfather. As we finished our shelters, Grandfather finally arrived at camp.

As we greeted him, he told us that this was going to be a spiritual camp and there would be no hunting, only fasting. Rick and I had glanced at each other and, without a word, continued with our work of building camp. Neither of us would dare tell Grandfather we had set traps, but we decided that after he was asleep, we would return to the trapping area and take them down. After dinner we sat around the fire discussing spiritual things until well into the night. Eventually, when the conversation trailed off, I started to work on a talking stick, Rick beaded a pipe bag, and Grandfather leaned back against a tree, apparently asleep. Slowly, Grandfather leaned forward but did not open his eyes. "Grandson," he said, now looking at me. "A rabbit has sprung your deadfall, but it did not get him." Pausing for a moment, he spoke again. Now turning towards Rick, he said, "Your snare got him." He slumped back against the tree and went back to sleep, or whatever it was that he did at night.

Rick and I were beside ourselves with confusion. How could he have known we had set traps? He had been miles south of us when we set them, and neither of us had mentioned them. And how could he tell when the traps were sprung, and that it was the same rabbit? We had set them several miles away, across two swamps, and it would have taken quite a while for any emanating rings of movement to reach him. Rick marked the time on his pocket watch, and we slipped from camp and ran to the trap area. I had reached my trap first, and to my utter amazement the trap had been sprung by a rabbit. We followed his tracks, which ended at Rick's snare site. There, high above our heads, was the rabbit. At that time in our lives, we could read a two-week-old track to within minutes of when it was made. These tracks were made at the precise time Grandfather had told us about the traps. It was impossible to have heard any concentric rings or nuances of the kill in that short a time.

Grandfather had been waiting for us to return to camp. There was no need for an explanation, for Grandfather had known the whole scenario. With great shame, I remember asking him how he had known exactly when the traps had sprung, what kind of traps they were, and that the same rabbit was involved in both. What he had said not only explained the world of Inner Vision, but also touched the "oneness" that he so often spoke of. He had said, "If a rabbit moved upon your back, could you not feel it? There is no separation in the force of nature, no inner or outer dimension; we are at once part of nature and nature is part of us." That had been my first of what would be countless encounters with Grandfather's Inner Vision.

Now my mind drifted back to the swamp where I sat. All the events of Inner Vision, of last night's prophecy, swirled in my head. I wondered to myself why Grandfather had not even attempted to teach us this Inner Vision, especially when he considered it to be the real and pure mind, the spiritual bridge. Possibly, I thought, that I might in some way be unworthy, or maybe Grandfather did not think I was ready. I also considered the fact that it could not be taught. Might it be a gift that only a few mortals were permitted to posses? I had been more than willing to learn ever since the first time I heard Grandfather speak of it, but whatever the reason, he was not going to teach me yet, if at all.

Rick and I went back to exploring the swamp, our senses attuned and moving, never resting for very long on any one thing. We wanted to make sure that we would know when the dogs were coming so that we would have plenty of time to climb trees and escape. Rick and I talked about the future dog encounter as if it were absolute fact. There was not a shred of doubt in our minds. We laughed to ourselves with the thought of trying to explain it all to anyone in the outside world. Surely, our friends, the whole of society, would think we were nuts. That would be, of course, until the dogs ultimately showed up. But even then, we did not think that anyone would truly understand what we had witnessed for so many years.

As we continued our search of the lower swamp, I began to get a funny feeling. It was not unlike the feeling of being watched, laced with a little apprehension and fear. Though unfounded in reality, it was still a rapt and apparent mood deep inside me. Without any hesitation, I yelled to Rick to climb the nearest tree. There was so much excitement and anguish in my voice that Rick did not hesitate, and we scrambled up two tall cedar trees near the edge of the spring. We clung to the branches for a long time without a word, each of us searching the landscape for evidence of oncoming dogs. There was no movement, no shift in the natural order of things that would send out even the slightest indication that dogs were around.

I began to grow perplexed as to why I had suddenly panicked and sent us both to the trees. Rick, after a long and searching silence, called over to me and asked where I had seen the dogs. I had no answers and all I could tell him was that for some reason I had felt uneasy and panicked. Sporting a nice array of fresh scrapes from the sharp branches, I felt like such a fool. The anticipation of the dogs' arrival had made me jumpy, I assumed, and that is what had sent me into a panic. I quickly apologized to Rick for my stupidity and began to climb down the tree. I guess he understood because he never said a word, and I know that he had made the same mistake many times before. We both had. Fear can cause an array of strange emotions and bizarre actions.

As I began to near the ground I was again filled with a sense of panic and fear. I yelled to Rick again, never questioning the feeling but just reacting to it with urgency. Up again we went, without hesitation, without question; that is, until we got to the top. After surveying the landscape again and finding nothing, Rick just looked over at me, laughed, and asked, "Did I ever tell you the story of the boy who cried wolf?" I could tell by the tone of his voice that he wasn't angry, but slightly amused. I felt a slight loss of dignity and credibility as we began to climb down again. Sure, I thought to myself, I had panicked in these situations before, but never quite in this way.

As we got to the ground, the fear and panic arose again from somewhere deep within me. This time I fought it back, for I had made a fool of myself now twice and I didn't want to add another. We began to walk away from the tree within a few steps, when again I was hit with the feeling, this time with incredible power. I stopped so abruptly that Rick looked over in my direction with an expression that fell somewhere between amusement and disgust. I listened to the landscape and looked for any sign of concentric rings of movement, but there was nothing. Still, I was held in place by fear, paralyzed by feelings I could not fully understand or identify. This time I had to force myself with difficulty to break out of the paralysis and begin moving.

We pushed out from the trees we had climbed and began to walk back into the deep recesses of the swamp. It was at this point that several things happened all at once. First the fear and panic returned, and secondly, I realized that the only two climbable trees were several feet away. They were the only real substantial trees in that part of the swamp, at least close enough to get to easily. It was then that Rick suddenly spoke up. With a trembling voice he said, "I have a real bad feeling about leaving the trees," and without hesitation we both ran back toward the two trees by the spring.

As soon as we reached the base of the trees there was a crackling of brush and a violence of movement not ten feet from where we had been standing. Excited snarls and barks followed and we had just hoisted ourselves into the trees when the dogs reached the base, trying desperately to bite at our ascending heels. We clung to the tops of the trees with a vengeance, trembling from our narrow escape. For a long time we said nothing, but just looked far below at the five dogs that circled the area. We were not amazed that we encountered the dogs, for we had expected them. I knew that there were five even before I looked down; there was not a question in my mind. I think that we were both relieved to be up in the trees, for one more step, or a few more moments of hesitation, and we would never have made it in time.

It seemed to take forever for the dogs to finally move away from the tree. Yet each time that we began to climb back down we both sensed the panic and fear, and quickly headed back up without a word to each other. Each time the dogs would quickly return, as if they were watching us from some unseen location. We never spoke to each other, for we knew from years of experience with dogs like these that the sound of the human voice only excited them more. Especially voices laced with fear. In fact, it was a long time before we could even look at each other. I suspect that Rick, like myself, was wrapped up in thought about the events leading up to the point where we had escaped the dogs. Both of us felt a certain confusion about how we knew the dogs were there when all physical evidence was to the contrary.

Finally the sun began to set on the horizon and at once a feeling of deep relief came over me. I looked at Rick and could tell by the expression on his face that he too felt the same thing. It was as if some invisible veil had been lifted from my body and I could finally breathe free again. All sense of dread and panic vanished and I somehow knew that the dogs were no longer nearby. I searched my mind for some sort of logical explanation, but there was none. All I knew was that I was certain that the dogs were no longer there, no longer a threat, and had moved far away. I could almost feel them in the distance.

Without a word to Rick I climbed down to the ground, listening to the landscape for any sound of the dogs' return. This time there was no bad feeling, no sense of fear or panic. I felt safe. Looking toward Rick's tree I was surprised to see him standing on the ground, also looking confident with his decision. Without a word to each other we began to stalk from the swamp, watching the darkening landscape and listening to the flow of nature. My senses felt overworked, as if they were about to burst, but there was no sign of anything wrong. Though very alert, I felt secure and relieved, especially when I finally reached the outlying trail and the tall trees.

We moved several miles from the camp before either of us spoke a word. Finally after sitting down to rest for a few moments we broke the hours of rapt silence. At first we looked at each other in utter amazement, not knowing what to say or how to say it. Somehow we had touched some greater awareness than we had ever known, but neither of us knew how to explain it, at least not in words. Rick finally said, "You were right from the start. Did you see how close those dogs were to us? Did you see how long they had been lying in the brush before attacking us? From the lay marks we passed, they must have been there for over half an hour. You knew they were coming close at least an hour before they lay down to wait us out. How the hell did you know? Nothing in the natural order of things was out of place and their tracks showed that they had stalked to the area. I should have listened."

I thought for a long time about what Rick said. I had seen the stalking trails to their lay area and I knew that the stalking had begun when I first got the funny feeling, the feeling of being watched, and the deep sense of panic and fear. However, I did not know how I got the feeling or where it came from. All I knew was that I could not explain in words what I felt. I knew that there were no physical concentric rings of movement, for the dogs had stalked to the area, then lay down to wait. What I did know was that the feelings were very real, so real that I had to obey them without question. In fact, they felt more real than anything I would have picked up with my physical senses. I told Rick that I must have gotten lucky, and just left it at that.

It was long after dark by the time we reached camp. We were both exhausted from our ordeal. We were so full of questions that we could not relax at all. Fortunately, Grandfather had a fire going and a fresh pot of stew and greens ready for dinner. I tried to come right out and ask him some of the questions that were festering in my mind. He wouldn't hear of it until we both had eaten and rested for awhile. Rick and I sat in silence as we ate. From outward appearances it looked like we were brooding, but inside we were churning with questions and emotions, lost in the workings of self, oblivious of the outside world.

I was jolted back to the reality of consciousness by Grandfather's voice. He said, "I had to wait until you had experienced fully and truly the feelings of Inner Vision. Though impure and imperceptible as it was, I could not teach you until you had this happen to you both today. It has been a long time coming, but you would not have fully understood these teachings, the wisdom of Inner Vision, until it reached you in the profound and powerful way you experienced today. How could I have taught you something that you could only vaguely understand? Though it has always been there with you, deep inside of you forever, it took a powerful event to plant the seed of wisdom, and from that the pure Inner Vision will grow."

It did not surprise me in the least that Grandfather knew exactly the questions flowing through my head, nor did it shock me that he knew exactly what had happened in the swamp. I was no more surprised that he knew my questions than I had been certain the dogs would come as he foretold. What did surprise me was that he said that Rick and I touched Inner Vision. I never realized that may have been where the feelings had come from. What I didn't understand was why he referred to it as impure and imperceptible. Did it not drive me up the tree and keep me safe from the dogs? Did it not also abate and disappear when the danger of the dogs finally disappeared? How then could it be impure and imperceptible, I wondered.

Again Grandfather's voice broke into my thoughts. He said, "If the Inner Vision was pure, then you would have known exactly where the dogs would find you long before you left camp this morning. You would have known exactly where they were when you first climbed the tree and exactly when to come down. Pure Inner Vision is without any logical thought. Not only would you have felt the dogs' presence, but you would have known about them moving both in the circle of the spirit-that-moves-in-all-things and seen them in the circle, the island of the world of spirit. As I have said, you have had this gift forever, it is your birthright, as does everyone else possess this gift. Now you must learn to purify that gift and let it become your guide."

"What do you mean that I always had this gift?" Rick asked.

Grandfather looked at us both for a long time, searching our questioning faces, then smiled and said, "You both know it so well, but it has been so weak and ineffective for so long. Your logical thinking mind has imprisoned it and smothered its power."

"But," I said, "I have never had feelings like I experienced today before."

"Maybe not with that rapt intensity," Grandfather then said, "but you have still had them. You just did not know what to call them or how to interpret them, thus you set them aside."

Rick and I sat in silence for a long time wondering what Grandfather was talking about. I know that I never had feelings such as those that I experienced with the dogs today. Any time I had feelings of panic before, they were never justified and nothing ever came of the feeling.

Grandfather said, jolting me back out of my thoughts, "Have you ever felt that you are being watched, only to find out that you have been? Or have you ever been passing along a trail and received an unfounded uneasy feeling, only to find at a later date that you passed by an unknown graveyard? And many times you have told me that you thought that you might be needed at home, only to leave camp and find that you were needed at home."

We both agreed that all of these things had happened to us before. Grandfather then simply said, "Then that is the impure form of Inner Vision."

I watched Grandfather get up and walk away from the fire, my eyes following him into the blackness of the night. It was customary with Grandfather to give us a piece of knowledge, then walk away for a while, allowing us to think it over before anything new was added. Sometimes it could be weeks, months, and even years before he added anything more, in that he wanted to give us plenty of time to understand or to practice what we knew before we could go on. Nothing with his teachings were ever rushed, but taken slowly. Sometimes he would even go to the extent of giving us just enough knowledge so that when the skill or teachings were put to the test, we would fail. That way when the final lesson was delivered, we could thoroughly understand, through our failure, when something had to be done a certain way. Many lessons could only be completed after much practice and sometimes only after failure. I hoped that this would not be one of those times. I not only did not know what to practice, but even where to start, and I certainly didn't want to fail. But that was his way and, as I knew from experience, his way of teaching was best.

Passing the concern for time or failure out of my mind, I began to think about all the things Grandfather had asked us. Many times I had the feeling of being watched, or a feeling of uneasiness, or even knowing that something was going on at home. There were those things and so many other things like that that had happened to me, but again, not as powerfully as the feelings I had experienced today with the dogs.

I still did not fully understand what Grandfather had meant when he referred to our Inner Vision as being impure. Yes, I could understand that the Inner Vision we had experienced was vague as to the whereabouts of the dogs, but it still had warned us early and was by no means subtle. What also troubled me was that I did not know where this Inner Vision came from or how it communicated with me, at least not in a logical way I could firmly understand.

It seemed like half the night passed before Grandfather returned to camp and sat down by the fire. Without waiting for my question he spoke, saying, "Inner Vision does not communicate to us in the words and concepts of man but through the language of the heart. Inner Vision speaks to us only through feelings and emotions, symbols, signs, dreams, and waking visions. The problem and impurity come when we try to put these communications into words that the logical mind can understand. It is when these things are interpreted that they often become distorted or are cast aside, unacceptable, by the logical mind. That logical mind, that overtrained part of the self that creates the prison of man's spirit, is what destroys or smothers the pure Inner Vision."

Grandfather waited for a while before he continued, giving us time to digest and understand what he was saying. He continued, saying, "The reason that your Inner Vision was so strong and apparent during your encounter with the dogs is because your logical mind was distracted by fear and the need to stay aware. It was during this time of distraction that the Inner Vision was allowed to come through in a very real and powerful way. It spoke to you not in words, but through feelings and emotions, and though unfounded with any physical evidence, you knew exactly what was causing these feelings. There was no question, just an innate knowing, but you did not know why. If your mind was stilled and the Inner Vision pure, then you would have known all these things from the very beginning. There would have been a clarity, yet there would have been no need for words or explanations." Grandfather stood, smiled at both of us, then disappeared into the night. As I sauntered off to the sacred area to pray, and then off to bed, I remembered my second Vision Quest, when I had learned to use the pure mind.

I had been sitting in my Vision Quest area for three days when I learned one of the most valuable lessons of my life. Up until this time, I felt that my first Vision Quest had been a failure. I could not understand the connection between the physical world and the world of spirit. I simply did not know how to meet the spirit world on its own terms. I could not fully communicate with that world, nor could I understand much about it. It was Grandfather who had told me that I had to believe purely. My problem was a lack of purity and an overbearing logical mind, though at the time I did not know what he had meant. He simply said that I was not looking at the worlds of nature and spirit in the right way, a pure way.

It was then, during the morning of the third day of my Vision Quest that I inadvertently wandered away from my quest area, unconscious of the fact that I was supposed to stay in the area. The question of purity hung heavy in my mind. I had been drawn to the edge of a nearby stream, as if directed by a force outside myself. As I sat by the water's edge, I thought about this question of purity while staring into the quiet waters. It was then that I noticed the pure reflection of Nature in the mirrorlike water, along with the reflection of myself. Then a light wind began to blow and the surface of the water began to stir. The pure image began to surge, flutter, then all reflection was gone. It was then that the word "thoughts" came rushing into my head and I had the answer to the question of purity.

I had learned that day the mind is much like water. When there is thought, analysis, words, and definitions, it stirs the surface of the waters and there can be no pure images. All is lost to the movement of thought. It is only when the mind is still and pure, without the need to define, that we get a pure reflection. I realized then there had to be a connection between the worlds of nature and spirit. I finally understood the purity of mind and how to communicate in a pure and real way. I learned that to see, to understand, and to communicate with these worlds the mind had to be still. I knew then that the logical mind only stood in the way of real communication, of really seeing and understanding. It was one of my grandest breakthroughs.

I spent all of the next morning and much of the afternoon working in the camp. The events of the past day seemed so distant, but the fires of desire to learn Inner Vision still burned within my mind. I had to continually force out of my mind all thought of Inner Vision, for I found it almost impossible to concentrate on anything else. I became so distracted at times that I began to foul up even the most remedial chores. Grandfather noticed my distraction and chuckled to himself every time I would mess something up. I guess that he must have known how it felt for he simply said, "Concentrate on what you are doing and we will return to the wisdom of Inner Vision tonight." With the huge burden of thought lifted from my back, I began to have fun again. Still I realized that I wasted the entire day consumed in useless thought.

I was cleaning up camp after dinner, trying to do the chores that could not be done after dark. Grandfather sat at the far end of camp, exactly where he had been through all of dinner. He did not move but appeared to me that he was waiting for something, such was his posture. Curiosity got the better of me and I walked over to him and asked if everything was all right. Searching me with his eyes, he asked, "Haven't you forgotten something?" I was taken aback by his question and my mind rushed over all manner of things that I had done throughout the day. It began to gnaw at my gut, as he questioned me with his eyes.

Saying nothing more, Grandfather stood and walked away, apparently in disgust. I remembered that Grandfather had asked me to do something earlier in the day, but for the life of me I couldn't remember what it had been. As my mind reached for answers, my gut tightened, and the feeling of having forgotten something overwhelmed me. I brooded over it for hours. All the while my gut was telling me that I had forgotten to do what Grandfather had asked, but what he had asked was just out of reach. I paced camp, well into the night.

As the night grew late, and camp became silent, Rick had gone off to bed leaving me to the silence of my searching thoughts. The deep gnawing sensation of forgetting pounded my gut and at times made me almost sick. My mind raced over the events of the day, thinking of all the conversations I had with Grandfather, but still nothing emerged. I knew very well that he had asked me to do something for him, and forgetting to do something for Grandfather, to me, anyway, was a cardinal sin. The act of forgetting actually tormented the center of my existence and my guts, my heart, ached for answers.

Somehow I let go of my searching thoughts and gazed into the fire, wrapped in the purity of my aloneness. I just stared at the fire, mindlessly playing with a small stick. I began to push around the coals with the stick, stirring the fire so that its blaze cut further into the night. My gut still ached for answers to what I had forgotten, but I had long since given up my mental fight. I lifted the stick from the fire and held it aloft, accented against the blackness of the night sky. Suddenly I saw the image of a torch and a huge burden was lifted from my gut, from my being. I had forgotten to bring a torch to Grandfather's sacred area!

The relief of finally remembering was overwhelming. I felt as if I could breathe again. I ran from the fire and over to the storage area of my shelter to get one of the torches I had made earlier in the week. Now, even though it was very late, I would bring the torch over to Grandfather's sacred area and leave it there for him. Perhaps, I thought, he would teach the lessons of Inner Vision tomorrow, now that I had remembered to bring him the torch. I just hoped that he would not be angry at me for bringing it to him so late, but, then again, Grandfather never seemed to get angry at anything. Either way, I was just so happy and relieved that I remembered. I never wanted to let Grandfather down.

I walked over to Grandfather's camp area, which was less than a mile from mine. Carefully working my way through the dark landscape, I approached cautiously. I did not want to disturb him if he was in prayer, but there was very little that Grandfather was not aware of. I chuckled to myself, thinking that he probably knew that I was coming to his camp even before I left mine. I stalked as I neared the area, but it was too dark to see if he was there. I slipped through the brush and placed the torch near the old tree at the back side of his sacred area. Just as I was about to turn and walk away, his voice shattered the silence of the night, surprising me. He said, "Sit down, Grandson, I've been expecting you."

I was so surprised and taken back that I nearly tripped as I entered his area. It wasn't often that Grandfather would talk to us from his sacred area, but when he did it was always a special lesson. My voice trembled with excitement as I apologized for bringing the torch so late. Grandfather laughed and told me to sit down, motioning to a grass mat near him. It was obvious that he had indeed been expecting me. I asked him how he could have possibly known that I would be coming. I hadn't even thought about going to his camp until I remembered the torch. He laughed and said, "I knew that you would remember the torch, as I knew that you would forget the torch in the first place. I planted the thought in your head so that it would be forgotten and then remembered."

I was confused, to say the least. How could he put something in my head that he knew I would forget, only to remember later on? Just as I was about to ask him, he cut me off. Speaking now with a sense of play in his voice, yet not in a mocking way, he said, "I asked you for the torch at a time when your mind was occupied with something else. I also made my request in such a way so that it was heard yet not fully part of your consciousness; thus you forgot. Yet you remembered you had forgotten something, but you could not find what it was you were forgetting. I only did this to teach you a lesson of Inner Vision. It is now that you finally remembered the torch that I can begin to teach you. I could not before this, not until you reached this point.

"The tightness in your gut when you tried to remember but could not was your Inner Vision trying desperately to talk to you. As I have said before, the outer worlds of the mind and those places beyond know all things. Deep inside your mind you knew exactly what you had forgotten. As your Inner Vision tried to communicate to your logical mind but could not, there was that tension. That tension, that deep gut feeling, is exactly how our inner vision tries to talk to us. Thus when the answer is finally found on a logical level, the gut reacts with the release of tension. Your greater self is so relieved that you have found the answer, an answer that it knew all the time."

"But I still don't know how the Inner Vision finally communicated with me," I said. Grandfather continued, saying, "Remember, I had told you that the Inner Vision does not communicate to us in words, but through symbols, feelings, waking visions, dreams, and intuition. When you held the burning stick aloft, it was a symbol of the torch, and your logical mind, with the help of your Inner Vision, recognized it as such. It is this same inner tension that you feel whenever you get the feeling of being watched or, for that matter, any time there is an attempted communication from the world of nature or spirit. So the inner tension is the way Inner Vision tells us that it wants to communicate and it is the release of that tension that tells us that we have found the answer."

Grandfather paused then, as usual, to give me a chance to digest what he had said. I had never realized before that this was the way that Inner Vision communicated with me. I had that feeling so many times but I did not understand what it was or where it came from. I was also well aware of the release of tension in the gut, and now I finally understood where that had come from and what it meant. What was still vague to me was exactly how I would go about communicating with all of this in a real and understandable way. I knew that it was the symbol of the torch that led me to remember, but how could that work with the worlds of nature and spirit? If, in fact, the torch was the symbol, then why could I have not arrived at it earlier? I thought that there must be a better way to ask that Inner Vision so that the answer would be immediately clear and understandable.

Grandfather continued, "Until you learn to purify the communications from Inner Vision, the process of communication will be a little vague and difficult. Many times, without a purification of that Inner Vision, the answers are weak and impure, and success is beyond reach. First you must learn how to make a strong connection to the communication of Inner Vision and then you must learn how to purify it to a point of perfection. You will do quite well even using the difficult and impure form of communication, but to get perfection all must be purified. Without that purification the answers could be incomplete and very dangerous."

"How can I practice the communication?" I asked. "The symbol of the torch was an accident and I can't see how I could make it a working process, even if it is impure." Grandfather said, "All of Creation has an instinct to survive. Every creature knows exactly how to hunt, what to eat, and where to find shelter. If a doe dies, does the yearling also die? Of course not, for it knows what to eat and how to live. Even when the doe is present, she shows the yearling very little. The instincts are there and the doe at best only brings out that instinct. You too have the same instincts. Deep in your Inner Vision you know all you need to know about survival. You know what plants to eat, which are medicinal, and which are toxic, even if you never have seen that plant before."

I was excited now about the prospect of knowing the use of plants. For all too long I had been searching through books for identification or asking Grandfather about the plants. Now, what he was telling me was that I possessed that information as surely as any other creature of the Earth. Grandfather's voice broke into my thoughts, saying, "This type of communication that you will first learn, without the purification, can be very dangerous, especially when dealing with the plant people. If the communication is vague or tainted in any way by the logical mind, then you could possibly make a mistake. That is why the purification is so important, for without it many mistakes can be made. Remember too that this Inner Vision not only reaches to our instincts and memory, but to the outer worlds of spirit and nature."

With those words, Grandfather took the root of a plant out of his buckskin bag and handed it to me. I had never seen such a root and did not know if it was even from the Pine Barrens. Grandfather collected many plants outside the Pine Barrens area and this could very well be one of them. I could see his smile, even in the dark, and the anticipation of what could follow made me tremble with excitement. Grandfather simply said, "Hold the root in your hand, close your eyes, and relax." I followed his directions, pushing the excitement out of my mind. Relaxing my body deeply and clearing my mind, I reached into what Grandfather called the "sacred silence."

I held that sacred silence for a long time, but nothing emerged. There was no tension in my gut such as I had experienced earlier on that night. Disappointed, I told Grandfather that I felt nothing. He said, "Of course you feel nothing! You have not asked the Inner Vision any questions yet! Now," he said, "I want you to pay attention to your deeper self, the area of that self where the Inner Vision first came to you earlier this night." I concentrated very hard, reaching deep inside to the area where I had previously found the tension, but again there was nothing. I must have sighed audibly so that Grandfather heard me, and again he told me that there would be no feeling until I asked it a question.

I reached back deep inside and waited. Grandfather then said, "As you hold the plant in your hand, ask yourself if it is an edible plant." As soon as my mind reached for the question, my gut tightened to the same point it had been earlier in the night, though this time it was a little stronger and more urgent. Grandfather then asked me to ask myself if it was a medicinal plant. Immediately there was a release of the tension and I knew somehow that this plant was medicinal. He then asked me to ask myself if the plant was poisonous and my gut tightened again. He then asked me to search my body, using my Inner Vision as a guide, and find the place that the plant would feel good on my body. As soon as I reached my eyes with my mind, the tension of Inner Vision disappeared once again.

I was astounded and could not talk when I came from the realm of the "sacred silence." Grandfather chuckled and said, "So now you know how to ask your Inner Vision, and you found truth. You did not know what the root was, for it comes from my homeland. You know now that this root is not edible, but medicinal. You also know that it is poisonous if it is not prepared in the right way, and most of all you know that it is used to fight eye infections. You do not know the name of this plant but you know everything else about it. You know its spirit." I could not believe that I had really done it, and began to laugh and cry at the same time. Grandfather also began to laugh, long and hard.

As we both calmed down, Grandfather continued, saying, "I must warn you again that you must not fully rely on your Inner Vision until you have learned to purify its message. One mistake with this root and you would have been poisoned. You can use this form of communication with less dangerous things, until you learn to purify that connection between self and Inner Vision." There was a sternness in his voice that told me that he was dead serious and I took that warning with the same seriousness. "But," he continued, "let me show you what else Inner Vision can do. You have received a message from your instinct through Inner Vision, now I want you to communicate with the world of nature, from a place beyond your physical senses."

Grandfather then told me to stand up and to face out into the swamp, letting go of myself and my thoughts, and reach a point of sacred silence. He then said, "Ask yourself where the nearest deer are bedded down on the far side of the swamp." As soon as the question hit my mind, my gut tightened up again. "Now," he said, "begin to slowly turn until the tension is released." Again I followed his instructions, and by the time I made a quarter turn, the tension was gone. "Now," he said, "how far? Let your mind work its way across the swamp and deep into the night." Again I followed his directions and when my mind reached the distant end of the swamp, the tension disappeared. I could see in my mind exactly where the deer were bedded down. Without hesitation, Grandfather ordered me to stalk to the area and find them, and I left without another question.

I plunged right into the swamp without a word. My mind raced over all manner of thoughts and especially doubts. First of all, I thought, this is the middle of the night and deer do not usually bed down now. I also knew the area to which I headed and it is not a likely area for the deer to be bedded down. Anyway, I could not see how I could have picked up their presence with Inner Vision. They were too far away to feel any physical concentric rings emanating from their position. It would take a major disturbance there to even reach my side of the swamp, and there had been none. Still, I pressed on through the swamp, with just a vague hope that I might be right.

As I drew near the area I had seen in my mind, I began to stalk. If there were deer there I did not want to have them take flight before I got there. As I reached the exact area where my Inner Vision had led me I slowed down even more, taking great care in stalking. To my absolute disappointment, there was nothing in the area. I felt so heartbroken; not only had I failed but I had made a stupid mistake. I knew very well that deer would not have been bedded down at this time of night, and especially in an area like this. Anger welled up inside of me and I kicked at the ground and cursed. Brush crashed just a yard behind me and two deer bounded off from their beds. I was so stunned by the action that I fell over backwards.

I came down on my butt hard and with a jolt. Certainly it hurt but I was laughing so hard that it never made a difference. I had done it, I had been right or, rather, my Inner Vision had been right even though my logical mind was telling me that I was wrong. I crawled through the brush, to where the deer had been. I wanted to make certain that they had indeed been bedded down and did not just happen to wander to me. With a heavy dose of skepticism I began to feel around the ground and to my delight I found their beds. There was no denying the fact that they had been lying there and, judging from the depressions, for a few hours at least. I still could not believe what I had done.

I didn't walk, but ran back through the swamp, my head filled with so many questions. How could that miracle have happened? I thought. There were no noises that I could have picked up at the far end of the swamp. There was no logical reason or proof that the deer would be in the area, but I had been right, despite what my mind had been telling me. Possibly I was just lucky and it was a weird coincidence. I knew it was late but I hoped that Grandfather would be waiting for me in his sacred area. My gut told me that without a doubt he would be there, and this time I was sure it was right.

No sooner did I sit down than Grandfather began to speak, "So, you wonder how you communicated with the deer and knew where they were even though there was no logical reason or physical evidence that they were there. As I have told you so many times before, all things of the Earth are connected to each other. It is this connection that we call the spirit-that-moves-through-all-things. You were able to communicate with that spirit through your Inner Vision. When you felt the connection, you became one with its power. That is how I knew, so long ago, that you had tried to trap that rabbit. You have done the same. Now you must learn to purify that communication so that it is clear and strong and there are no mistakes." Grandfather continued, "You have already received part of the answer through the wisdom of the still waters, the pure reflection of the mind, with the disturbances and distractions of logical thought. But you must go beyond that wisdom and now learn how to purify your Inner Vision. This can be done only when you have spent some time alone with that question of purity. You can only find it yourself, for I cannot lead you there." With that, Grandfather left and I wandered back to camp.

I wandered slowly, almost in a daze. I was so caught up in my thoughts that I blundered into brush and tripped frequently. I was amazed at what I had done and how easy it had been. Yet I could finally understand why Grandfather had waited so long to teach me. I had to learn so much before this night or I would have never fully understood. As I neared camp, rapt deep in thought, my gut began to tighten and I felt a powerful sense of being watched. Instead of letting the feeling pass, I stopped and began to give in to it. In my mind I began to run through the images of all manner of animals, but none broke the tension. Then I thought of Rick and the feeling suddenly vanished. I called his name. In a surprised voice he called from the bushes. "How the hell did you know I was here," he said. I laughed long and hard and simply said, "Go ask Grandfather," then went to bed.

3

Quest for Purity

I sat for a long time in the swamp trying to understand what Grandfather meant when he talked of the purity of Inner Vision. I knew I had three possible answers. It could be like the purity of mind which I learned on my second Vision Quest, or it could be the purity found in the sacred silence, or it could be the purity found in wandering alone, without time or destination. It also could be any combination thereof.

I wandered aimlessly for hours, randomly stopping, lying down, and relaxing whenever the feeling moved me. I eventually sat down for a while but I felt the wrongness. Suddenly I felt as if I needed to be directed to go somewhere, but I didn't know where. I decided to quiet my questioning mind. I was trying to reach the purity of the still waters that was so necessary to the process of opening the mind and self. Everywhere I thought of going felt wrong. I wanted to venture down through the rest of the swamp but was overpowered by the wrongness. I thought maybe I should continue wandering aimlessly but that also felt wrong. Then the quiet waters came to mind.

I didn't understand why, it just felt right to go to the quiet waters and that was all there was to it. I began to accept the fact and could no longer allow myself the luxury of knowing why. Many times, especially around Grandfather, it was not important to know why something was right, but that it just felt right. So many things, so many miracles, defied analysis or description. Analysis of any sort would only distort the events, and as always, the active mind would only become an enormous distraction. Distraction is the least of what I needed right now, for I had to keep my mind free and open to find the answers. After all, I thought, this is why Grandfather wanted me to be alone and free of distraction altogether.

I finally arrived at the exact place I had sat during that third day of my second Vision Quest, but nothing happened. I knew it felt good to be in this place and right now that was more than enough. I tried to stare into the quiet waters once again, just as I had done in the Vision Quest, and could feel their wisdom return to me, but there were no new insights. Yes, I understood the pure reflections of the pure mind, but there was nothing given to me beyond that initial lesson. All I knew was that I was drawn here for a reason and the reason had to be found someplace in the reflective surface of the waters, or in the wisdom of pure mind. At least, I thought, that was the only reason I could have been led back to this place.

As I sat and gazed into the waters, I got the feeling that there had to be more to the reflection, this purity. There had to be something beyond what I had learned during my second Vision Quest. Possibly, I thought, there was more to the lesson, something I was overlooking, or something I already possessed but could not understand. Every time my attention was diverted from the water or I looked away from the surface, I had the feeling it was wrong, and I quickly refocused on the water. This was my surest indicator I was onto something, but I did not know how to find it. I just continued to gaze at the waters, at times almost unconsciously, other times searching with rapt attention. In a glimmer of immediate insight, not knowing where it came from, I felt there was more than just the reflection on the surface, for the water had depth.

Depth, I thought! The feeling of the word "depth" hit me so hard and in such a profound way that I knew that I must be coming close to the answer, or at least part of the answer. I looked past the surface of the water, past the reflection, and into the darkened depth. I could see minute currents moving, bits of debris floating by, and myriads of countercurrents, swirls, and whirlpools, all moving beneath the surface. All these deeper movements seemed contrary to each other, yet born of each other. Some were caused by the ebb and flow of the current; fast-moving areas stirring against slow-moving areas, or by currents pushing against the banks or acting upon all manner of debris, sticks, and blocks. All of this was contrary, but all moving eventually in the direction of the current. I felt as if I was looking into the very movement of my own mind and spirit.

Again the feeling of finding the answer overwhelmed me as my mind fought to put it all into words. The stirring of the logical mind and the spiritual mind in the deeper self, yet still moving in the flow of life, were just like the undercurrents of the stream, I thought. As I let go and gazed deeper into the waters, I imagined myself looking up to the surface, as if from underwater. There too, if there is movement, contrary movement, the view from underwater to the outer worlds are obscured. So then it must not be enough to quiet the surface of the waters, but one must also quiet the inner waters of the very spirit, or there is no complete purity. But, I thought, how do I reach this inner purity, and suddenly it no longer felt right to be by the water.

I began to think about the feeling and then it became clear to me. What was driving me was my Inner Vision, and suddenly I had the feeling that I could leave the area. The total realization took me by complete surprise. In essence, not only was I guided to this place by my Inner Vision but also to the place of the quiet waters. I began to wonder if in fact my Inner Vision could not only guide me to the deeper answers I needed, but if it could also, in some way, purify itself. So, to this point, I had learned that I not only had to still the surface waters of the mind, but also the deeper waters of the soul. I also learned that the Inner Vision was guiding me to the answers, and ultimately to its own purity. Everything to this point had been random searching, but now I had a strong ally in my Inner Vision.

Since my Inner Vision had helped thus far, I decided to sit down right away and contact it. I settled in right where I was and drifted into the sacred silence, trying to clear my mind as much as possible. I guess I was too excited at the time, for the process that would normally have taken just a few moments took the better part of an hour. Finally, I felt free enough of my mind and body and asked my Inner Vision what I should do next. Two images flashed into my mind. One was the image of Grandfather sitting waiting in his camp, and the other was an image of myself in a Vision Quest area. I immediately discounted these images because I knew before that the way Inner Vision came to me was through a tension in my gut. In frustration, I decided to try a different approach. I went back to the place of sacred silence and asked my Inner Vision exactly in what direction I would find the answers. Turning the landscape in my mind, I finally reached a direction where I had a complete release. Again I asked and again it answered in the same way. Without hesitation I began to walk, most of the time without even using any trails or landmarks. Each time I veered from my direction, the feeling of wrongness, as I began to call it, drifted into me.

As the trek wore on, the Inner Vision grew stronger, almost demanding that I quicken my pace. I had to follow its urging, for every time I slowed, I was overwhelmed by this feeling of wrongness. I began to enter a place where the brush was so thick that I had to crawl along the small animal runs and trails. Finally I could see an opening up ahead in the brush and quickened my crawl. I burst from the brush, as if finally released from confinement, and stumbled right into Grandfather's camp.

I was amazed, for I hadn't even realized I was anywhere near his camp. I had entered the camp from a way I had never used before, although it shouldn't have been any surprise. I jumped when Grandfather's voice said, "Come sit with me. I've been expecting you." "Expecting me!" I said in amazement. "Up until now, I didn't even expect me," and we both laughed. Grandfather continued, "Your trip would have been a lot easier if you simply followed your Inner Vision. Instead you took the longer and harder route." "But I did follow my Inner Vision," I said. "No," Grandfather said, "you followed your Inner Vision in its desperate attempt to get you back to my camp, since you wouldn't listen to it the first time."

I thought about what he said for a few moments, but it didn't make any sense. My Inner Vision only directed me once, not twice. Without waiting for me to ask the question, Grandfather said, "Well, at least it got you here, didn't it?" Still confused, I asked Grandfather what he meant. "You were given two images when you first went to your Inner Vision. One image was of me and the other image was of a Vision Quest." Without hesitation and in absolute amazement, I asked Grandfather how he knew that. He laughed and then said, "Because at the same time you asked your Inner Vision, I asked mine about how you were doing. I had the image of you talking to me here in camp, and an image of you in a Vision Quest. How do you think I know what your questions are before you ask?"

I did not want to pursue it any further. There were too many other pressing questions that needed answering and I didn't need more questions right at the moment. "Then what you're saying is those images were not images at all but a communication from my inner vision?" I said. Grandfather answered, "Remember, I told you that Inner Vision speaks to us through feelings, emotions, symbols, signs, dreams, and waking visions. Well, your Inner Vision decided to communicate to you through a waking vision, or image of what you needed to do." Grandfather paused for a moment, probably to let me think, then said, "You know now what you have to do. First we must talk and then you must take a Vision Quest. As to where it will be and how long it will be is what your Inner Vision decides. It is your Inner Vision that teaches you and guides you now, not I."

This last statement frightened me for I thought Grandfather would no longer be my teacher. Grandfather broke into my thoughts, saying, "Inner Vision is but the beginning of a long road. Once mastered, you still have so much to learn. I will be your teacher for a very long time. It is now that you have an ally to help you in your struggles." Up until this point, I considered Inner Vision to be the ultimate awareness, now only to find that I was just beginning my spiritual path in life. It seemed like every time I learned something and thought that it was all I could learn, a whole new world of things to learn opened up.

Grandfather's voice broke into my thoughts, saying, "You have learned to look deeper into the purity of the still waters and you were drawn close to an answer. You now understand that the Inner Vision is your guide, and before the Inner Vision is entered you know that there must be the sacred silence. But you still do not know how to purify this Inner Vision. You know what is necessary, what are the main elements, but you do not know what lies beyond that wisdom, of things you have yet to learn about purification. This is why your Inner Vision now leads you to take the Vision Quest, to discover the final answers, the final purity. What now does your Inner Vision tell you to do about your Vision Quest?"

Grandfather's question took me by such surprise that I hesitated to answer. I had not, until this point, even consulted my Inner Vision. Without a word I closed my eyes and went to the place of silence, and then to Inner Vision. "The Inner Vision tells me to go now," I said. "And how long will you be gone?" Grandfather asked. "As long as it takes," I said. "Then you have learned to listen well," Grandfather said. He then stood and smiled, and went about his business around his camp. I immediately felt uncomfortable being there and left camp, without a word to Grandfather, not out of disrespect, but because we both knew the conversation was done. I knew what I had to do and there was no need for further discussion.

I decided to go back to camp and get some things I needed for the Vision Quest. Since most Vision Quests lasted four days, I needed to have water. My Inner Vision said otherwise and I was on my way, to where I did not know. All I knew was that I had to Vision-Quest to get any more answers, and that was all there was to it. I searched my mind for a place to quest, but nothing made sense, nothing felt good. It didn't take long before I realized that I should not be thinking about it, so I went to my Inner Vision for the answers. I drifted to the sacred silence and then to the Inner Vision and asked where my quest was to take place. Quickly, and in a startling way, the image of the place of quiet waters came to me.

Without any thoughts about the image, or trying to validate it with any further logical explanation, I just went on, trusting my Inner Vision to know exactly what I needed. The thought of trust overwhelmed me. Not just trust, but a blind faith, and I knew somehow that I had gotten another part of the answer. There was no need to question that feeling, for I knew it was absolutely right. I still did not know how it all fit together, however, and I continued my journey to the quiet waters.

I arrived at the water's edge during the last part of sunset. I sat again in the same area I had sat earlier that day, the same place I had sat during that time of my second Vision Quest, but it did not feel good. The area felt good but the exact spot didn't. For the better part of the evening, I searched with my heart for the right place to sit, but none could be found. The frustration and fatigue of the day began to cast shadows of doubt in my mind. I began to think that I must not have listened to my Inner Vision and I really should not be here. Or possibly my Inner Vision was playing tricks on me, in that it still wasn't purified. But none of those explanations felt right. Now, in total exhaustion, my mind swirling with all manner of doubt, I lay down and went to sleep.

My sleep was fitful and broken. My mind dreamed so many dreams, but mostly of birds flying or sitting in trees. Sometimes the dreams would produce strange nightmares, where at once I would be soaring above a grand landscape, then suddenly plummet to the Earth. Every time, nearing the ground

in my fall, I would awaken with a start, my body out of control
with fear, my heart pounding in my chest. I would quickly fall
back to sleep and then be soaring again. All the time I would
feel the freedom of flying, as if I were disconnected from the
problems of flesh. Soaring, all things were perfect and I could
look down and see the chaos of the world from afar and see
it in a detached but pure way.

I fell from my flight again, and awakened with a start. This
time something was far different. Not only was it dawn, but
I stared into the upper branches of the huge old grandfather
cedar tree that stood near the quiet waters. There in my gut
was the release, and it felt so right. I had to go and climb the
tree, for that is where my Inner Vision said that I had to be.
There was no doubt now. Even the Inner Vision of my dreams
was of birds, flying, and lofty heights. That too is why the
quiet waters had felt good, yet the place, any place, I chose
to sit did not feel right. It was because I had to be in the
tree. The relief that washed over me was beyond description,
though I did not know how I could possibly spend an entire
Vision Quest clinging to a tree.

As I climbed the tree, all manner of thoughts swirled through
my head. I began to devise a number of ways to stay up in
the tree for the next four days. I was worried that I would
eventually fall asleep, lose my grip, and fall. I began to wonder
if that wasn't the message carried by the past night's dreams
of repeatedly falling. That might have been so, but my Inner
Vision overrode all the negative thoughts. I decided that I
would only worry about it when night came again and I grew
tired. My Inner Vision somehow told me not to worry about
it at all.

It was quite a struggle getting past the branches, but once
there, it was quite comfortable and secure, though I still had
my doubts that I could rest there without falling. The view of
the surrounding landscape was absolutely breathtaking. I did
feel like a bird in a way, perched high above the problems of
the world. My dream seemed to come hammering home, now
in full life.

As I looked around the landscape, I gazed back down toward the base of the tree. There the waters ran by like a ribbon of silvery reflection across the green carpet of sphagnum moss. As I looked up and down the stream, I could see the harmony and balance that it struck with the landscape. I peered over the edge of the branches and down to the area of the quiet waters. There was the most absolutely beautiful reflection in the surface. It appeared more like a mirror than at any other time. I could see myself looking down from the towering tree, and I was even more amazed at the purity of its reflection. It seemed to reflect every detail. I tried to look deeper into the water. It was then that I noticed that I couldn't see the turbulence, at least not from this high up. The feeling of having to be in the tree vanished.

I was startled by the absence of the need to be in the tree and how quickly it had left me. I did not remember getting any insights into the answers to purity, but I felt that I must have gotten something. I climbed back down the tree and returned to the original sitting area, and now it did feel good to be there. I began to think about the waters and what they now told me, but there was no clear message. As my mind mulled over the questions, the recurring dream seeped back into my thoughts and I had the answers. Simply, when viewed from afar, the spirit is purer, problems vanish, and there is no turbulence. But when viewed at close range, there is that turbulence. The problem was that I could not see how it could fit into the overall picture of purity that I was building.

I could understand the need for the sacred silence and the guiding force of Inner Vision. I could definitely see the need for faith in Inner Vision, and I could see the necessity to purify it all, but I could not see the need for the lofty heights. Unless, I thought, that we must somehow remove ourselves from ourselves, our problems, and the problems of the world, like being up and away from it all. As the winged taught, sometimes you have to fly high above all things to put them into proper perspective and to understand how all things fit together. Possibly, to find the purity of Inner Vision we had to rise above it all. After all, in my dreams I felt whole and pure when I was aloft. Only when plunging back to the Earth did I feel the turmoil.

That answer, at least, felt partially good. But I knew that it was not a complete answer, for like the other, I did not know how it all fit together. I did not know how to achieve this lofty position without climbing a tree. I chuckled to myself, thinking that there must be a way to climb a tree within ourselves. I thought about this dilemma all day, right into sunset, without moving from where I sat.

I watched the setting sun until it disappeared behind the distant treescape. With its disappearance, I could feel the waves of heat leaving as the colder night air moved in and pushed it out. Soon, columns of mist began to rise from the swamp and water, drifting about like a gathering of apparitions from the spirit world. The sounds of the night, especially the insects, intensified to a grand symphony. The night was a gorgeous display of life, mist, and water, that interplayed with the symphony, like a well-choreographed dance. Mists began to gather in gauzy curtains and move from the swamps, carried on the wings of the cooler air. Each time the mist moved through my area its cold touch would quiet the insect voices, at times making everything grow silent. It seemed that at these times the world stopped, everything stood still, and there was purity.

Then it struck me, an ultimate knowing struck me hard. The mists were much like the "veils" of the sacred silence. As Grandfather so often explained, when we pass through these veils we reach a deeper part of ourself. We go then beyond the self and into the outer realms of nature and spirit. It is the veils of the sacred silence that will ultimately bring the purity. That is why Grandfather had me enter the sacred silence before I even attempted to communicate with the Inner Vision. So then, I thought, the sacred silence must be the vehicle to the outer worlds and it is the Inner Vision that communicates with these outer worlds. The purer and deeper the sacred silence, the more powerful the Inner Vision, the purer the communication. Above all, it is the absolute faith which then gives it power.

I ran from the quest area, caring little that it was late and I had only spent one day there and not four. I had to find Grandfather and tell him what I found. I was too close and there was much swirling in my head. If I waited until the morning, I was afraid that I could not put my insights into words.

I ran off into the night, but was suddenly stopped by some unseen force deep inside of me. It was the feeling of wrongness emerging again, not only telling me to stop, but also driving me back to the quest area. I tried to resist, but the command of the Inner Vision was now much more powerful. I reluctantly walked back to the quest area and sat down. I was confused, for I knew that something outside myself had guided me to talk to Grandfather, the feeling was undeniable. As I sat, I grew tense and upset, afraid that if I did not get to talk to Grandfather this night I would lose or confuse the insights that I had been given. My head was already beginning to surge with more questions than I could handle.

I sat for a long time, trying to put together again all that I had learned. The mind began to distort the insights, so in a desperate attempt to purify I went to the place of sacred silence and then to the Inner Vision. As soon as I reached deep inside myself an image quickly emerged. I could see Grandfather sitting by me here at the place of quiet waters and I was talking to him. Almost in an unconscious way, more out of habit than by will, I began to talk to Grandfather in my mind. The conversation felt so real and the answers that he was giving me so important and viable. I could feel a wave of relief come over me, then suddenly I lost the image of Grandfather in my mind. I heard his voice again, echoing through my thoughts. He said, "So why did you call me to you, Grandson?" Startled by the reality of his voice, I opened my eyes, only to find him sitting directly in front of me.

I gasped in utter amazement, as if he were some sort of ghost or spirit. "No, Grandson," he said, "I am real." "But how did you know that I needed to talk to you?" I said. Grandfather smiled at me for a long time, to a point where I could even see his teeth in the dark. He then said, "Did you not want to see me? Did you not call to me through the universal voice of Inner Vision?" "I did see you when I went to the place of Inner Vision, but I thought that the image just came to me," I answered. "But is not that what you wanted?" he said. "But," I said, and he cut me short. "Grandson, remember that Inner Vision works in both ways. Not only do we receive communications from the outer worlds, but we also send our voice and desire to the outer worlds. That is how I knew that you wanted to talk to me. You communicated to me through the voice of Inner Vision."

Grandfather paused in his conversation, again to make sure I digested all that he taught. I literally shook with excitement. I never realized that we could have our desires heard in the outer worlds through the voice of Inner Vision. The concept, at least, excited me because this meant that I could communicate to everything of flesh or spirit. It meant that I just did not have to listen. I was more than amazed and excited. Before I could ask the question Grandfather said, "Why do you look so surprised at all of this? Did you not ask your Inner Vision a question before it answered? And the Inner Vision sometimes communicated to you from your deeper mind, sometimes from the world of the spirit-that-moves-through-all-things, sometimes from the world of spirit, and sometimes from the world of man, who is also part of the natural world."

Again I mulled over his words. "Then why," I asked, "have I never gotten a communication from you?" "You did, yesterday, when I told you through your Inner Vision to come to my camp," he said. "The reason you never heard me before was that you did not listen to your Inner Vision. I told you again tonight, but your Inner Vision was still impure and weak, yet growing stronger with what you have learned so far in this quest. You have learned that you must have faith, that you seek the veils of the sacred silence for purity, and that you must remove yourself from yourself in order to allow the Inner Vision to grow strong and pure. Now your Inner Vision tells you that you must remain in this quest and learn the wisdom of communication, so that the communication works both ways."

With those words Grandfather walked off into the night, leaving me stunned yet excited. It was just as I had imagined it would be. Just as I began to get things sorted out in my mind, there was more to do. Inner Vision reached beyond anything I ever dreamed it would do. I was beginning to understand the process of purifying the Inner Vision, but I was not sure how to go about communication with the outer worlds so that my voice could be heard. I was not sure how I had called Grandfather to the area this night. All I knew now was that I had a lot of work to do, not only on purification of Inner Vision, but also on the two-way communication that Grandfather spoke of. At this point in my thoughts, I lay down and quickly fell asleep, mentally exhausted.

4

Communication

I awoke to a brilliant dawn. Birds in grand voice created a symphony of sound that mingled with the splash and gurgle of countless streams and springs that dotted the swamp. The magic of the morning, mingled with the excitement of the past night, jolted me into immediate consciousness. All the fatigue, both mental and physical, vanished. I had slept so soundly that I didn't even remember a dream. I remembered what Grandfather said about dreams; "Dreams are only important to those who do not know how to communicate with their Inner Vision on a daily basis. Dreams are only for those who do not listen on a conscious level to the worlds beyond self. It is then in desperation that the Inner Vision tries to communicate to them in dreams. To those who listen, there is no need for dreaming, except in times of need or warning."

With those thoughts, I realized why I had not dreamed anything important. It must have been because I had been in touch with my Inner Vision so much in the past few days. The night before I had dreamed about birds flying and of lofty places, but then there was a need, because I had not communicated purely with my Inner Vision. It felt good, not only the night's sleep, but somehow the feeling of being connected to all things, even Grandfather. As I began to think over the past days' events, especially to the communication I had had with Grandfather, my mind began to fill again with all manner of thoughts and questions. I had to find the final purity of Inner Vision, and I had to find out how to communicate to the outer worlds, not just to listen.

I knew that this quest, no matter how long it would eventually be, could not be approached through the mind. At this point in my life, especially with all the lessons learned over the past few days, I knew that it was not enough just to go with the quiet mind. There had to be more. All must be pure and guided by my Inner Vision. Most of all, I knew that there were still parts of the truth missing, and that is what I had to find. The first thing I decided to do was to go to the place of the sacred silence and contact my Inner Vision, and allow it to guide me. There was in my mind no other choice, for I could think of no logical approach to the problem. This quest could have no logical guides and I had to follow my heart.

I prayed and meditated before doing anything else. Each sunrise and sunset was a time for prayer, to relax, reflect, and plan. I then slipped into the place of silence and asked my Inner Vision what I should do. All I received was an image of me sitting exactly where I was, staring off into the swamp. The place was right, but the communication gave me no advice as to what I should do. I felt that the first thing that I should do was to approach the problem of purifying Inner Vision. Logically I knew that had to be purified before I could get a solid communication with anything. I somehow knew that if I tried to speak to the outer worlds, my voice and desires would be impure and vague. However, I still did not know how to find the purity, and my Inner Vision just said to wait where I was.

I sat in the area all day, my mind going out of control with all manner of thoughts and questions. The only relief would come when I would gaze into the place of quiet waters, and even then there was no real letup in the questions. My mind concentrated on the sacred silence. I knew that it was a vehicle and somehow a purifying agent, but I did not know how. Grandfather often spoke of the veil of the sacred silence, and mentioned veils beyond that silence. But up until now, we learned nothing except to touch the first veil and enter the silence. Yet I knew that there was something beyond that first veil. I could almost feel it, see it, yet not understand it or reach its power. It felt like the veils of mist in the swamps the night before. I had to reach the next veil, but I did not know how. As my mind began to relax, I started to remember my first lesson on the sacred silence this past summer.

I sat naked and alone, atop a small hillock, watching the late summer rains hissing through the pines and splashing on the lake, casting the surface into a misty frame. Not a breeze stirred the lower oaks, only the constant trembling of leathery leaves in sync with the raindrops. Birds were silent, except for some lone forlorn calls telling their friends of a good roost for the night. As the skies grew a deeper gray, a small chorus of frogs drifted on the thickening misty air, foretelling oncoming darkness. Most animals seemed to be hiding, waiting for the storm to pass rather than venturing out into the relentless rush of water. I felt bitter, left out of the natural order of things, as I sat unprotected, wet, and chilled by the oncoming night air. I fought back the small shivers that ran down my spine as I remained absolutely motionless. I was as silent and still as an old tree stump, at least to all outward appearances.

My inner rhythms and thoughts, however, were in a turmoil, fighting to mark time with my body and seeking that same inner stillness. My mind surged to fight the cold, to rise above stray thoughts, and to remember the reasons I was there. I had mastered the outward silencing of my body through many months of watching animals, but it was the inner silencing and stillness that Grandfather now wanted me to master. Consciously, it was easy to minimize the movement of the body, to control breathing and heartbeat and to allow the elements to flow through me rather than fight against them. But the inner stillness, the silencing of all thought, and the passing into the void of nothingness, of oneness, now seemed so impossible.

Grandfather called this inner silencing "passing into the veil," and to him it was the most important training Rick and I had yet received. To him the mastery of this skill was a kind of doorway, a rite of passage into the spiritual realms. Even though I was not yet nine years old, he thought it time enough for me to understand the veils of the spirit and their grander lessons and uses. I had found difficulty in controlling my body at first, and even in the process of fusion and inner voice, but they were easy compared to what I was trying to achieve here and now. I could see the reasons for most things that he taught, but for the veils, this profound silencing, he gave me no clear or understandable explanation. With some explanation I thought I would do much better, but I had no idea that these things could not be explained until I personally, actually touched the veil and understood what it was. All Grandfather said was that the silencing was what happened to the body when the stillness of the veil was touched. It was a perfect balance and equilibrium of nothingness, an absolute pure and fertile ground from which spiritual things would grow.

I remember, vividly, the conversation around the fire the night before I went to the hill. Grandfather was trying to explain the world of the spirit and how it was entered, but it could not be understood logically; it could only be understood by listening with the heart and abandoning the mind altogether. Grandfather lived in a world far different from the superficial world that most people existed in. He always seemed to be listening to voices far away, to things we could not hear or understand. His vision penetrated deeply into life, into levels we could only dream of. There was an aura he walked within that could not be experienced with the physical senses, and Rick and I desperately wanted to live in his world. He could read beyond the physical landscapes into the past or future and communicate with the spirits of nature in a real way. There was something about his every action that made us understand that he never walked alone but lived in a world far deeper than we knew. In his manner of speech and action, we knew that there must be much more than just the physical realms. We instinctively knew that there was a grander scheme of things, a force, a time, and a space beyond anything we could yet comprehend.

Grandfather had often described what he perceived as the plight of modern society, a society deceived by its shallowness into confusing material acquisition with fulfillment and yet in turn frustrated by its haunting sense of lack. There is a spiritual world beyond the material existence of modern man, a world of the unseen and the eternal, a world that most people never really understand or seek to know. Certainly, he said, there were the meager attempts by modern man to reach this spiritual world, but at best they were superficial, all too complicated with customs and traditions that no longer seemed to work. Most of modern society has lost its ability to see beyond the flesh and logical thinking, which is its guiding force. Yet society so desperately seeks fulfillment outside the realms of that superficial flesh. It seemed to Grandfather that after man acquires the comforts of flesh and heights of learning, he is then left lost and searching for more to life. He acquires more and more of the false gods of the flesh and mind, and he soon finds that the acquisitions of the flesh can give him no more. He seeks wilder forms of entertainment and toys, and nothing fulfills his most desperate yearnings or the emptiness inside of him.

Grandfather felt that somewhere in man's ancient history, society lost its communication with the spiritual world and with the spirit-that-moves-in-all-things, the life force. Grandfather knew that man was a duality, part logical and physical, but mostly spiritual. The problem is that man has concentrated on developing the logical mind, while allowing the spiritual consciousness to atrophy. Grandfather felt that man found it difficult to deal in the realms of the spirit and sought the logical, as it was more provable, probable, and less work. This pursuit of the logical then followed mankind through the centuries and into modern times, where now man believes only in things manifest in science and knows nothing based on faith. Thus logical man began to persecute and eradicate all who dealt in the spiritual, considering them pagans, insane, or lunatics. The spiritual way of life interfered with man's science and explanation, and showed the shallowness of society's meager attempt at being religious.

Grandfather clearly showed us how society today has become lopsidedly strong in logical things but weak and ineffective in the matters of the spirit. Modern man, then, is but half a person, unable to comprehend the spiritual world, or the intensity of real faith. His world has become shallow and unfulfilling. His desperation now has brought him to the brink of destruction. His thirst for fulfillment through logic, science, and technology has made the Earth a graveyard for his grandchildren. He has removed himself from the Earth and has become an alien on his own planet. Without the connection to the Earth and her laws, he can never know fully the spiritual worlds. And so Grandfather began to guide us away from the spiritual world of society and to the greater world of the spirit and the life force, guiding me to that hill where I now sat, so desperately trying to break free of the shackles of society's demands.

To modern man what I was attempting to do would be called meditation, but it was far greater than what he considered meditation. Grandfather had taught me to meditate many months before. First he had taught meditation through movement. The combination of fox-walking and wide-angle vision, plus the easy-flowing motion and absolute concentration on nature would produce a wondrous meditation. Other times he would have us sit and watch a track very carefully, until there was nothing but us and the track, until there was no consciousness of outer dimension. The track in essence had become our mandala, and the closeness to the Earth produced an absolute meditation. These meditations we knew very well, for they were at the seat of our power, the power of Inner Vision, of primal mind, and of absolute body control. But what Grandfather now wanted was far greater than any meditation. It was the absence of all thought, of consciousness of time, place, gravity, or body. It was an absolute nothingness, an equilibrium, and a limitless void. The veil was the absence of self, totally, and absolute purity of existence and nonexistence.

It was in this void, this veil, that Grandfather said all things of the spirit would be found. It was there that we would have total understanding and transcend the physical plane of man's existence. It was there that the primal self could be found; it was the abiding place of the life force, the spirit-that-moves-in-all-things, and all the spirits that inhabit our worlds. It was also where we could find all knowledge, create realities, and touch the Creator. In this veil was the apex of the power and the world of the shaman. Here was the world we should live in, for it is the grandest and greatest part of man's existence. Here and only here can man find absolute peace and the deepest meaning of life.

I so desperately wanted to penetrate that veil as I sat shivering on that hill. I could feel myself slip in and out of reality, but my mind would never fully let go. There was always something there, something left to stand in my way and yank me back from the brink of nothingness. With each surge back to reality, I tried harder to break into the veil, and the harder I tried, the more difficult it became. As the night skies closed in fully, I completely lost control of my body and began to shiver uncontrollably. There was no turning back into myself, and I was cast off the hill.

I remembered walking back to camp, heartbroken that I did not accomplish what Grandfather had asked. I remembered vividly what he had said. "Trying creates impossibilities, letting go creates what is desired. You believe that penetrating the veil is impossible, because that is what you have been told to believe. You have created that reality based on other people's beliefs that there can be no world of spirit. Somehow, you think that it must be difficult to enter this realm and that you must suffer and try hard to get there. This then is what you have created. But when you have absolute faith, learn to let go completely and purely, then, and only then, will you touch the veil." The walk back to my quest area had filled my head with all manner of thought as I contemplated the word "trying."

I thought deeply about what Grandfather had said. As I concentrated and searched out each apparent and deeper meaning, I lost consciousness of my body and my place. There was nothing in my world other than his words and my thoughts about them. Eventually these things slipped away, and I found myself floating in a void of absolute darkness, having no awareness of time or place, or even an existence outside the world. Though it was only for a moment, it felt like an eternity that I was there, where time had stood still. As I opened my eyes to the night, I felt a deep sense of relaxation wash over me. I felt pure, my mind free and absolutely clear. I was there physically, but then again, I wasn't there, at least not as I normally felt. As I gazed across the piney landscape toward the lake, I understood many things, things I could have never known by just the physical senses. I saw rhythms and cycles, the nuances of nature combining and creating a splendid force. I became part of that force. I could feel myself move within wilderness and wilderness move within me. At once I knew where all things were, physical and spiritual, form and space, action and reaction. I was really here, now, and conscious of the spirit-that-moves-in-all-things in a real way for the first time.

My mind returned to this current place in time, to the quiet waters, and to this Vision Quest. Since then, I have learned so much about this world of the veil we now call the sacred silence. I understood that the veil was what had to be passed through when we entered the world of silence. That veil, in essence, was the transcending of the physical self, the logical mind, and our fleshly connection to the world. Certainly there was a purity, but now I knew that there had to be deeper levels, deeper veils, as Grandfather had told me so long ago. The words "letting go," not "trying," still thundered through my mind. I thought that what must be true then, must also be true now.

Even with all the events I could clearly remember from the past, I could not see a clear way of going deeper into the sacred silence. What I was attempting to do now was to go beyond what I had learned and practiced for the past year. Not trying, I knew, would be a big part of it, as would belief and the act of transcending self. I had to somehow go deeper into the turbulence of the deep water, and the only clear path seemed to come from my vision in the tree. I had to rise above myself in order to transcend self. Somehow, I had to climb that internal tree, if there was such a tree. I had to find a way of going inward so that it really moved me outward and beyond self, expanding and purifying my spiritual consciousness.

At this point I felt lost in my mind, with no direction or place to go. There was certainly nothing logical that I could do, nor would my Inner Vision answer. All I knew was that every time I went to the Inner Vision I would see myself sitting exactly as I was, staring off into the swamp. The only difference I could tell between the Inner Vision and my flesh reality was that when I had the image of myself, it was at night. I could plainly tell that the place where I sat, though foggy and dark, was by the quiet waters, for the water and the shape of the area were easily visible. Possibly, I thought, it meant that I might have to wait until nightfall before any more was revealed to me.

Night had not fully come and I could see a clear reflection of myself and the oncoming night skies in the water's surface. It was then that I got a very weird sensation—nothing planned, but spontaneous. For just a moment, I lost dimension and place and could not decide if I were really seeing my reflection in the water or if it was me looking from the water to my physical self. The experience became so intense that I lost my equilibrium for a moment and almost fell into the water. The splashing of my hand by the water's edge pulled me back to my physical consciousness.

I was at once frightened and fascinated. Never before in my life had I experienced such a conflict in duality, where I didn't know where I really was. It felt so real and valid, yet seemed so accidental. It just happened and I didn't know why. All I knew was that every time I tried to reexperience the feeling it fell short of reality. It was then that I decided to sit back down and think things through. I began to run through all the events immediately leading up to the experience, but nothing seemed to make any sense. It was then that I realized I had entered the sacred silence before the experience, though the entry was more by accident than by choice. I wondered to myself if that was the only thing that was needed to reexperience the imagery and have it feel real.

I decided that I should go into a deep sacred silence, and take my time so that I could be as free as possible from myself. This way my mind would reach a deep state of purity. Then I would try and reach back to the experiences and see if I could recapture that bizarre reality. I first began the process of clearing my mind to the pure reflection, free of thought, like the reflection of the pond. I began to lose myself, to a point of deep silence, where the flesh was transcended. It was then that my Inner Vision hammered through to me in a very profound and real way. I began to imagine myself wandering across the mud flats that lay beyond the quiet pond. I visited places I had never been, and even imagined that I had found a deer skull with a deformed antler that pointed downward. It wasn't a feeling of seeing myself wandering, but actually wandering in all its reality.

I began to feel a sense of freedom and detachment from the world. Vast realms seemed to open before me and the forests and swamps came alive with animals and spirits, all watching me wander. I felt so free and pure, the guiding force of my Inner Vision strong and pure. So, too, as I walked, I began to pass through misty veils, and with each imagined passage I felt more free and pure. Here there were no restrictions, no time or place, and here all things seemed possible. The communication between flesh and spirit, between nature and man, became absolute and powerful. There were no doubts in the communication because it was at once real and reciprocating. I walked on, finally coming to a part of the swamp that felt evil, and immediately I was cast back into my physical consciousness with a shock.

I jumped from the sitting position without thought, my body stiff and sore from holding that position for so long. What I experienced was incredible, for I felt as if I had really lived it, yet I knew that it was my imagination. I was still elated because I had achieved what I was looking for, the purification of Inner Vision. Even though I had imagined the journey, I still understood clearly what it was telling me. I had to reach deep inside of the sacred silence, beyond the surface, and deep into the depths of turbulence where the spiritual waters could then be stilled. I felt so good, so enlightened, and I wanted to run and tell Grandfather, but my Inner Vision begged me to sleep. No sooner was my head against the flesh of the Earth than I was asleep.

I awoke to a gray dawn. Though the skies did not appear to carry any rain, it still looked threatening, and the day was warm. Hardly a breath of wind could be felt. I felt so good, so at peace, that I just sat and enjoyed the dawn landscape with its constant ebb and flow of life. I stood to leave the area and go back to camp, but again my Inner Vision held me there. It did not feel right to leave. What did feel good was to explore the swamp and mud flats. I had never been there before, except in my imagination, and I really wanted to see what it looked like. It felt so good to finally leave the area of the quiet waters, but it was much like leaving an old friend.

As I began to cross the mud flat area I had the strong feeling that I had been there before. Though the landscape looked very familiar, I knew logically I never explored beyond the place of quiet waters. Certainly I had been above and below the quiet waters area, but not on the flats. It is just too difficult normally to cross mud-flat areas, and this one was no exception. The further I traveled, however, the more I began to realize that somehow I definitely knew the landscape. I even knew where the cross logs lay before I got to them. This baffled me to a point where I began to wonder if another mud flat I had been in was similar to this one.

As I pushed on, I began to wonder if somehow I had really traveled this landscape, and it wasn't just my imagination. It was exactly as I had pictured it to be last night in my mind. There was no difference between this landscape in its flesh reality and that which I had imagined. Then it occurred to me that I could have easily looked across the mud flats a few days before when I was up in the tall tree. I knew that the mind never forgot anything and I would have certainly cast my gaze across the flats, though I do not remember any detail. I began to accept that explanation as the only alternative; that is, until I reached the small thickets and islands at the far end. Just as I did when I imagined the trek the night before, I crawled up on an island and there, partially hidden by some brush, I found the deer skull with the bent antler that pointed to the ground.

I could not believe my eyes. My thoughts became overwhelmed with excitement, to a point where I could no longer think clearly. I wheeled around and looked back in the direction of the quiet waters, but they were well hidden by a high wall of brush. I then looked up to where the huge grandfather tree would be, but the whole tree was hidden on the horizon by other tall cedar trees. I could not have seen this skull from that tree! I hardly remember what happened from that point on other than that I wandered back across the mud flats carrying the skull. I was in a daze, almost a stupor of disbelief. As I traveled back to the quiet waters, I kept looking for the tall tree, but it never became visible until I was nearly at the waters. I could not have seen the flats from the tree at all. As I made my way along the edge of the quiet waters and back into my sit area I had the overwhelming need to talk to Grandfather. I knew that he would know what really happened.

When I sat down to rest in my sit area, I had the feeling of being watched. It was as if something was behind me, watching my every move. At once, I got the image of Grandfather standing behind me and whipped my head around. There behind me stood Grandfather, smiling, that usual smile that told me that he knew exactly what I was feeling. He simply said, "Yes, the Inner Vision also allows us to take spirit journeys, but now is not the time or the place to discuss such things, for this will come later. What you must do now is to work on the communication with the worlds of Inner Vision, so that your voice, your desires, are clear and strong. Yes, Grandson, you did see the skull as your spirit wandered the mud flats. It was not your imagination. But again, another time, for you have work to do." With that he wandered off, leaving me tormented by my thoughts.

What does he mean that this is not the time or the place, I thought. How was I going to concentrate on communication when he had just told me that I had made a spiritual journey? My first spiritual journey—and it had been a powerful success. What Grandfather had just told me confirmed my deepest beliefs and fears, and I was so overwhelmed that I cried like a baby. Yes, right now was not the time and place, for I was just too excited and overwhelmed by the whole experience. As I tried to race back over all the events in my mind, the deep feeling of wrongness hammered into my thoughts, to a point where I could not even think of spirit journeys. In frustration, I resolved to focus my attention on that communication which Grandfather had directed me to. I knew deep inside that must be mastered first.

The few communications I had over the past few days were more by accident than by design. Each time I had communicated with Grandfather through the Inner Vision, it had been so spontaneous, almost out of my control. It felt as if it was directed by a force far outside myself. I know that I did not consciously will the communication, and that was my problem. How could I consciously will the connection, and what chain of events would ultimately lead up to that communication? Those were a few of the more pressing questions on my mind. Again, I did not know where to start searching for the answers. All I knew was that it could not be through the mind, but through the Inner Vision.

I remembered that Grandfather had told me that Inner Vision reaches to the deeper self, to the world of the spirit-that-moves-through-all-things, and to the world of spirit. Knowing that, I decided I would try to communicate with the huge old grandfather cedar tree that grew by the edge of the quiet waters. I figured that I was close to this tree because I had climbed it and it had taught me so much. I moved closer to the tree and sat at the base and gazed up its trunk and to the uppermost branches. Certainly I felt close to this tree, and was thankful for the lessons that it taught me, but my looking, gazing, and staring, produced nothing in the way of any communication. For some reason it just didn't feel right.

I ignored the wrongness feeling and tried again, but again there was no communication beyond the physical beauty of the tree. Exasperated, I moved over to the water's edge and gazed into its quiet surface. The water was still and beautiful as always, but besides that there was nothing in the way of deeper communication. Surely, I thought, this water has something more to teach me, for it has been the center of so many teachings. I passed aside my feelings of wrongness and tried again, but to no avail. The water stood mute, almost in a mocking way.

I began to think that possibly it was not working because I had failed to enter the veils of the sacred silence, thus obscuring any communication. Convinced that this was the problem, I went back to the tree and again sat at its base. I relaxed, and slipped deep into the place of silence, almost as deep as I had been the night before when I took my spirit walk. The feel of the landscape and especially the tree had changed, but there was no communication. Nothing at all, except for the pure, expectant silence of the soul. I tried again, this time going deeper, but again there was nothing but the purity of spirit. Convinced now that I was not hearing the tree, I turned my attention to the quiet waters and entered the place of silence. There too, like the tree, was no communication. I grew very frustrated, almost angry.

As I moved back to the center of the quiet waters area, I began to lose my patience. I began to also think that all that I had learned was still not enough. Either I was not doing something right or there was another piece of the puzzle missing or overlooked. I could not understand how it had worked so well in the past, and now I could not communicate at all. To complicate things even more, my Inner Vision was of no real help, other than to tell me that everything I tried to communicate with was wrong. Again I went back through all the steps in my mind, trying to decide what, if anything, I had left out. I tried all manner of approaches through the rest of the day, but nothing seemed to communicate, or wanted to communicate with me. I felt that these things may not really have anything to say to me, as if I was unworthy of their time.

All day long I continued to try and communicate with the world of flesh and spirit but with no results. I tried the grandfather cedar tree, the quiet waters, the swamp, and many other things, but nothing spoke. Every time I tried and failed, my gut had the feeling of "wrongness." I really began to get angry and frustrated with the multitude of failures, now growing disillusioned with my Inner Vision and its ability to help. Finally, in desperation, I asked my Inner Vision what it wanted me to communicate with, rather than my dictating to it what I wanted. As soon as I asked, a clear image of Rick popped into my head.

The image appeared so suddenly that it took me by surprise. I hadn't really thought about Rick for the past several days because I had been so consumed by my searching. I began to wonder how he was doing, in that he was also working on the problem of Inner Vision. Unconsciously I began to slip into the place of silence and listen to the voice of my Inner Vision. I began to think of Rick again, and the image of him sitting downstream from where I sat filled my mind. I imagined myself sitting with him and talking. It would be so good, I thought, to talk to him and find out how he was doing. Possibly we could even discuss our successes and failures and put our minds together to find answers. Anyway, it would be good to have some company.

My mind began to drift back over all the events of the past several days, back even to the past year. Most of all I thought about the spirit journey I had the night before and all the questions I wanted to ask Grandfather. I don't know why, but I began to get filled with all manner of self-doubts, probably because of all the failures I had this past day. I began to think that the whole journey of spirit was just a coincidence. But then again, a skull like the one I found is rare and it would have been some remarkable coincidence. Still, my insecurities tugged at my gut and made me uncomfortable with any more thought about the Inner Vision and all that it entailed. I began to just enjoy the night on a physical level and let go of all else.

Brush rustled behind me by the trail and as I looked around, Rick appeared in my area. Without a word he sat down and asked me how I was doing. So, desperately wanting to talk to someone and unload all my insecurities, I began to tell him the story of the past several days, mostly of the Spirit Journey, and even to my failures and confusions of this day. As Rick looked at the deer skull he told me of his journeys to the Inner Vision. Ironically, not only did we have similar experiences, but we also were exactly at the same exasperating roadblock in learning. He too was in the process of trying to communicate and, by some miracle, was trying to communicate with me not even an hour ago. He told me that he was calling my name from his place of silence, but there was no answer. He said he had an urge to find me and had an image of us talking that just popped into his head. His Inner Vision had demanded that he find me.

I told him that I did not hear him calling my name, but I had the image of wanting to talk to him. I related the story of how it all came about and, to my delight, he said that he had been flooded by that exact same image, though it wasn't of his doing. We talked well into the night, trying to understand why my Inner Vision allowed me to call to Rick, but Rick could not call to me. We took things apart in our conversation, analyzed the techniques, and helped answer each other's questions. Yet we still could not decide how I had been able to communicate with Rick, but not he with me. In a glimmer of enlightenment, I finally had the answer. It wasn't a problem with Inner Vision, but rather how we had attempted to communicate. I had imagined, envisioned, the communication, but Rick had only used words.

It was so very simple. Grandfather had said that the Inner Vision does not communicate in words, but in signs, symbols, feelings, dreams, and waking visions. Why I had gotten success and Rick had not was I used the images and he used the words. That is why the image came to Rick so clearly but I did not hear him call my name. We both agreed that the communication could not be in words but through some kind of controlled imagery. Grandfather had often spoken of seeing things in his mind, calling it envisioning, and now it made sense why. At this point we both decided to try and communicate with the quiet waters and sat down side by side near its edge. We both slipped into the place of silence and began to communicate with the waters, creating all manner of images in our mind. We both met with failure.

We began to talk again, trying to decide what we did wrong. Almost at the same time we both felt that we had to talk to Grandfather, for we knew he would have the answers. Without a word to each other, I imagined Grandfather coming to us, little knowing Rick was doing the same thing. I could feel my gut uncoil and the feeling of "wrongness" vanished, and was replaced by a feeling that I had done something right. I looked over at Rick and he had a look on his face that told me he had done the same thing. Smiling at each other, we turned toward the trail and waited for Grandfather to arrive. No sooner had we both turned than Grandfather stepped into view.

He sat down by us, without a word at first. He had that look on his face that told us we now understood the power of communication. After a long moment he finally spoke to us and said, "You both have learned how to purify Inner Vision so that the messages are clear and powerful. However, distractions of the mind and body can make the message weak. Great care must be taken to go deep into the place of silence during these times of turmoil and distraction, otherwise the communication becomes impure. You have learned also that the sacred silence is the bridge to the outer worlds, a bridge which purifies. And so you have learned that communication works both ways. You have also learned that to send a voice to the outer worlds through Inner Vision, you must envision the communication, not talk, for the worlds beyond self do not speak in the tongues of man."

Grandfather paused for a moment, but did not allow any questions. He continued, "Now you question as to how to communicate. As you have found, it is not enough just to want to communicate with the worlds of nature and spirit. You may want it very badly, but that does not mean that any entity wants to communicate with you. It is spiritually arrogant to believe that every entity of Earth and spirit has something to say to you. Unless you are directed to communicate through your Inner Vision first, then all else will remain mute. There can be no communication. But when your Inner Vision draws you to something, then the communication is clear and strong. This is why you both failed to communicate with the waters. Right now the waters have nothing more to teach you. Possibly at some other time, and only when you are drawn to them through the power of Inner Vision, will they speak to you."

Grandfather paused for a while, waiting for our minds to assimilate all that he had taught. I knew exactly what Grandfather was talking about. The communications that I had that were a success came easily, spontaneously, and directed by Inner Vision. There was no "trying" necessary, for it just happened. Grandfather continued, "You just go about life as usual, not looking, but just remaining open to all the voices of the Earth and spirit. You will be drawn to communicate when the time is right and when something wants to teach you. But you must always walk openly and listen to the voice of your Inner Vision."

Grandfather continued, "Now it is time to explore the world of spirit, where at once you walk in flesh and at the same time walk in spirit. There are two ways to make any journey; one is on a physical level and the other is in the spirit. Both of you have borne witness to the impossible. You made imagined journeys only to find that you had somehow really taken that journey. The proof is in what you found when you took the journey again in the flesh. That you can not deny. It is not imagined but real, as you have proven to yourself. Now, the week is growing old and you must still explore this world of spirit travel. You must go back now to spending time alone, and to walk the spirit trail."

With that, Grandfather wandered out of camp, not long after I began to wander upstream. I knew that Rick was going to stay by the quiet waters, for that is what my heart told me. They would now teach him as they taught me. He would receive different lessons, for the quiet waters speak to each individual in a way he can understand. I had no idea where I was going to go, but I did not care. My Inner Vision would guide me to my next lesson and beyond—to wisdom I knew existed somewhere, though, for right now, out of reach.

5

Journeys of the Spirit

I walked well into the night, paying little attention to where I was going or to the fatigue that caused me to drag my feet and to occasionally stumble. My mind literally swam with all manner of thoughts, questions, and expectations. Before I began any new exploration of the spirit worlds, I wanted to make sure that I understood all the things I had learned. I did not want to make any mistakes. Time was growing short and in a few days I would have to return home for a week or more. It was always so difficult to practice spiritual things in a world away from the wilderness. There is no purity in man's world, only distraction and pollution, pollution of the spirit. I felt an urgency now, for I had to understand spiritual journeys before I went back home. I was too close now and I didn't want to chance losing what I had.

I began to think about the power of the Inner Vision. I could understand now why Grandfather had said that it was not only the voice of the world of nature and spirit, but also the very voice of the Creator. With the many successes and failures of the past days, I realized that the Inner Vision had never been wrong. Yes, at times it had been weak and impure, and at times I had interpreted the messages wrong, but in the final analysis it had never been wrong. After all that had gone on over the past days and all I had seen Grandfather do, I knew now why he would always consult his Inner Vision before doing anything. It was the main guiding force in his life and I wanted to make it mine. I could also finally understand why the Inner Vision was always followed even when the evidence on a physical level would dictate the opposite direction. The logical mind was fallible but the spiritual mind, the Inner Vision, was never wrong, only tainted sometimes by our impure thoughts.

After praying and honoring the Creator, I decided that I had to practice this spiritual travel. I felt that I had assimilated all the knowledge of the past days and now was ready, more than ready and eager, to practice what Grandfather had asked. I slipped deeply into the sacred silence and in my imagination, just like I had done before, I wandered through the swamp. Somehow the trip did not seem that real for I was not walking in my imagination but watching myself walk, as if from the outside. I never really could shift my consciousness inside my imagined spiritual body. There was a certain removal from the whole picture and the more I concentrated the more removed I became. It just wasn't real and my Inner Vision was of no help.

I emerged from my place of silence and back into my full physical consciousness. I then took a walk into the swamp, taking the same route I had imagined. Nothing appeared to be the same as I had imagined. Nothing was even close. Disappointed but undaunted, I went back to the area where I had been sitting and tried again. This time I took great care in getting to the place of silence and I concentrated fully on the imagery. Though it felt better, a little more real than the time before, there was still something missing. I just wasn't in the picture. I just wasn't there and I knew it. The physical trip to confirm my spiritual journey again produced utter failure, and now I became very frustrated. My Inner Vision still was of no help for it was neither pro nor con, only benign and unmoving.

It felt as though it no longer cared to communicate or cared if I failed or not.

By the time I got back to the sit area the sun had set. Clouds had moved into the distant horizon and appeared as smoke wafting from the huge fiery ball of sunset. Again the oncoming night had brought a feeling of relief for I had done so well before at night. I hoped now that it would help again. I continued making the imagined spiritual journeys followed by the physical journeys of confirmation, but they all met with failure. As it was with the day, the harder I tried the more removed from the imagined picture I became. These journeys felt more unreal than those of the day. Each time I tried to contact my Inner Vision, I was met with the same feeling, a feeling of complacency. I grew very frustrated because it felt as if my Inner Vision was inattentive or asleep.

Grandfather walked from the brush and sat down near me. He said, "Grandson, I know that you are frustrated and angry at yourself, but you did not listen to all that I had told you. In order to do anything it first must be directed by your Inner Vision. As you have witnessed when you tried and failed to communicate with the various entities of nature and spirit, there must first be direction from the Inner Vision. So, too, when we travel the realms of spirit. That too must be directed from a place outside of self."

"But," I said, "my Inner Vision has shut down or gone to sleep. Every time I have tried to travel in the spirit there has been failure."

Grandfather answered, "Inner Vision never sleeps. The reason it has not communicated to you on your spiritual journeys is that it is not yet time to take such a journey. There is no purpose and right now nothing calls you to take the journey."

Grandfather was right, there was no Inner Vision direction to my spirit journeys and, like my attempts at communication, the journeys had failed because there was no inner direction. What I didn't understand was what Grandfather had meant by purpose. That word had come up so many times before. In the silence, as Grandfather waited for me to digest what he had told me, I began to think back to the past winter when Grandfather had talked of purpose. At that time we had been trying to understand the way to walk in the spirit, where we could be protected from all things of the flesh. We had attempted and failed to complete a long journey which could only be done in the spiritual consciousness. It was then that Grandfather first spoke of purpose. A time and a conversation I remembered now so vividly.

We had asked Grandfather about entering the world of spirit and he answered saying, "I have taught you how to enter the world of spirit. What I must do now is to show you how to work within that world and allow that world to work within you. The cycle of man's existence is that the I and ego are a prison. Then there is the world of the life force. That which you already know. Beyond that world is the realm of the spirit, and we must learn to use the power of that world. You got to the world of the life force, the primal mind and instinct by concentrating on that world, letting go all logical thought, and through belief. It was a conscious effort, a dynamic meditation which brought you to the world of the sacred silence. This sacred silence became the vehicle which expanded your existence into the world of the spirit-that-moves-through-all-things.

"Now you must learn to enter the world of the spirit and to work within its power. It is a world which brings you closer to the sacred 'oneness.' For when a man becomes all circles and all cycles he is then one with all things. It is not enough to get into these realms but you must know how to work within each power, so that you become the power and the power becomes you. What good is it to dwell within a world if that is all you can do. Getting to that world is just the beginning, the vehicle, but what you do there begins the cycle of power. This world of spirit is closer to the Creator, it is the world where all healing is found, where there is no time or place, a world where the body no longer exists and you transcend all flesh. When we walk in spirit, the body then falls away, and there are no limitations. The body is protected then, through the spirit, and the spirit has fused with the body.

"To get to this world of spirit, you first must know where you are going. You then must believe that you can get there. It is the unwavering faith that becomes our doorway, and it is this faith which gives us power in the world of spirit. To enter the world of spirit, you must have purpose, and a purpose beyond the self. If the purpose is selfish, then the spirit realm cannot be entered."

Back then I had thought long and hard about what Grandfather had said. I could understand that to enter the spirit world, there would have to be a direction. The direction I knew now lay in the wisdom of Inner Vision. I also understood that there would have to be pure faith, for nothing is done outside oneself without that faith. What I didn't understand at the time was the purpose, a purpose without self. This then would not allow any exploration of the spirit world for practice and learning, for that learning is for the self.

I had asked Grandfather if we could enter the world of spirit just for the purpose of learning. He then had answered, saying, "If you were to try and enter the spirit world for your own personal learning, then the spirit world could not be entered. But if you entered that world with the purpose of bringing back what you knew to share that knowledge, then the purpose would be pure. If there is just self and no sharing, then the world is not yours. The spirits will know if your motives and heart are pure. That is why great care should be taken to define the purpose before an attempt is made to enter that world. This way, when the purpose is clear and powerful, we can easily enter that world."

I remember asking Grandfather how I could justify entering the world of spirit just to learn to undertake that long journey. I had asked if that too would not just be for self. He had answered, saying, "If the journey was your sole purpose, then you could not enter, but if it is something you can use to help another, then that world is yours."

Again I had thought about that purpose. How could I be sure if a purpose was really pure and free of self, and how could I ever use it to teach someone? How, I thought, could I make a difference in life by learning this, or was I just deluding myself? I could not see how walking that incredible journey could help anyone but me. It was then that Grandfather had broken into my thoughts, saying, "If you had to go and help someone who was many miles away, and you had to get to him using a journey such as this, would you make it there? Probably not, but if you did you would be too exhausted to be of any help. Living in the spirit helps us transcend the limitations of our own bodies so that the distraction of pain and exhaustion will not stand in our way. Ultimately, even in practice, you learn these things just to help someone. Your purpose then becomes pure and clear. Your purpose then transcends self."

I then asked Grandfather if we could use the fusion of spirit to save ourselves in a dire survival emergency, or would that be too much for self. He had answered, saying, "The purpose is still pure. It protects the temple of the Creator. Remember always, you are the temple of the Creator, as is everyone and everything else. The Creator dwells in all things, equally."

It was then that Grandfather continued with a certain warning in his voice, explaining the things that were important to me now as they were then. He had said, "A man who attempts to enter the spirit realm, the world of the unseen and eternal, and does not return to help others, then he has only selfish purpose. The spirit will be denied unto him. Thus if you attempt to run to wilderness and hide from your responsibility of helping others, you will never fully understand the power of the spirit worlds."

I remember asking Grandfather why so many people in the past ran to the wilderness. He had answered, saying, "Anyone can enter the world of spirit, especially in the purity of wilderness. The spirit world then speaks to each person individually, with more power being added unto those who seek that world for the enlightenment of others. Thus if man's purpose is to selfishly run away and seek spiritual enlightenment for himself, then the spirit world will not give much of its power. But to those who seek that world purely and with a grand purpose, beyond the self, the power will be freely given unto him."

I remember Rick asking Grandfather what good it was to live in wilderness, if someone could be given more power living in the world of man. Grandfather had answered saying, "It is in the purity of wilderness that we must learn, free from the distractions of man. It is wilderness that brings us close to the Creator and to the realities of life. Here in the bosom of Creation all spiritual things are born, for Creation is our temple, and it obeys the Great Spirit's every command. It is not a world built by the hands of man, or influenced by the laws of society. Once the learning process in wilderness is over, however, a man must make frequent journeys into the world of man to share what is taught by the purity of wilderness, for wilderness is where their spiritual fires were born. It is then, in wilderness, that man is given a choice. If he chooses to hide and seeks spiritual enlightenment only for himself, then his education is finished or limited at best. But for the one that leaves wilderness to give freely of the wisdom, there are no limits."

I remembered a long period of silence back then as I sorted through all the things Grandfather had taught. I thought it didn't seem fair to me that the power of the spirit world be given unequally. What Grandfather was saying was that if I chose to stay in the wilderness, then I would never fully know the powers of the spirit world no matter how badly I wanted that power. I would always remain an outsider. But if I chose to bring this knowledge to the world, then there would be no limits to that power. I couldn't see why both could not live equally in the power of spirit, especially if both were totally committed to spiritual enlightenment. I remember Grandfather's words back then, saying, "The power of the shaman, the power of the spirit world, is given only unto those whose love is strong for his fellowman. To know the spirit-that-moves-in-all-things is to know that if one part of that spirit is sick, lost, or searching, then all is sick. To work only for the self is to know not the spirit-that-moves-in-all-things. If one does not know that spirit, one does not know love, and thus cannot transcend self."

My mind rocketed back to this time and place as Grandfather's words broke the silence of my thoughts. He quietly said, almost in a whisper, "Grandson, it is now you realize that if the command comes from the purity of Inner Vision, then the purpose is pure. For the voice of Inner Vision comes from worlds outside of self, and thus can contain no self. This is why you must wait for the Inner Vision to speak to you and tell you when a spiritual journey is necessary. All other attempts will fail, for attempts that go against Inner Vision are impure and full of self. As I have told you before, the world of spirit cannot be easily entered when the motives are strictly selfish. You must wait until the Inner Vision guides you to take such a journey. Then and only then can you accomplish what you desire."

With those words, Grandfather slipped away into the night. Inner Vision directed, I thought, and the purity comes along with it, for it is the Inner Vision which is also pure. I could understand now what my problem had been. As with the communication failures with the entities of nature, if there is no Inner Vision direction, then it will fail and did fail repeatedly. It was nice to know, however, that the Inner Vision would give me purpose beyond self, for that is a question I had struggled with since the past winter. Now at least I had some help with that problem because so often it was difficult to remove the self from many of my spiritual endeavors. Now, as Grandfather had said, all I had to do was to sit and wait for the Inner Vision to move me to spiritual travel.

As the night deepened and grew very late I let go of all searching and just relaxed. I knew that I needed a break from all the learning, so I just slipped into my place of silence to clear my head. No sooner had I reached the silence when a powerful image came hammering through to me. It was the horrible image of a small pack of dogs stalking the quiet waters area where Rick sat. So too did I get the immediate image of Rick, unaware of the approaching dogs. The image so terrified me that I jumped out of the place of silence and back into conscious reality, carrying with me the image and the fear. All

I knew was that I had to get to Rick right away and warn him. I tried to get up from where I sat but this time my Inner Vision hammered me back to the ground and literally held me there. I began to panic, but for some reason I could not move. It was like being pinned to the ground.

I struggled for a while, almost out of control with panic, when I finally realized that this was my chance to travel in the spirit. It was a dangerous chance because if I failed, Rick could be badly hurt. In desperation I searched my Inner Vision as it spoke to me very clearly. I had to go, not in flesh, but in spirit. Resolved to take this dangerous route, I sat back up in my area, the ground finally releasing me. I rushed to get into the sacred silence, but I was amazed at how easily it was obtained. Normally, under stress conditions, the sacred silence is quite difficult to reach and takes a lot of time to get as deep as I was now. I imagined myself walking out of my body and heading down the trail to where Rick sat.

This time the imagery was so real. There was no need to try, for it happened so easily, as if driven by a force far outside of myself. I was no longer back in my physical body but fully entrenched in what I perceived as my imagined spiritual body. I was totally there. I could feel the ground, the sounds of the night, the heaviness of the air, the aromas, and the feeling of movement, all of which created a reality beyond even being there in the flesh. I traveled quickly and easily. I moved through brush like a whisper, never moving a single leaf. There was no sound from my feet, nor did the many animals I passed flee at my approach. I felt so alive, free, and pure. It was as if all things were possible, with none of the limitations of the flesh.

I quickly reached Rick's sit area by the quiet waters but he was nowhere in sight. I looked around desperately and all I could find was my deer skull with the bent antler hanging from some branches. I could sense the closeness of the dogs, but I could not find Rick. It was then that I imagined that if he was not there then wherever he was he would be safe, so I began the journey back to my sit area. Again I traveled quickly, and without restriction. However, I was still concerned to the whereabouts of Rick and the stalking dogs. As I imagined myself walking along the final trail that would lead back to my sit area, I sensed someone coming. I imagined myself standing and waiting along the trail's edge when suddenly Rick walked up to me, looking upset.

I was absolutely shocked by the image of Rick for I had not planned it, for it had just happened. Without hesitation he said, "I couldn't find you in your area. Dogs are coming from the far edge of your swamp and I felt that you were in danger." I then told Rick that I too had seen dogs stalking his area, but I couldn't find him there. Rick said, "That's because I moved to the other side of the quiet waters." I told him also that I wasn't in my original area but deeper in the swamp. I also said that we had both better get back to our bodies and protect them. That statement really shocked me, for I did not know where it came from. Somehow my imagination was working overtime and coming up with things that I could never have dreamed up.

I imagined myself running back to my sit area in a panic. I could see the dogs stalking me. I ran so hard that I flew right into my body and my physical body responded by immediately climbing a tree, without a question as to whether the incident was real or imagined. As I clutched the upper limbs of the tree it was a while before I could separate my physical consciousness from my imagined spiritual consciousness. Finally regaining a full physical foothold on reality, my logical mind came back, and it was then that I realized that there was a rather large group of dogs running around the base of my tree. Their barks and growls were real enough to make me understand that part of what I had imagined must have been true. I didn't care whether Rick had really talked to me or not, for he had saved me and I somehow hope that I had saved him. The reality of the moment preempted any further thought.

The dogs lingered for nearly two hours until they finally slipped off into the night, their barks slowly disappearing in the distance. I clung to the tree until my Inner Vision told me that it was safe to leave, and by the time I reached the ground so had the morning sun. The first thing I did when I got out of the tree was to sit down for a few moments and try and make sense out of all that had happened. I still didn't know whether the trip was real or imagined. All I knew was that somehow it had saved my life. The most pressing question came from the fact that when I first got up to climb the tree and escape the dogs, I felt as if I was coming out of a dream. Possibly, I thought, it was my dreams and nothing more that saved my life. But what I couldn't fully understand was why I had such a hard time separating dream from reality.

I decided that I should go over and see how Rick was doing; after all, he in some way had saved my life. As I walked, I really began to doubt the validity of the experience, feeling that it was nothing more than a dream, rather than the imagined spiritual experience. After all, I thought, it was the symbolism of the dream that comes from the Inner Vision and it was probably the Inner Vision that sent the message, not Rick. I began to approach Rick's area, cautiously, just in case there was a glimmer of validity in what I had dreamed. I walked into the area but Rick was nowhere in sight. As I looked, I spotted my deer skull hanging from some lower branches of a tree, just as I had imagined it in my dream. This really shook up my initial thoughts about it being a dream.

Branches rustled high overhead and Rick shouted down, "Thanks for the warning old friend." He sounded as doubtful as I had been, but in the searching manner of his voice, I could tell that he was dropping his theory of dream. As he got to the ground, I thanked him too, for saving my life. We talked for hours, almost through the entire day, and didn't leave his sit area until sunset. We found that we had both envisioned the same thing. Every detail, even the conversation we had was the same. I found too that Rick hung the skull in the tree earlier in the day, as I had seen it in my imagination. So too had we both not been in the areas where we were supposed to be when the other came to warn of the danger. The whole thing was too miraculous for further discussion, and at the same time we both knew that we had to go and talk to Grandfather.

We reached Grandfather's camp at full dark and found him sitting by the fire waiting for us. Finally, after all that had happened over the past several days, I understood how he could know what was going on, even to the questions that we were about to ask. For him, it was as simple as being in constant touch with his Inner Vision. It was comforting to know that since we had met Grandfather he had always been there for us. Either in the flesh or in the spirit, it made little difference, for they were both as powerful. So many things came together in my mind, so many questions that had festered over the past few years were finally answered. So much was clarified, but again, there were new questions, and so much more to learn. At that very moment, however, if I were to learn nothing else, I had now understood and used one of the grandest gifts in life: the gift of Inner Vision.

We sat down near him, waiting for him to speak, knowing that he would know exactly what we needed. He smiled at us both for a long time, with a look that said he was very pleased with our progress. Then his face hardened a bit as he spoke to us, saying, "Again you did not listen fully to your Inner Vision. You have been both so caught up in your success that you overlooked the yearning of the Inner Vision that told you both to go on. I have nothing that I can teach you now. Not until you complete what your Inner Vision dictates can you understand all that I must tell you. You both have to go now, back to the quiet waters together, and find out what it is that you have overlooked. Remember that joy and success, at times, can also be a distraction that stands in the way and weakens Inner Vision."

Somehow I felt that it had been wrong to go to Grandfather at this time and I knew that Rick felt the same way. We were just so overjoyed with our success and the many questions that we had that we ignored the Inner Vision that tugged at both of us. We walked back to the quiet waters in silence, both searching our deeper selves for what it was that our Inner Vision had been telling us to do. It wasn't until we got back by the quiet waters and both sat down that anything truly stirred inside of us. Before I said a word, Rick said, "My Inner Vision tells me that we have to take some kind of a spirit trip together, but Grandfather had said nothing about traveling together, and I suspect that it may be wrong." I confirmed what Rick had said because I too had felt the same thing, but, like Rick, I didn't think at the time it could be true, or even possible.

We both discussed the possibility of taking some sort of spiritual journey together, but we had no idea of how it could be accomplished. It had been hard enough to take the previous journeys by myself, in that the imagination had to be so powerful that there could be no distraction. It had to feel and be real. The only real time we had met on the spiritual trail was more by accident than by choice. There was no struggle to it, for it had just happened spontaneously. However, we thought, if it could happen by accident once then it could possibly happen again. It felt good to both of us to go on this spiritual journey together, so at least half of the battle was won. We knew that when the Inner Vision wanted something it was easy to accomplish.

For the next hour or so we talked, thought, and stared off into the night. The hesitation in undertaking our spiritual journey together was due to the fact that we did not know where to go or how both of us could go. We discussed all the possibilities. First we thought that we would both imagine each other being there, but it was hard enough to concentrate on the self, far less two people. We discounted that way because it just didn't feel right. We both decided that when we imagined the trip we would do it alone, but both go to the same area. That way, if the other showed up in the imagination it would be by accident. That problem resolved, the next thing we had to do was to find out where we should go—a place that felt good to both of us. We knew that it had to be the same place, otherwise we would fail.

It did not take us long to locate a place that we both felt good about, though we did not know why. It was the place that I had gone to in my imagination shortly after finding the deer skull. It was the same place that scared the hell out of me and catapulted me back into my physical consciousness. I had no idea why my Inner Vision would direct me to go back to a place where I felt uneasy, a place that reeked of evil. Rick too had chosen this same place. He had gone there the day before in his imagination and had been driven out with the same sort of panic and sense of evil. We knew we had to obey the Inner Vision, but we put off the trip further, out of fear. It seemed the more we hesitated, the more our Inner Vision drove us to take the journey. Finally, we decided that we had better get it over with since the night was growing very late and dawn would be fast approaching.

We sat side by side, by the edge of the quiet waters, and gazed off into the direction of our imagined travels. I could feel the deep apprehension arise within me but that was over-shadowed by my Inner Vision's drive to go on. We both slipped deep into the place of silence as we quieted our logi-cal minds. Almost immediately I found myself, or imagined myself, walking out in the middle of the swamp. It was so real that I completely lost the concept of my physical body. As I walked toward the chosen area, I could sense something moving up ahead. At first I was anxious, but soon found to my surprise that it was Rick, wandering just up ahead. I called to him as I ran up to his side. We said little as we walked, other than to discuss the fact that in our imagined journey it was full daylight, yet back in our physical reality it was night. We couldn't understand why, and for a moment we thought that we had really failed.

Deciding that it didn't matter what time of day our imagina-tion said it was, we pushed ahead. As the journey progressed, there was a sense of reality to it that I had never experienced before in the past few journeys. In a way, I grew worried about the safety of my physical body, but that soon passed. As we walked I noticed that there was a strange feeling and look to the landscape. Yes, it was similar to the real landscape, but slightly different. I could sense things moving out in the distance that I knew were not animal. Strange lights, sounds, or gauzy apparitions would appear out of the corner of my eye. But looking directly at them they would disappear; only the sense of their presence lingered. It was at once fascinating but at the same time strangely frightening. Two landscapes, one real, one imagined, similar but very different.

We walked on, rarely speaking, and slowing our pace as we neared our destination. Both of us could feel the fear erupt into our throats as the sense of evil began to increase. Along with the ever-increasing sense of evil was the increasing power of our Inner Vision driving us on. At times they both struggled against each other, at once wanting to run and at the same time to go ahead. We both now stalked toward the area, as if the quietness of the stalk would prevent the evil from finding us and keep us safe from the imagined danger. We could see a clearing up ahead, at the far side of the swamp, and instantly I knew that was where I was supposed to go. Up until this time we only knew the direction and the area in general; now we knew the exact place.

We cautiously entered the clearing, the sense of danger and evil now pounding in our heads. I walked on the edge of running panic but, as usual, my Inner Vision held me there. We looked across the clearing. Nothing grew from its surface. It was as if nature had forgotten this circle, for there was only sand and gravel. Not even the sounds of the natural world seemed to penetrate this place. In the center of the circle, his back toward us, was what we assumed to be a man. He was hunched over, apparently asleep. I knew deep inside that this man, this thing, was not a man at all but some kind of evil presence. I looked toward Rick and I could tell by his expression that he was feeling the same thing about this presence that I was.

As we gazed in horror at this thing, it turned abruptly toward us, as if for the first time realizing that we were there. The face of this beast was so horrible that I couldn't look. Its head was all that we could see—rotted and maggot-ridden flesh barely covering bone, more skull than anything else. It began to

seethe and growl, the likes of which I had never heard in
reality. Suddenly, like a pouncing cat, it leapt toward us in
a frenzy of spitting and growling. We could take no more
and ran terrorized back toward the quiet waters. At first we
thought it was following but when I looked around it appeared
to be confined to the clearing. However, its growls and screams
carried to all edges of the swamp and fed our frenzied panic
even more.

Suddenly Rick and I both emerged from our imaginations,
physically screaming. The panic had followed us all the way
back into our reality. I looked around for the thing, but the first
fissure of light from the advancing dawn told me that it had all
been imagined, or a dream. The swamp and everything around
lay as it always had. It was then that I remembered Rick's
screams as I had come out of my dream. Those screams were
reality and not imagined. We sat for a long time, catching our
breath, before we could even talk to each other. The whole
experience was so terrifying and so real that it took quite
some time to come back to a full reality. I know that my
mind was trying to explain it as a dream or a free flow
of my imagination, possibly even a hallucination. But I still
could not explain the fact that Rick and I both awoke from it
together.

We began to talk about the experience, reluctantly at first,
for the fears and anxiety had not yet vanished. We were both
amazed to discover that we had experienced the same things.
We remembered conversations, though not many, and even as
to where we had walked. The clearing was vivid in both of our
minds, and Rick's description of this thing we saw was exactly
as I experienced, even to the panicked run. We talked for the
better part of sunrise, the light of day driving away the fears
that were still locked in the darkness of our minds. We felt
more relaxed, but questions pounded into our conversation.
We could not understand why we had imagined the journey
as being the day, rather than the night. Most of all, we could
not figure out why our Inner Vision would lead us there in the
first place.

As we got up to leave the quiet waters area and head back to Grandfather, we were both hit hard by the "wrongness" of it all. We glanced at each other and, without saying a word, we both knew what we had to do. We had to retrace our trip in full physical reality. This did not appeal to either of us in even the slightest way. If in fact that place was out there, then so must be that thing. We were not sure as to the power of this entity or if it could exist in our flesh reality. Reluctantly, because we so wanted to talk to Grandfather, we headed out into the swamp to find the clearing we had found in our imagination. There was still the feeling that it could all have been a dream, no matter how real it seemed at the time.

We slowly worked our way across the swamp. The travel of the imagination is so much easier than the travel of the flesh. It took hours to do what we had done in only moments of the imagination or dream, I still was not sure which. We went beyond the area we both knew in flesh reality and on into the areas we only imagined. As we walked we began talking a lot, nervous talk about the landscape, because we both saw the exact landscape in our travels. It was exactly the same, except we did not feel the presence of anything other than animals. As we drew closer to the clearing we began to slow our pace. My anxiety created such a nervousness that I began to physically shake.

We entered the clearing as we had before, and just as we imagined there was nothing growing. It was just a vague circle of sand and gravel with no tracks to decorate its surface. It was as if nature had turned its back on this place. We edged around until we could get a good view of the entire clearing, but when we could finally see it all clearly, to our relief, there was no being in its center. The only thing was an old blackened tree stump, marking the place where we saw the thing. We approached the stump very cautiously and we both sensed a deep evil. When we got to within ten feet of the stump our hearts began to pound and I could feel a terror overtake me. Suddenly our Inner Vision let go of its hold on us and we ran blindly from the area, just as we had done the night before.

We didn't even stop at the quiet waters, but ran right past and into Grandfather's camp.

Grandfather was in his sacred place praying when we found him. We dared not disturb him, for that was a universal law. No matter how pressing an issue, no one was to be disturbed while in the sacred areas. Without opening his eyes or moving his head he motioned us to join him in the area. He then went back to his prayers, for what seemed forever. While he prayed we realized what he was telling us to do. In our haste to discover the spiritual traveling and our subsequent success, we had forgotten our morning and evening time of prayer. It was also law, that no matter what we were doing or how pressed we were for time, there was always time taken to honor the Creator. There was rarely an exception to this rule and now was not the time to argue the point.

Grandfather finally looked up from his prayer. He looked toward us and saw that we had finished. In fact, I do not think that I had prayed for more than a few moments. He said in a rather matter-of-fact voice, "So, the Creator gives you the gift of Inner Vision and of Traveling in the Spirit, and you cannot honor Him with a little of your time. Inner Vision is your birthright, everyone's birthright, granted, but we can only understand that voice through the Creator's love. If we do not take the time to honor and thank the Creator for all of these gifts, then why should we assume that he will help us in times of need or confusion?" Without a word, Rick and I closed our eyes and went deep into prayer. A deep prayer of thanksgiving, and we passed all the pressing issues out of our minds.

Finally Grandfather spoke again, saying, "You now understand the wisdom of journeying through the spirit. Though you still cling to your disbeliefs, you cannot deny that you have borne witness to the fact that the lands you have seen in your imagination exist also in flesh reality. What you do not understand is why and how all of this is possible. You assume that you imagined or dreamed the journey, yet when you explored in the flesh you found them to be almost the same, yet different. This, I know, has confused you, but that is the way it must be right now until you fully understand the way of the spirit world. It is not important whether you believe that you have imagined or really lived it, for it is the end result, the final analysis, that makes it real. You have known things that you could not know on a physical level."

Grandfather continued, "As I have told you so many times, man is a duality. Man lives in the world of flesh and at the same time lives in the world of spirit. The reason that society does not see this duality is because it does not know or accept the realms of spirit or Inner Vision, even though it is their birthright. So too have I said that man only becomes 'one' when he walks in both the spirit and the flesh, and can see and exist within both worlds. The world that you saw is not just flesh reality, but also its spiritual counterpart. That is why you could feel various entities moving far off in the landscape. That is why you could see the demon while in the spiritual world but not in the physical world. For a moment in time and space, you have walked the duality and have seen both worlds. That is the world that you should live in always, walking between both worlds, and becoming 'one' with them both."

Grandfather fell into a state of silence and closed his eyes. I suspect that it was to give us a chance to digest all that he had said. I could easily understand all that he taught, but what I couldn't understand was why our Inner Vision had led us to a place of evil. I could not see what that could have taught us. Without waiting for the next obvious question, Grandfather spoke again, saying, "When you enter the world of spirit, it is only similar to our world of flesh. There is a strange and beautiful difference. It is not only a world of images of our flesh reality but there too is a vast spiritual domain where the entities of the spirit world exist. You felt them moving and you knew them to be real. So too does the world of evil exist in this place, as you have seen with the demon that chased you from his area of death. In the spirit world there is both good and evil. There is also no time or place as we know it to exist, and there, as in the flesh, mankind must make a choice between good and evil."

Again Grandfather paused, giving me much-needed time to understand his words and teaching. Still, there were three things that I could not fully understand. First, why was I led to the demon? I still could not understand what my Inner Vision and the spirit world was trying to teach me. Second, I still did not know why I saw the landscape during daylight when in my flesh reality it was taking place at night. I understood when Grandfather had said that the spirit world knows no time or place, but if that were so, then what time and place did my spiritual journey represent? Finally, I could understand when Grandfather told us that we must walk the duality of flesh and spirit, but I could not see how it could be done simultaneously. At best, the physical body and mind had to be put at rest, deep in the silence, before the spirit could emerge.

Grandfather continued, saying, "The world of spirit and the voice of Inner Vision guided you to that evil place and to the demon to teach you that these things exist. It taught you that great care must be taken when venturing into the spiritual domains, for evil there can hurt you. If you are not guided to take the journey by the Inner Vision, then your spirit becomes very vulnerable to these demons of evil. But if you are guided there and your purpose is pure, then you are less vulnerable and more powerful. As you have witnessed the evil of the demon, you will also soon witness the goodness of the spirits. It is these spirits that you find on your journeys that will teach you and guide you, as I guide you in both flesh and spirit. So too, as you have seen many times before, evil can also be a teacher, if you look at the wisdom of its negative power."

Without waiting for a response, Grandfather again continued, saying, "You are also wondering how it is that a man can walk the duality of flesh and spirit at the same time. You have, up to now, found it very difficult to get into the spiritual realities without first quieting the body and mind. So too have you found that when you reenter the flesh reality, for a time it has been difficult to separate the logical mind from the spiritual mind. It takes some time for the logical mind to come back to full consciousness. It is at these times that you are living in both the flesh and the spirit. You have been fusing your flesh reality with that of the outer circles of power. With each entry, you will weaken the walls more, until one day you will walk the duality. Until then, you must continue seeking the sacred silence first, before any spiritual journeys begin."

"Finally," Grandfather said, "you most of all wondered how you witnessed the spiritual reality of your journey in full daylight, when in flesh reality, you existed at night. As I have told you, the spirit world knows no time and place. All things that ever existed will still exist back in spiritual reality. Every song ever sung, every word ever spoken, every act ever committed is floating back there someplace. Fortunately the acts and meanderings of common people lack any real power in the spirit world. That is why so often you can go back in time and learn how things were. That is why you sometimes come back singing sacred songs that have not been sung in the flesh for centuries. All things that ever were and are, now exist in the land of the spirits."

He paused for a moment, a long moment, then continued, saying, "So too does the world of spirit contain all the possible and probable futures. As I have told you before, there is not future, just probable futures. When man is given a choice in life and in spirit there is no law for future. The now is like the palm of your hand, with each finger pointing to the direction of possible futures. But there is only one finger that seems to be the strongest: the finger in which the flow of life seems to be heading, and it is this future that we call the probable future. Many times the spirit world warns us of the probable futures, the way in which the course of events will surely take us. At any time, man can change the probable future to another probable future, as if pointing with another finger. What you saw then in the daylight of your spirit journey was the probable future. And as you saw when walking in the flesh, you began to live the probable future and it became your now. The only way you could have changed that future was if you did not walk into the swamp this morning."

I sat for a long time in absolute silence, thinking over all that Grandfather was telling me. It felt like my mind was overloaded with too much information to assimilate. So many questions had been answered, but now I could feel many more emerging. The thoughts of being able to talk to spirits really intrigued me, as well as the ability to travel back in time. But what really fascinated me was the ability to go forward in time to explore the possible and probable futures. The concept sounded great to me, but how to get there, how to call up the futures or the spirits still remained a mystery. I knew that at the base of anything we tried to do, there had to be the direction of Inner Vision and a pure purpose. I did not think that one could do anything anymore just for fun and learning, and somehow I knew that everything from this point on had to be directed by the powers of Inner Vision.

Grandfather emerged from his silence and spoke to us again, saying, "Now it is time for both of you to separate and to go back to the world of spirit. That world still has much to teach you before you go back to your homes. You must now make manifest in your lives all that you have learned. So too must you understand the entities of the spirit world and the wisdom of possible and probable futures. What you have learned in the past week is so important, but it cannot end now or be broken by a long separation from the purity of wilderness. Again, time is running very short and you must complete your journeys into the world of spirit. You must go back now." With those words, Grandfather gave a wave of his hand to Rick and pointed in the direction of a distant forest. To me he pointed back to the swamp.

6

The Possible Futures

Without a word to Grandfather or to each other, Rick headed upland into the forest and I walked back into the swamp. My head literally pounded with an overflow of information. All that happened during the past few days and all that I learned up until now overwhelmed my mind. There seemed so much I couldn't even sort it all out, nor did I really know what to think. I bounced from one thing to the other at random, never fully finishing a thought. The past several days had at once seemed to fly by so quickly, almost in a flash, and yet at the same time seemed an eternity. It had been the most intense spiritual teaching of my life, overwhelming, mystical, but very real. The excitement and rapture of it and all the possibilities overwhelmed me. I cried like a baby, praying to the Creator as I walked, thanking him for all of the gifts and for giving me back my birthright. As far as I was concerned if the teaching ended right here, I had enough for a lifetime. I couldn't even conceive of any more, yet Grandfather had said we were merely beginning.

I wandered for hours, caring little of where I was going. For some strange reason my thoughts seemed to be cleared from my head, all the questions vanished, and I began exploring the swamps again. I drifted about the swampscape, following track after track, diverting my attention from a flower growing in the rich damp carpet of sphagnum moss to the lofty crowns of the cedar trees. My head filled with the laughter and chatter of birds and all around me life and nature were in constant motion. I had never seen the swamp look so gorgeous, and afford such a splendid escape from the mind, and fill my very soul with its beauty. It was truly the temple—a place of enlightenment, where man and nature fuse as one, where one could touch God.

There is a splendid consciousness found in nature that seems to seep deeply into the very soul. It becomes a cleansing, healing, and awakening, as if all rush and turmoil of life is washed away and there is nothing but purity. I don't believe that anyone can walk in wilderness without nature casting off the burdens of life. Anyone can truly walk with the spirits of nature and here is found all truth, all rapture, for nowhere is one closer to the Creator than in the temples that His hands have made. This day, this swamp, this walk for me was so needed, for it cleansed me of my burdening thoughts and I could finally think clearly. I lost myself in the rapture of it all for hours. On unconscious journey through pure consciousness, I was reborn.

It did not occur to me that I had work to do until I saw the sun setting on the distant horizon. Grandfather had sent me to the swamp but I had no real indication of what he wanted me to practice or how to go about getting any practice. The three things I had questions about had been answered, but I suspect also that he wanted me to discover them further. There was the communication with the spirit entities, the possible and probable futures, and to rethink all that I had learned. All I could do now, so late in the day, was to rely on my Inner Vision to guide me to the next place, the next lesson. But here and now my Inner Vision was content to just have me walk and wander, right into the belly of the night. And it felt so good.

Finally I came to a place at the distant end of the swamp—a place I had never been before. This area was located high on the north bank of the swamp. The little rise that I sat upon afforded a vast view of the entire swamp. The stars seemed to come down and touch the very tops of the distant tall cedar trees while the smaller closer trees appeared to be a dark carpet, surging with life. It was there that my Inner Vision told me to sit down and rest, to wait, and to listen. I had not been seated for more than a few moments when I lay down on the ground and went to sleep. There was no argument from my mind or heart because I was past exhaustion on every level of my existence. The night was warm and beautiful, so comforting and peaceful that the sleep was profound and virtually dreamless.

I awoke with a start, hearing the approach of a small group of deer going down into the swamp. At first I had no idea what was rustling the brush. Fear rushed up into my chest and I unconsciously held my breath as the image of the demon in the swamp from yesterday flashed through my mind. It didn't take me more than a moment to identify the sound and in that same moment all fear vanished. At that point I had no idea how long I had slept but it was still full dark. Judging from the position of the stars in the sky it was still quite a few hours before dawn. I could not go back to sleep without much effort, but my Inner Vision would not allow it and the startled awakening had left me energized. I didn't feel tired, but refreshed.

I knew that it was time to get to work, for my Inner Vision was tugging at my heart, and that was the powerful force keeping me from sleep. I sat for a long time staring off into the swamp, intermittently praying, asking for guidance. I guess that in a strange way I was hesitating, for the fear of the demon still hung in my mind, though I did not want to give in to that fear. I somehow knew, though not in a cognitive way, I would have to go into the spirit world for my next lesson, although I did not fully understand what that lesson was. As I prayed and procrastinated, I could make out the faint sound of insect wings, but it wasn't an insect at all. It was more like a chainsaw, but there was no reality to it, for the swamp still sang its night song. I knew that I had put it off long enough and now had to follow my Inner Vision to my next lesson.

Again I thought about the spiritual journeys and again the fear of the demon arose within my heart. I remembered that Grandfather said as long as I was guided by my Inner Vision and my purpose was pure, the demons would not be so powerful, but somehow that did not make me feel much better. The lesson of the demon that Rick and I encountered did what it was supposed to, it gave me a healthy respect for the world outside the flesh. I was damned sure that I was not going to take any chances and try to explore that world for fun. I would only go there if my Inner Vision came to me in such a powerful way that there could be no doubt as to why. With that thought my Inner Vision hit me so hard that it seemed to flood my heart, and I had to obey, fear or no fear.

I again gazed off across the swamp, its beauty overwhelming. I prayed for guidance, then slipped deep into the realms of silence, still not sure as to where I was going or what I was searching for. It did not take long to reach deep into the quietude of the sacred silence, and in a flash of clarity all body and mind were gone. I emerged into the dazzling brilliance of the swamp at full light. In my imagination the swamp took on a new feel, a feel that reached into the consciousness of my very soul, purifying and healing. All around me was the flow of life unlike what I had ever experienced before. Green carpets of sphagnum moss, tranquil pools full of frogs and fish, choruses and movements of all manner of birds, other animals dancing to the rhythm of the Earth, and a sense of beauty the like of which I had never experienced before.

I wandered this wonderland of my imagination for what seemed to be hours, but no time at all, for time did not matter. I began to play in the swamp, dancing across old logs and perching on stumps like some imagined human bird. I stalked deer until I could touch them and stroke their backs. They would respond by arching and stretching, appreciating the scratching. Birds would land on my shoulders and head, I could speak the language of the herons, the fish, and the turtles. The swamp had turned into a paradise, a Garden of Eden, where my world became perfect. There was no disease, no pain, no hurt, just purity, strength, and, most of all, peace, love, and boundless joy. I felt whole, alive, and pure.

I lay back on a carpet of emerald-green sphagnum moss in my imagined world and let nature flow into me. I could feel the spirits all around me, as if watching and waiting, but I was not anxious. I could not feel any accusing or scrutinizing looks from the entities of spirit. It was as if they were just watching and waiting, while they too enjoyed the tranquility and cleansing love of the swamp. I could not see them but I could sense them, powerful, waiting, watching, and loving. I had never felt so whole and pure in my entire life. This, I thought, is the way that man should walk upon the Earth. I was not hungry, thirsty, tired, or lonely. There was no death or disease in this pure world of swamp, just the purity of Creation and the presence of the Creator's love.

My world was shattered again by the grating buzzing sound that I had heard before I traveled into the spirit. At first it sounded like angry mosquitoes or bees, but then I realized that it must be the sound of chainsaws. I was dead certain when the animals began running from the sound. The crackling death of trees could be heard resounding through the swamp, and the crash of their bodies hitting the ground shook the very soil. Suddenly there was no peace, nor joy, nor purity, for everything was in chaos, death and fear were all around. I could feel the cedar trees all around me trembling in fear, and the fear reached every beast, plant, and spirit, in this once-pure paradise. I tried to flee with the animals and spirits, but I was held fast to the ground, unable to move, unable to run, imprisoned by the soil and defenseless as the trees.

The dying bodies of trees crashed around me as I saw a small group of men with chainsaws nearing me. At first I thought that they were going to cut me from the ground, but they passed and cut the trees behind me. They could not see me at all and thus went about their cutting, while I desperately tried to reason with them. They could not hear my voice and I felt as helpless as the trees that they were cutting. The whirring saws moved from me and deeper into the swamp. The cutting went on for what seemed to be hours, as the swamps resounded with the cracking of trunks and the falling of the cedar giants. I could see the trees all around me dying, their life slowly seeping from their open wounds. Trees, I knew, did not die when they are first cut, but in a slow process that could mean nothing but agony.

The noise of the chainsaws finally quit, and quiet once again took over what was left of the swamp. I imagined myself walking through the tangle of fallen trees, and looking out across an area that encompassed several square miles. Where the cedar giants stood in these once lush swamps was now open land, tangles of brush, dead animals, and dying trees. It was no longer the spiritual paradise that I had imagined but a living hell. Gone were all the animals, the trees, the tranquility, and purity. Gone was this cathedral of God. All that remained was an open wound, festering on the flesh of the Earth. Gone too was the passion and love I had felt, along with all hope. I had no idea why these people cut the forest here, because it was state land and should not be cut. My head swam with surges of anger I had never felt before. All was now lost, all hope was gone, and I could not prevent it from happening.

I sat for a long time on the dying trunk of a tree, and gazed across the massacre. I felt so sick. It had all happened so fast, faster than it would normally have taken to cut the forest. It was as if these people were rushing on purpose, and I did not know why. New sounds of man penetrated the forests. This time it was the sounds of cables and winches, yanking the trees from where they lay. The sound of chopping axes filled the air, accompanied by the rumble of big trucks. The frenzy of the men's voices could be heard shouting back and forth to each other with such rushed intensity I knew they must be in a hurry. This went on for hours, right into sunset and well into the imagined night. Then, as suddenly as it all began, the last truck rumbled off into the distance and the silence returned. A dead silence where not an animal or leaf spoke, for all had run away, all were dead.

I lifted my head in anger to scream, and my screams now came from my physical body. I had awakened from the horrible dream, and the forest was still alive. I was so overjoyed I ran right down the deer trail and into the bowels of the swamp. The cedar trees still grew uncut and everywhere was the sound of animals. I began to wander the swamps, touching and hugging trees, thankful that they were still alive. It was like a reunion to me, the gathering of old and cherished friends. When the first shafts of daylight accented the trees against the horizon, I fell to my knees and prayed with a fervor. My heart was full of thanksgiving. Dream or not, it all seemed so real. There was no question in my mind that it was all a dream, for the forest had remained uncut and alive.

I began to slowly drift out of the swamp. My heart told me that I should go back to Grandfather's camp but I felt I had more work to do. After all, I had not gone into the possible future as Grandfather had asked and I did not want to go back until I had something to talk about. As I walked from the swamps that still clung to the dawn mists, I hugged the last big cedar tree. As I did, the winds began to pick up and all the trees of the forest began to dance and wave. I hugged the tree hard, when suddenly I heard a soft voice, like a faint whisper in my ear. It seemed to say, "Wood bandits, that's why they rush," but then all fell silent. I had to shake my head to get the voice out of my mind. Truly it had been a thin line between flesh reality and the reality of the spirit.

I wandered far from the swamp, and did not stop until mid-afternoon. I decided to climb a hill that lay to the south of our camp area to pray. It would be a good place, I thought, since Grandfather had always called this place Prayer Hill. I loved it there because even though it was not high it still afforded a grand view of the Pine Barrens. As I climbed to the top and sat down, my gut felt a sense of "wrongness," but it was not extreme. I had forgotten about consulting my Inner

Vision through most of my walk because my mind was still thinking about last night's dream. Now in this place of silence and prayer, my Inner Vision was beginning to come through. Still, I thought, I had much to do and I felt this place would be best to continue my searching. I still did not want to go back to Grandfather, despite what my Inner Vision was telling me.

I stayed on the hill well past sunset and into the early evening. Everything I attempted to do in the spirit, even in prayer, had failed and I grew very frustrated. Nothing was working, except that my Inner Vision was strongly directing me to find Grandfather. The more I put off listening to my inner voice, the more powerful it became, until I had to give in and go back to Grandfather's camp.

It was very late when I finally arrived at Grandfather's camp. It had been more than a day since I had the dream of the swamp and it became a distant memory, lacking the power it once had. I decided, before I found him, that it was not even important to mention it, for I felt a little embarrassed that I had nothing other than the dream to report. As I neared his sacred area I felt that I would just tell him my Inner Vision had not guided me to any new lessons, which, as far as I was concerned, was the truth. I eventually found him; he was not sitting in his area, but off to the side by the swamp. Without looking up he pointed nearby for me to sit down. Not a word was spoken, and I could feel that he was upset with something. I saw by the tracks on the ground that he had been sitting there for a long time.

After a long time without a word, he stood up and I followed him. He entered the lower area of the swamp and began to penetrate its depths. We eventually passed the quiet waters area and pushed on, following the same route I had taken the day before. It was a difficult journey for me, not because of the terrain, but because I wanted to speak to him, and I felt that in some way he was mad at me, though he gave no indication through his actions, only his silence. He would stop frequently and listen, not with his physical hearing, but with something deeper, something more profound. Then he would go on again, still without a word. I knew that he was searching for something beyond the flesh, listening with his Inner Vision. My inner voice at this time seemed to be numb.

As we neared the part of the swamp where I had sat, I suddenly heard the distant rumble of a large truck, and the thoughts of last night's dream came hammering back to my reality. At the same time I was struck with a grave sense of loss that I did not understand. All I knew was that it came from deep within the realm of Inner Vision. I felt almost sick to my stomach, but for no physical reason. I followed Grandfather right to the base of the deer trail that would lead to the area where I had sat. I knew now that Grandfather was taking me back to the same area where I had the dream. I could sense something wrong with the forest, a feeling that I had not felt the night before. It felt as if I had failed in some way, and neither the trees nor animals would speak to me.

We traveled for a few more yards and then suddenly emerged into a huge clearing that I did not remember from the night before. At first I felt disoriented, unclear as to where we actually where. It was then that Grandfather stepped aside and waved his hand for me to gaze upon the clearing. It was then I realized that the clearing was one of destruction. All the trees had been cut and the forest was no more. It was the same forest I had seen cut in my dreams, but it was fresh, butchered during this very day. I grew violently sick to my stomach as the feeling of failure washed over me. I was too upset to speak and just followed Grandfather up to the place I sat the night before. It was all so real now, exactly as the dream, but not a dream at all. This was a probable future that had now become a reality.

We sat for a long time in absolute silence as I gazed across the cut and barren landscape. Wood bandits, I thought, that is why they were in such a hurry. I felt sick for I had seen the possible future and did nothing to prevent its reality. No, I did not know what I could have done, for I was only a boy, but at least I could have warned the authorities or someone. Possibly, I thought, if I had listened to my Inner Vision and stayed there, they might not have cut the forest. After all, they did not want any witnesses and if they saw me there they might have left.

Nonetheless, I felt horrible, I felt responsible, as if I too had taken part in the destruction of the forest. By not trying to stop them, I was also guilty. I was too self-absorbed at the time to care of anything but myself.

Grandfather's voice broke into my thoughts, though it was not accusing or angry. He said, "For many suns now you have learned to listen to and consult your Inner Vision. Yet on this past night you failed to do so. Your logical mind saw no proof that the dreamed image was real because the forest lay uncut. If you had listened to the inner voices you would have known what you witnessed was the reality of the probable future. You heard the voice of the trees' spirit telling you that it would be tree bandits, but again you passed it off as imagination, or the whisper of the winds. You did not fail this forest, for I doubt if you could have done anything to stop the cutting. What you did fail to do was to recognize the voice of the probable or possible futures, but now you know it well. I doubt that you will mistake it again for dreams or fantasy, as now your mind can see the results."

I did not answer, I could not answer, for I still felt responsible, no matter what Grandfather said. He was so right. I assumed it was all a dream because when I awoke there was no physical evidence the forest had been cut. I had allowed my physical mind to overrule my spiritual mind, discounting the voice as a dream. Grandfather then said, "As you have seen, many times there is no physical evidence for what the Inner Vision tells us. With me, I always follow my Inner Vision, no matter what my physical mind thinks it knows. The Inner Vision, the spiritual mind, knows all things, beyond anything the mind of the flesh can even dream. You have learned a valuable lesson. Listen to the spiritual mind whenever it speaks, for it is truth."

Silence again. My problem had been the satisfaction of the physical mind. Since there was no evidence, there was no accepted truth. I knew that it was real, but my mind would not accept that reality, or possible reality. Instead the mind came up with all manner of explanations, excuses, and self-absorption, to distract me from the truth. Grandfather spoke again, saying, "By seeking explanations or evidence to feed the physical mind you have made the spiritual mind impure and weak. As you see now, the mind of the flesh becomes at once our greatest enemy and our greatest ally. Many times we have to just accept what the Inner Vision tells us as truth, and set aside our need for explanation or proof. Faith, remember, is part of the power."

Grandfather paused again, then said, "You have not finished. If you listen to your inner voice it will tell you to remain here and learn. There is still much you have to understand before the night is finished." With that Grandfather left the sit area and wandered back across the butchered forest. I sat feeling absolutely humbled by my failure. What bothered me even more was that I tried nothing to prevent it and as far as I was concerned I was as guilty as those who cut the trees. I had allowed my physical mind to rule, set faith aside, and had not listened to my Inner Vision. Now I had to pay the price. The forest was lost, the temple destroyed, and I was guilty.

I sat numb against the night as I gazed across what was once a beautiful swamp. I knew it would take years for the forest to grow back to what it once was. I would never see it in my lifetime. Nature struggles to hide the scars of man, but it is a slow process. At this point I became so heartsick and disgusted with myself that I felt not only had I allowed the destruction of the swamp, but I also failed the Creator. I had allowed one of His temples to be destroyed. I prayed for guidance, but I felt unworthy to speak to the Creator. Almost at the moment of my deepest sorrow and self-ridicule, my mind seemed to clear and I slipped into a deep place of silence. Again, I felt at peace and cleansed of all my sorrow. I felt loved.

I looked out into the cut and barren swamp. The silence was overwhelming, but not accusing. There was still the sadness over the loss of the forest, and I still accused myself, but not in such harsh terms. Possibly I could not have done anything, but I should have tried. I felt a little kinder toward myself and my failure. I then caught some kind of movement out of the corner of my eye. It was just a movement, but I knew that it wasn't an animal, it was more like a human, though there was no sound. I looked closer, trying to pierce the dark with my eyes, and I saw what at first appeared to be a clump of brush. My Inner Vision immediately told me to go to it, and I obeyed without hesitation. I did not want to deny that voice and make the same mistake again.

As I worked my way to the center of a cut area, I saw what was not of bush at all, but someone bent over a fallen tree trunk, as if in prayer. I did not feel the fear I had experienced with the demon of the clearing a few days before, but I felt strangely at peace. I also knew that this man, if it was a man, was not of flesh, but of spirit. I was confused because I did not remember entering the spirit realms for any kind of travel. I felt fully awake and in my physical consciousness. It became very difficult at that point to decide whether I really was in my physical body or in my spiritual mind. But somehow it did not make any difference, for I was too interested in this spirit and wanted to see what he was doing.

I drew closer to it, but there was no fear. I saw that he, or she, or it, was in the process of planting a small cedar tree and praying over it in a very loving way. Very slowly it stood and turned toward me in such a manner I knew it had known I was there all along. As it stood and faced me I was still too far to see its face, but it beckoned me to come closer without a word. As I drew near I saw that it was an old man, in a very old and weathered blanket. At once I thought that he might be Native American, though the features of his face defied any racial identification. He did, however, have the actions and mannerisms of an ancient one, as he pointed to a tree stump and motioned me to sit down.

There was a long silence as he seemed to scrutinize me with his big sad eyes. It reminded me so much of the way Grandfather would sometimes look at us. His mouth was without expression, and I felt a little uncomfortable. Then he spoke to me in a very kind and loving way, and said, "I am not the voice of the tree people that spoke to you on this morning, but I am the voice of the spirit world, the keeper of this forest, of many forests. You are not to be held accountable for the destruction of this forest, for you could not have done anything to prevent its death. These men who cut without love or knowledge would have hurt you, for they have hurt others who have stood in their way. You have only now learned to listen to the possible futures and to the voices of the spirit. There has been no failure."

He paused, then sat down solemnly on a tree trunk. I hesitated, then said to him, "That isn't true. If I had been here I could have followed them to their camp and then reported them to the police or the wardens." His once expressionless mouth now smiled lovingly as he said, "You could not have followed them, for their place of hiding is many miles from here and over many roads. The wardens have been looking for them for many months now, but with no success. I know them well, for they have destroyed many of my forests. But now you can help, for I know where their hidden camp is, and you will direct those who seek them." "But what will I be able to do, and who would believe me?" I asked. The spirit spoke again and said, "They hide at the old pond, near where the broken mill is found. It is there that they butchered the trees for market, and it is there they can be found."

Suddenly, I awoke back in my physical body, and the spirit was gone. I did not care whether it had all been a dream or a reality, I just knew what I had to do. I was not going to give my mind a chance to discount what I had just heard or what I imagined I had done. After all, I made a mistake before and I could not take the chance of ignoring the information, whether real or not. I would not allow myself the luxury of doubt. At this point I did not care if I looked foolish, or if in the end I was wrong. My Inner Vision had not lied to me yet, and now it told me that the imagery and information was true. However, I did not know what I was going to do. Convincing someone, some authority, that I knew about an illegal lumber operation that was many miles from the camp would be hard to do.

I did not hesitate but began walking right back to camp. As I walked I began to think about all that had happened. If it were all true and not imagined, then not only did I reach into the possible future, but also communicated in a real way with a spirit. I had encounters with the world of spirit before, but they were not called for. The encounters were more in dream, and by accident, than by choice. As I continued walking, I began to think back on the time that I first received a message from a spirit. We were on a long trek when that spirit came to me in a dream. During the first night of our trek, we had built debris huts and fell into a much needed sleep. It was then, as I so vividly remembered, that the spirit appeared to me.

Sometime during the night, I had a vivid dream. It stood out from all the others because it had seemed so real, so urgent. I first had images of walking along the trail that we were to take the next day. The landscapes I passed were very clear, the travel was easy, and the day was far warmer than it had been on the previous day. I could see every detail of the landscape and of Grandfather's and Rick's presence there. I then dreamed of approaching the stream, one that we usually drank from, and the first we would pass since the beginning of the journey. I could feel the rush of emotion and relief as I drew close to the edge of the water. I could feel the anticipation of my thirst being quenched after such a long and hard journey. The stream produced images of pristine beauty, a soothing energy, and a gift of life from the Creator.

In my dream, as I bent to drink the water, I was taken back by the image of an old Indian reflected in the stream's surface. I looked up across the water, and there stood the same Indian looking back at me. He looked very old, older than Grandfather, yet he still stood very straight, strong, and regal. He waved his hand, palm down, across his chest in greeting, then sternly spoke his warning. "Do not drink from this water, from this day forth. You must also deliver this warning to your grandchildren, and their grandchildren to come." With that he motioned upstream and then said, "They have poisoned the stream for all things. Do not be deceived by the clarity of the water." Before I could have asked any questions, he had vanished, and I had then fallen back into a deep and dreamless sleep.

I remembered so vividly waking up the next morning, the dream had stayed with me, but I would not tell Grandfather or Rick. I knew that some dreams were important, but most were merely imagination and logical static. Even then I did not want to take the chance of making a fool out of myself, no matter how important the dream had seemed. As my mind drifted back, and I reached the midpoint to Grandfather's camp I realized it would not be the last time I would make the mistake of not telling anyone about a spiritual encounter. I had made the mistake of not telling about the oncoming destruction of the cedar swamp and had subsequently lost that temple, for fear of making a fool of myself, just as I had done with my first spirit encounter. I was more determined now not to let it happen again. I set aside my pride and my fears of failure.

As I continued walking, I remembered vividly what had transpired not long after leaving the camp that morning after my first spirit encounter. The day had grown warm fast, far warmer than it had been the day before. The clarity of dawn caused the surrounding forest to stand out in bold relief, and travel had become easier. It was exactly as I had dreamed, and the urgency I felt during that dream began to intensify. As we drew closer to the stream, I wanted to tell Grandfather of the dream, but still I felt reluctant and let it pass. I walked toward the stream as I had seen in my dream and began to kneel beside the water. Rick and Grandfather did the same. As I looked at the clarity of the water, I realized what a fool I had been to think that there was something wrong with the water. It looked so clear, pristine, and beautiful. As I cupped my hands to drink, the image of the old Indian appeared momentarily on the surface, just as I had seen in the dream. Without thinking, I had yelled at Grandfather and Rick not to drink the water.

Rick had stopped for a moment, then ignored me, then had raised his hands to his mouth to drink. I dove for him and knocked him back from the edge, water flying everywhere.

He had come back at me quickly, and we wrestled in a rage. Grandfather had quickly broken up the fight, settled us down, then asked me what it was all about. Reluctantly I had then told him about the dream, giving great detail to the events, how they were the same that day, and the old Indian's face reflected again on the surface of the water. I had told him that I didn't want to tell him because I thought it had been my imagination. Rick had readily agreed and had gone back to the water to drink. Grandfather held him back and said, "First we will look upstream." Rick reluctantly agreed, had given me a dirty look, and muttered to me as I passed, "Great imagination." When he said that, I remembered how very foolish I felt.

I remembered how we began to walk upstream, Rick complaining the whole way that the water looked fine to him. I remember too that Grandfather had told him that the water was sick, and had pointed out the wilting vegetation. Eventually we found that upstream several barrels of some kind of clear chemical had been illegally dumped and were seeping down the banks and into the water. It was only then that my dream was confirmed and I no longer worried about feeling foolish. I knew now that Grandfather had known all along about my dream and that the water was poisoned. I knew also that he wanted to test me to see if I would say anything about it to him or Rick. He wanted to see if my pride would stand in the way of the truth. As I thought back, I realized that if I had said nothing then we could all have been poisoned, possibly killed by the water. That same fear had cost the temples of the cedar swamp.

I finally reached the trail to Grandfather's camp, but walked right by. I was not afraid to tell him, but rather wanted to go right out of the Pine Barrens and tell the authorities. I believed enough in my encounter that I did not need to run it by Grandfather first. I just wanted to get out of the Pine Barrens and tell someone as quickly as I could, for the sooner I told someone, the sooner something would be done about the wood bandits, I hoped before another temple was destroyed. I gave no thought at the time as to who I was going to tell or how I got the information. That hadn't even crossed my mind; my Inner Vision was just too strong and overwhelming to allow for any other thoughts to get out and stop them.

I knew that just at the edge of town was a small house that was owned by one of the local game wardens and I thought telling him would be my best bet for getting something done. I finally got to his house and knocked on the door. As I heard him approach the door, it was then that the thought of what I was going to tell him struck me. I had no idea what I was going to say or how to tell him where this information came from. I could not even dream of telling him about the spirit, for he was an outsider and would not understand in the least. I could not even mention how I had found out and, if he asked me, I would tell him that I heard someone talking about it. I just couldn't tell him who. Grandfather had taught me to deplore lies, and I figured that I would not be lying as long as I did not tell the warden who had told me.

The game warden opened the door in a manner that appeared angry at someone disturbing him. I could not understand why he wasn't in the woods on such a beautiful day, anyway. He was a heavy man with a big belly and appeared to be thoroughly out of shape. His face was reddened and dripping with sweat from the heat. In his hand appeared to be what was left of a pork chop which made his hand glisten with grease. He looked at me with a look that was somewhere between arrogance and authority, as if I was some sort of scum and beneath his interest. Before I could get a word out, or even say hello, he snorted, "What the hell do you want, kid?" I was so taken back by his appearance and words that I began to stutter.

Finally I got up the courage to tell him about what I had seen. He listened in a disinterested way, never showing any indication that he was listening to anything I had to say. In fact, he looked more interested in his pork chop than in stopping the killing of the trees. To my relief, however, he never asked me where I got the information. He just told me in no uncertain terms that he was a game warden and that he had nothing to do with trees, in fact he wasn't even a full-time warden. He also told me there was no way that anyone could be at the old mill because that old road had not been used in years. He also said everyone knew about the illegal tree-cutting but no one seemed to care about doing anything about it. He told me I should just run along and play and not to bother him again with things that did not concern him. With that he slammed the door in my face, never saying good-bye.

I was shocked by what he had said. How could this man be a warden and not care about the trees? Trees have everything to do with the game, and so much else, for that matter. He looked too out of shape to do the job of a game warden, and even his boots showed no wear that indicated travel in the woods. They were worn by the action of sidewalks and roadways, not by the woods. I thought to myself that a game warden should love the woods and not become a warden because it was a job. Knowing that he didn't care about the trees really upset me, not only because it was beyond my comprehension someone couldn't care about trees, but also because of what he had said to me and how he said it. Anyway, I had no idea where to go next. Certainly he was not going to do anything.

I began to walk back to the woods when the image of an old family friend rushed into my head from nowhere. The friend was an old state trooper named Joe. At first I discounted the image because I knew that troopers patrolled the highways and had no interest in the trees, but the image persisted. I knew, however, that Joe loved the woods and possibly my Inner Vision was directing me to him because he could help in some way. Anything at this point was worth a try. I had to save the trees, I had to exhaust all options before I returned to camp. At that point I turned back toward town and walked over to Joe's house, hoping he was home.

I knocked on his door, and before I could tap three times the door swung open. Unlike the game warden, Joe greeted me with his huge warm smile and told me to come in and sit down. He was a big man, tall and strong, in a way intimidating, but very warm and sincere. He asked me how I was and how my folks were doing, and finally asked me what I needed. Without hesitation I told him the story of the trees, again leaving out the part of the spirit but rather saying that I overheard someone talking about it. He listened intently as I spoke, showing great concern. Even when his phone rang, he told whoever was on the other end that he would call back, because he was tied up gathering evidence for a case. This made me feel really good. I didn't know if he was humoring me or if he was really concerned. My Inner Vision told me his heart was true.

He asked me several times about where I had heard about the wood bandits' camp and each time I told him the same story or dodged the question. He told me that he wouldn't ask me again. I knew he thought I was protecting someone; he was right. I wasn't protecting the spirit, however, but only myself so that I wouldn't risk embarrassment. Joe then made several phone calls and returned to me. He said he had checked with the main office and that the police and other officials were investigating the wood bandits, but they could not find their camp, nor did they know who they were. There were suspects, but no one had been arrested because nothing could be proven. He said if what I told him were true it would have been the first real breakthrough for the case. Then he shocked me by telling me that he wanted me to take a ride with him to check out the area of the old mill.

We drove for the better part of an hour to where the spirit had told me I would find the wood bandits. We stopped the car at the beginning of the trail and walked along the old road. The road had overgrown so badly that we had to duck for most of the journey. When we finally reached the sight of the old mill there was nothing to be found. No one certainly had used the old road and there were no signs of any trucks or cut wood. I felt sick to my stomach, for not only had the spirit been wrong, or imagined, but I had cost Joe a good part of his day off. Without accusation he just said that the information I heard must have been wrong, but credited me with at least trying to help. I did not know it at the time, but that was the start of a long friendship and Joe would be the man who got me started in police tracking just two years later.

Joe drove me as far up the trail as his car would allow, said good-bye, and dropped me off in the woods. I was too upset to go right back to camp, because I didn't want to face Grandfather. Somehow the Inner Vision and the look into the future had been wrong, or tainted in some way, and I wanted to find out why. So, too, my Inner Vision had lied to me in a way, because it had said I was doing the right thing all the way along. I worried that I was losing the ability to communicate with my Inner Vision, and tended to blame it on the trip back to civilization. Possibly, I thought, I wanted to make amends for allowing the swamp to be destroyed in the first place, and I had dreamed the whole thing up in that desperate attempt.

Somehow my wanderings had now brought me back to the very place where all of this had started. I looked out across the cut and barren swamp and began to cry. I not only cried for the swamp and my inability to save it, but I also cried for myself, fearing still that I had lost the purity of Inner Vision. I was so embarrassed. Not only had I wrongly believed my imagination, but I had also made a fool of myself in front of Joe. Even though it sounded as if he appreciated what I had tried to do, I suspected he was really laughing at me. As I looked up and out across the fallen swamp, I caught a motion to one side, and very close. Turning my head abruptly, I saw again the spirit that had told me about the wood bandits. Before I could even react or think, he simply said, "Thank you, warrior," then disappeared.

His words had really taken me by surprise; in fact, the whole appearance took me by surprise. I had not willfully sought out any spirit travel, yet as clearly as ever the same spirit had appeared to me. What shocked me where his words. I had no idea of what he was thanking me for, or why he called me a warrior. As soon as the shock of it all wore off, I began again to discount the whole encounter. After all, the spirit had been wrong and definitely imagined, for if it had been real we would have found the wood bandits' camp. I decided then not to say a word to Grandfather when I returned to camp; I just did not want to let him know I had failed. I would try again to reach the wisdom of the possible futures after I had a good night's sleep. I slipped into camp very late and just went to sleep in my shelter.

I awoke abruptly the next morning to Rick calling my name. I crawled out of my shelter to find Rick standing there with his buckskin bag, looking as if he was ready to take a hike. He told me he was going to go home a day early, so he could come back a day earlier, and he asked me if I would walk out with him. I said I would, and then said that I was going to tell Grandfather where we were going, but Rick said he would rather not, looking a little worried and embarrassed. As I looked at Rick I could tell something was bothering him deeply, but I couldn't tell what it was. It wasn't like him to leave camp to go home even a second earlier than he had to. It appeared to me that he was trying to hide something, and I suspected it was from Grandfather.

It was at that moment I felt I wouldn't want to face Grandfather right now, especially after my failure. Without a word or fuss we both left camp and hiked back to the main trail that would lead to our houses. We never said a word the entire trip. I once asked Rick how he had done with his quest for the possible futures, but the subject was quickly changed. I was glad of the change, in a way, because I was afraid Rick would ask me the same thing. From that point on the only conversation was small talk, usually about what we were going to do when we got back out into the woods on the next weekend, and also of what we were going to do that coming week. Even though I was going to wait until tomorrow to go home, I wished I was going home now so I didn't have to face Grandfather.

We finally reached the tar road and started across when we spotted a state police car parked on the other side of the road, just down from the trail that would lead to my house. As we got closer, the door opened and out stepped Joe. He came right up to us, hand extended in a gesture of friendship. He shook my hand and then Rick's, thanking us for the tremendous tip which led to the arrest of the wood bandits. We were both baffled. Confused, I asked Joe where they had been arrested, and he said they were at the same place I had taken him yesterday. "But they were not there then," I said. Joe then said that he knew, but when Rick came by an hour later and told him the same story he started to take it all more seriously. He then felt that he should stake out the area, and just after dark the bandits arrived and dropped off several loads of wood. They had not been there before, but this was going to become the site of their new operation, he told us. He also said that whoever told us about it knew they would be using that place soon. Thanking us profusely again, he got back into his car and drove off.

We both stared off toward the departing car, still in utter shock over what had happened. We began to dance around like fools, hugging each other, congratulating each other, and laughing until it hurt. We didn't really have to discuss anything, but turned and began to walk back to camp. I knew why Rick had wanted to leave. It was the same reason I wanted to leave. Neither of us wanted to face Grandfather with what we thought was a failure. Now realizing the spirit was right, and we had prevented further wood cutting, we could face Grandfather without feeling that we had failed him and ourselves. We talked all the way back to camp, barely taking time to even breathe or to stop for any reason. We were both too excited.

We both discovered we had seen the same spirit, though we were at opposite parts of the woods. I was in the swamp and Rick was still sitting on the hill. He too had seen cedar trees falling in his mind, and that was when the spirit approached him, telling him that I needed his help. The spirit actually directed him to Joe, but the spirit had been very specific about the time that he should go. Rick had felt like a failure when Joe had told him he had already checked out the area and found nothing. Joe said nothing to Rick about me at the time. That is why Rick had felt so bad, because I said nothing about needing help or of even going out to Joe's house. We both made solemn promises we would tell each other everything from that time on, no matter how absurd, so things like this would not happen again.

We reached Grandfather's camp by mid-afternoon, but he was nowhere to be found. We decided to sit down and wait for his return, still being far too excited about all that happened to us. As we sat talking, Grandfather's voice broke into our conversation, saying, "The only embarrassment you should have felt was not that you thought you had failed, but for not believing in what had happened as being true. You have both seen the power of Inner Vision work, even when all physical evidence seemed to the contrary, but this time you could not accept it as being true. Is it that you both are still allowing your physical mind to dictate what to believe and what not to believe? You both must have realized by now the heart can never be wrong, only our interpretation of what our heart is telling us."

Awaiting no answer, Grandfather continued, "You were to seek the wisdom of the possible and probable future. Did you not realize the keeper of the forests was telling you of the future and not your now? You must understand that you have touched upon a wisdom few people will ever know, far less believe. Not only have you both seen into the future, but you have also been told the future by the spirits. You can see now when the spirit thanked you both, that the line between flesh and spirit is becoming very thin. A duality in your perception, in your existence, is now becoming a reality. The spirit called you both warriors, because you sacrificed yourself, your pride, to help save the forest. A warrior is always the last to pick up the lance but the first to lay down his life for love."

I thought long and hard in the silence Grandfather had left after his words. I felt honored, but also still a little upset because I had not believed in my Inner Vision fully. I had again allowed my mind to decide what it thought was true and what wasn't true. I had allowed physical evidence and the now to sway my opinion, thus tainting the truth of the Inner Vision. If only I could have known that the spirit spoke of the future, I could have waited a day and told Joe on the day it would have happened. Grandfather broke into my thoughts and said, "There are two lessons still to be learned before you return home. You first must learn how to choose the time of the possible futures and you must begin to live the duality of flesh and spirit. Only then can you understand all of this. Go now, for you have only two sunrises left." We walked from camp a short distance, then drifted off separately, each to his own searching.

7

Time

I wandered off back into the swamp, now heading downstream
for quite some distance. I was caught up in the thoughts of what
I had to do and the possibility of what lay ahead. I had little
more than a day to complete the last lesson. I had to find out
how I could dictate to the Inner Vision the exact time and place
in the possible futures I wanted to go. I had learned so much
over the past several days that I could not imagine learning any
more. My head was already filled to a point of overflow and I
felt in danger of forgetting much of what I had learned. I did
not know how to identify a specific time or date in the future
and go to that place, but I had to find out. Grandfather must
have had his reasons for pushing us so hard. After all, I learned
more in a week than I had learned in the past six months.

As I wandered, I began to think about a similar time when I
had been struggling with time and dates. It had been at the end
of the past summer when Rick and I were first discovering the
wisdom of the "veil," which we now knew was the entrance
to the place of silence. Grandfather had told me then the veil
would unlock the secrets of the universe. In the veil there was
no time, place, or space, only the purity of all things. It was

at the same time when I was also having trouble using a particular hunting weapon, and asked Grandfather how it was used. He had answered saying, "If you want to know how a skill was used, go and watch the ancient ones use it, then you will know firsthand." I then asked him how that could be possible. I remembered him laughing and saying, "Why, through the veil, of course. It knows no time."

I had been amazed at what he was implying. Could it be, I thought, we could time-travel by using the veil, or was that one of Grandfather's coyote lessons? Rick and I had discussed the possibilities of looking at the past, not with absolute belief, but in a rather joking way. We had hoped it was true, but it was too farfetched for absolute belief. We fantasized for many hours, talking of dinosaurs, ancient man, atlatls, and all manner of forgotten histories. Actually, what we ended up doing was talking ourselves into faith, washing away many of our doubts by talking about what we believed or didn't believe. We decided to pick a date in the past and go out and meditate on that date before entering the veil. We wanted to pick the same date so there could be a chance we would end up at the same place at the same time. We chose May 15, 1500, when the woods would be full of Native peoples, before white intervention.

We had chosen a likely place and sat down several feet from each other, overlooking a small swamp. For several hours, we had tried to enter the veil, or think about the date, but absolutely nothing happened to either of us. We had again tried to carry the date through the veil with us, but each time the veil was touched we would lose the date and all other thought. I remember then going to ask Grandfather why I could not get through the veil with the desired date intact. Grandfather had simply said, "First there must be absolute faith, and second, you must not try to carry the time or place back with you. You cannot pass into the veil carrying any baggage. Instead, tell it where and when you would like to go and allow the 'all-knowing' veil to do the rest." Rick and I had been so excited about the insights that Grandfather had given us, because we remembered how hard it had been to concentrate on the date while entering the veil. Now we didn't have to carry any baggage, but enter the veil purely. We decided we should try again the next day.

It was near the end of that same day, I remembered, that just before sunset I had gone out to pray. I noticed not far from me Rick was also doing his evening devotions and prayer. I had relaxed for a while, thinking about what Grandfather had said, and trying to digest every last detail so it would become forever part of me. I had prayed again for a while, then slipped into a period of absolute thoughtlessness to meditate and rest. I awoke to the sound of voices coming through the woods. The sound had startled me because it was nothing I could understand. I remember opening my eyes to look and the entire landscape had transformed into a place I could barely recognize. There were huge pines where there had been none before. The vegetation was thicker, but the roll of the Earth remained the same as it had always been. Just several yards in front of me was a narrow and worn path I had never seen before.

I heard the voices again, coming closer, and I began to distinguish footfalls, much like the sound of Grandfather's walk, though many more. From the thick brush that was groaning by the edge of the swamp, there emerged an Indian, young, strong, and sinewy. He carried a club in his hand and across his back was an unstrung longbow. Others had soon deftly followed, smiling and carefully watching the landscape as they went. Many carried bundles in their arms and on their backs. Near the end of the line an old man had appeared, walking quieter than the rest, listening to the deeper voices of wilderness. I instinctively knew this was a man of power, and as he passed by me on the trail, he nodded and smiled at me. The rest of his party paid no attention to me, as if they didn't see me.

A few other people followed the old man, and I could remember vividly that at the very end was a young girl. She carried a bundle in her arms and a larger bundle on her back. Loosely strung from the backpack was a small stone berry masher attached to a sapling handle. As she turned at the edge of the trail to look at a large tree, the berry masher fell to the ground, landing on the edge of the trail. I instinctively yelled to her, pointing to the berry masher, but no one paid attention or seemed to hear me—that is, except for the old man, who abruptly turned around and smiled at me. I remembered looking toward the part of the trail where the masher had fallen, and as soon as I began to move, I felt the landscape surge. It was as if the whole scene flickered, went out of focus, then fell to blackness.

I opened my eyes only to find myself back in my original position, Rick not far away, and the landscape the same as I had always known it. I was amazed at the intensity of my imagination and subsequent daydream, it had all seemed so real, so vivid. I walked over to where Rick was sitting, but he didn't move at my approach. Instead, he sat there staring at a large tree in the distance. I laughed and said, "Looking for Indians?" He looked at me coldly and said, "Berry masher." His words silenced my laugh and shook me in my tracks. We sat for a long time discussing what each of us had seen. It wasn't long before we realized we had both witnessed the same thing, or at least had the same dream. It had not been odd for us back then to tap into the same thought, since we spent so much time together, and had frequently practiced a form of telepathy that Grandfather had taught us. We then decided to tell Grandfather about our experience.

Each of us told Grandfather our stories in great detail, giving the description of the landscape, the Indians, their clothing, the old man, and even the dropping of the berry masher. We also told him the whole thing was some kind of daydream we both shared and that we were very excited we could communicate that well. I had expected Grandfather to tell us how delighted he was with our shared thoughts, but instead he said, "Go dig up the berry masher." Rick and I looked at each other, both startled at his reply.

Without question, and with great speed because of oncoming dark, we went back to the area where we thought the berry masher dropped. We soon found a long, troughlike depression in the ground that must have been an old trail. I then drew a line from where I sat to the place I saw the berry masher fall and Rick did the same from his original position. Where the two lines crossed we began to dig.

It had been our experience with what we saw, that there were no trees close to the path. But next to where we wanted to dig now grew a huge old pine. We dug feverishly until full dark but found no berry masher. Just as we were about to give up, I decided to dig beneath a large dead top root of the grandfather pine. My stick clicked, then slid off something just beneath the root with a thump. It was a sound much like hitting a snapping-turtle shell beneath the mud with a probing sapling staff. It was also the sound of solid rock. I quickly cleared around the area of the root and out fell a berry masher head. It was cleanly pecked from a smooth river rock, the type found along the Delaware River. It was clearly identical to the ones used by the Indian people indigenous to this area and frequently carried on their migration routes to the bay and seashore area.

I had been so astonished back then, not only because I never found such a large artifact before, but also at how I had found it, and where. Because of topography, I knew there were no ancient camps in the area. Here was a celt head, many miles from any known campsite. We ran back to Grandfather carrying the berry masher head and placed it in his lap. He smiled and said, "Why do you look so surprised? Has what you have seen changed your beliefs?"

Rick and I talked until dawn, taking turns fondling the artifact, while trying to recall every detail of what we saw. The energy and elation we felt would not allow sleep. As our conversation trailed off with the rising sun, we both made a solemn promise never to tell anyone how we found the head. No one would understand or believe us, anyway, for everyone outside the temples of the woods lived their own fleshly reality and disbelief.

As I now continued my walk downstream and well into the night, I realized that the first encounter with time and the berry masher had much to teach me. Things I did not understand before now became clear. I now realized the old man of the Indian group was living the duality. He walked in the flesh, but he saw life in the spirit. This is how he could see me sitting there and no one else could. That also meant, when we go back in time, our presence could be felt by spiritually sensitive people, like the old man. What astounded me was that he did not appear to be using any lengthy technique to bridge the gap between flesh and spirit, but to him it had become a natural act. In essence, what the old man was doing back in his time and place was to spirit-walk into the future—just as grandfather had taught us several days before.

I also hadn't realized until now that what I had done when we saw the berry masher fall was a spontaneous form of spirit journey. Though we did not know the mechanics of how it happened then, I did now. What we had unconsciously done by accident back then, I could now do at will, providing it was right with my Inner Vision. I knew there had to be some purpose beyond self. I knew also why the landscape had surged and disappeared when I tried to warn the young Indian girl that she had dropped her berry masher, in that I had not yet learned how to move within the world of spirit, only look into it from afar. I also knew the same principles of going back in time must also apply to going ahead in time to the possible and probable futures.

As I wandered on, there was something that confused me deeply. I could see how a date in the past could be decided and then how to get to that place and time. What I couldn't understand was how one could go to a future that was not yet lived. There were too many possibilities to choose from. Not only would I have to know how to choose a future time and place, but I would have to know all the future possibilities and then choose one of those possibilities to explore. In other words, I would have to choose the possible futures of things that could happen, or I could choose the probable future, if things were left unchanged. It was all so baffling and confusing. I had an idea of how it could all work, but no clear-cut way to make it work. It was all still a vague theory, a theory without real direction.

I knew every event, every thought, action, song, and skill were recorded for all time in the past. Some of these recordings were more powerful than others, and some just floated about randomly and with no power. These lesser deeds were like peripheral thoughts that lacked any power to really affect anything. Could it be, I wondered, if all the possible futures floated about in the same way, lacking any real power, but when combined with the events of now, produced a more powerful thought or energy that would eventually become the probable future?—much like knowing that two plus two equals four. But then again, what would happen to the possible futures that were finally passed by the now of the probable futures? Did they just dissipate, or did they still contain enough power to show the searcher how things could have been? The complication of it all just seemed to overwhelm my mind and I had to sit down to rest.

I searched the wisdom of the Inner Vision for hours, but there were no real answers. I tried to logically reason, but that only produced more questions and confused the issues. What did happen was that suddenly and without warning I was hit with the overwhelming desire to go back and talk to Grandfather. Though the Inner Vision was forcing me to go to him, I had no real idea of what I was going to ask him. After all, I had not even come to grips with my own assumptions. All I knew was now I faced a wall, some sort of block, I could not get around. I also knew I had to go to Grandfather, possibly because he could help me bridge that wall.

Ironically, when I finally got to Grandfather's camp, Rick was also arriving. Looking at each other for a long moment we both realized that we had been simultaneously called here, but neither of us knew why. It was strange, but neither of us had to say a word to make the other understand that we were both at the same place, at the same wall. Grandfather was nowhere around, so we sat down and began to speak. It was ironic, but not surprising, that we both had the same experiences with what we called the wall. Neither of us knew which way to go or how to find the answers. Almost at the same time we felt we had to visit Grandfather, but we did not know what to tell him or what to ask him. After we talked for a while, we realized we had come to the same wall, though through different circumstances; it was still essentially the same wall. So too did we realize there was a bigger picture that neither of us could understand yet, but we had faith we would eventually get there, though where *there* was, we did not know.

Grandfather's voice shattered our conversation, telling us to sit down. After motioning us to draw closer to the fire, he said, "You have both reached a place within yourselves where you think you can go no further without help. That is only partially true, for if you had a limitless time to spend searching, you would eventually go beyond that wall. Part of that wall is created by your logical minds, and your inability to grasp the concepts of the future with your physical minds. You do not understand how it is, when something is not yet lived, it can still be found in the world of the spirit. You think you must understand how this could be true on a physical level, before you could accept that truth on a spiritual level. As I have told you, many things in the realms of spirit cannot be understood by the logical mind or the flesh."

Grandfather paused, then continued, saying, "In the spirit world, the place of the possible futures does not really exist in the same way as the past. The futures are like unformed thoughts that float around without any power, yet still they contain an energy all of their own. When the events of the now grow stronger, then these possible futures grow in power, combining with the now and other energy until they become the probable future, then finally the reality of now. Once lived, the now becomes recorded forever in the spirit world. However, what could have been the future is still recorded, but not as powerful. They are like the higher thoughts and dreams of common man that are never lived. They are still there, like signposts, to show what man could have become."

Grandfather paused for a long time to let the wisdom sink in. I could understand all of what he was telling me, but I still did not understand where the possible futures came from. It had to be more complicated than two plus two equaling four. His voice broke into my thoughts, saying, "The possible futures are born of the consciousness of now's events. They are like the unlived thoughts of man. The energy of the *nows*, combined with the entire consciousness of the spirit world, the world of the spirit-that-moves-through-all-things, and the wisdom of the Creator, creates these possibilities. It is because of these possibilities that man can have a choice; without these possibilities, man can have no choice. The future is not law, only choice and change are law. So care not where and how these possible futures exist, for your heart knows, and your Inner Vision will guide you there. So too will your Inner Vision know the pure purpose. Let go then your need to let your logical mind understand things that cannot be understood, except by the spiritual mind."

With those words, Grandfather motioned to Rick and me to leave camp and go back to where we had been. Rick and I walked together in silence until we reached the stream that cut through the swamp. We sat for a long time thinking about what Grandfather had said, but we did not talk at first. Both of us had to understand what Grandfather was trying to teach us before we could ever hope to discuss it with each other. So many thoughts raced through my mind, so many questions yet not formed, though I somehow understood, but on a deeper level—a level that was out of the reach of common logic. I wanted so badly to understand the possible futures on a logical level, at least to put my thirsting mind to rest, but I knew that could never be. So many times I remembered Grandfather saying that many things we would encounter in the spirit world could not be explained, and this was a damn good example. Exasperating, but a good example.

I decided to wander, following the stream. Ironically, there was no longer any need for thought. The passion for trying to understand the possible futures with my logical mind had ceased to exist and I felt so relieved. My inner vision was driving me someplace, but I did not know where. All I could do was to follow and ask no questions. Even the wandering felt good now despite the fatigue of the body. I did not walk, but drifted about the swamps, allowing my mind to do the same. Somewhere deep inside I felt a purging process going on, as if something was being purified and enlightened. In a way I felt I was on some sort of a long, walking Vision Quest, but the quest was not of the body and mind, but more to do with the spirit. Somewhere along my walk I had transcended the self and now there was no more fatigue. It was as if something else carried me along, gathering exhilarating energy from some unseen outer force. It was not unlike being fueled by the spirit-that-moves-through-all-things, the life force, which now empowered me.

I had traveled quite some distance when the sun reached high into the sky. I could no longer feel the urgency to learn and understand, but at the same time I knew I was being led to some greater understanding. I had wandered so far that I could now hear the distant drone of traffic, clearly meaning that I was drawing close to civilization. Though I did not want to go anywhere near the world of society at the time, my Inner Vision still directed me toward it. I had no idea why my Inner Vision would lead me back out of the woods. I could not see how society was going to teach me anything about time and the possible futures, but just possibly there was more to it than just going to the edge of civilization. Maybe, I thought, I wasn't going back at all, but beyond to the estuaries of Barnegat Bay. That would be a real treat, but I still feared my Inner Vision had plans other than to play in the estuaries.

I knew my primary purpose was not to seek the worlds of the possible futures so much as it was to understand the time, place, and dates involved in getting to those futures. After all, I had already been to the places of the future and now what I had to do was to find out exactly how to go to a particular time in those possible futures and, in some way, choose to do so. I guess that was what my problem was in the here and now. I still could not see how I could make a conscious logical choice and make that choice free of self completely. If in fact the Inner Vision directed me to a certain possible or probable future, then that was a pure purpose, but to have the mind do so would only taint it in some way. That was the problem I was wrestling with while I continued to follow the stream down to the threshold of civilization.

Hours slipped by, and with each passing hour I could hear the drone of traffic getting closer. The stench of society began to permeate the purity of the forests. At times the smells almost became choking, covering even the strongest of the natural scents. Animals appeared more alert and skittish. The flow of the forest and the natural order of things were way out of balance. I knew this stream must intersect two huge highways, but I also knew there were no houses around, for this part of the Pine Barrens still remained untouched by development. Eventually the stream would pass the highways and pour out into the estuary systems of the bay, which was wild again. At least it was a comforting thought to know the only civilization I would encounter would be high-speed roadways and nothing else. People traveling that fast, I knew, never even looked out of their windows. To them, the forests that surrounded the roadways were alien, and all they seemed to want to do was to get through them as fast as possible.

Eventually I came to the first big roadway. It cut through the outer edge of the Pine Barrens like a knife, leaving a huge open and infected wound in the Earth. Along the edges of the roadway was the usual sea of garbage where people had tossed things unconsciously out of the window for years. The collection of garbage in some places literally covered the Earth. It was not unlike a cancer, spreading from the wound of the roadway. Even more disturbing was the exhaust that reached deep into the forest and caused the very bark of the trees to reek. The only way around the road was to enter the water and go under the bridge, for to try and walk across the road would be suicide. Anyway, I did not like the feel of tar on my feet and chose to swim, rather than to go across.

I had to pick my way through all manner of garbage, car parts, and wire that had been thrown into the water. The plants along the edges of the stream looked sick and wilted, so unlike the upper reaches of the same stream that cut through our camp. Even the water had a caustic feel to it and, in places, especially in the eddies, there was the iridescent coating of oil. It made me so sick to think such a beautiful stream had been defiled and nearly destroyed by society. It was so clear to me that people didn't really care about the pure and natural world. Anything that stood in the way of society's progress was destroyed, no matter how beautiful. All people seemed to care about on this roadway was to rush to other places, passing by blindly some of the most awesomely beautiful wilderness found in the state. It was as if they were traveling from island of civilization to island of civilization and everything else in between had to be rushed through.

I decided to stay in the water until I got through the second roadway. Most of the animal trails I had been following downstream now disappeared. Wildlife had almost vanished from the area in between the roadways, and travel on land would become difficult without the help of their trails. I floated or swam for the next several miles, the once pure water now dark and turbid. The farther downstream I drifted, the more caustic and defiled the water became. Garbage along the banks and in the water had now grown in volume, and I feared I would either be tangled in it or cut myself on broken glass or sharp metal. It became a real test at times to get through some of the more littered areas. I wanted to turn and go back to camp so many times, but my Inner Vision kept driving me downstream. I hated the thought of spending my last day in the woods in such a defiled area. In fact, I felt cheated.

Passing under the second roadway was even more sickening than the first. This second road had been around for decades and the collection of garbage around it showed its age. On the other side of the road, lying partially in the water, was the carcass of an old wrecked car that someone had abandoned. The stench of oil-laced water and the smell of exhaust intensified to a point where it actually made me gag. I felt like I was bathing in a cesspool, a cesspool of man's ignorance. Fortunately, at this point in the stream the water had deepened and I could swim without touching the bottom and risk getting cut. I did not, however, want to put my face in the water, for fear of getting any of the oil in my mouth. So too did I begin to look for a place where I could exit the water and begin walking again, not only because of the feel of the vile water but because I was beginning to get very cold.

Finally, a mile downstream, I found a place to get out of the water. Though the stream still reaked of garbage and oil, the banks of the stream and surrounding forest were growing lush again and full of wildlife. It wasn't long before I found a deer trail and continued onward, the going now easier than it had been. Even though I was well beyond the roadways now, floating garbage and oil slicks could still be seen all along the stream. The animals seemed to avoid the stream in that there was no evidence of watering spots where they would drink. Instead, the watering areas were around seeps and the natural springs that could be found all along the stream. Even here, miles from the roadways, man had affected the flow and natural order of life. All here was defiled by his touch.

The forest finally quit, abruptly, and I found myself standing on the edge of a huge estuary system, beyond which lay the bay. It felt so good to be in the estuary for it was so full of wildlife and gorgeous plants. Only the stream contained the pollution of man, all else was pure and natural. Except for the distant drone of power boats and the sight of sails on the bay, there was no other sign of civilization. I always loved the estuaries for their abundance of wildlife, and every time we would go to visit there was always such a sense of adventure. To me, the estuaries held so many secrets, and an abundance of wildlife. So too could I see the effect they had on Grandfather, for he loved them as much as we did. It was always a welcome change to explore the open estuaries, feed on fish and clams, and do as the ancient Native Americans once did when they migrated yearly to the bays.

I sat at the edge of the forest for a long time, gazing out across the grasses, sedges, and reed islands of the estuary. Again, I was overwhelmed by exhaustion, this time more powerfully than before, and I lay back to sleep for awhile. Lying in the warm sun and smelling the pungent aroma of the bay quickly lulled me into a deep and much needed sleep, but the sleep would not last for long. I no sooner drifted off into a dream than I was quickly awakened by a tremendous sucking sound, the likes of which I had never heard before. I sat up abruptly and looked around, trying to find the origin of the sound and shake the sleep from my mind. For a moment I had lost time and place and did not know where I was. It wasn't until I saw the bay that everything came rushing back to me, but the sucking sound intensified and actually began to vibrate the very Earth.

From where I sat I could not see the origin of the sound but knew it was coming from the other side of a small forest that reached out into the estuary like a finger of land. As I made my way to the peninsula and pushed through the vegetation I could see the top of a rather large crane. Emerging from the other side of the forest I gasped at a most horrid and sickening sight. A huge dredge was pumping out the estuary, deepening the channel and creating high banks of muck and sand atop what once was the estuary. Bulldozers were moving around the muck, building up the banks of the channel. Further back into the estuary I could see a network of roads and lagoons dredged deep into the estuaries and into the very forests. Houses and docks were in various degrees of construction and the smell of newly laid tar roadways permeated the air.

I was at once frightened and sickened by the whole butchering affair. The life of the estuary had been destroyed and I could do nothing about it. I had to get away from this frenzy of destruction and turned to run. As soon as I moved, the landscape surged and I awoke in the area where I had originally lain down in the first place. It had all been a dream, frightening and deadly, but still a dream. I breathed a sigh of relief, for the estuary was still intact. Still bothered by the dream, and remembering the incident in the cedar swamp, I decided to go to the same peninsula of forest I had seen in my dream. Like in the dream I pushed through the vegetation and out to the other part of the estuary where I had seen the construction. To my relief it had remained as always, untouched, pure, and vibrating with the essence of life. The relief was so overwhelming I actually cried. It had all been a dream.

I turned to leave, but was immediately struck motionless. To my horror, not five feet in front of me was a surveyor's stake with a flag attached to its top. Looking around, desperate to know where it came from, I saw hundreds more, each bearing a marking flag. As I looked at the whole area I could clearly see that the stakes vaguely marked out the same pattern I had witnessed in my dream. Though there was no construction or dredging, the markers of the future roadways, the lots, and the lagoons were clearly there. I was sickened again as I realized my dream was a step into the future. I also knew I could not change this future, for everything appeared legal. These people knew nothing of the importance of the estuaries for breeding fish and all manner of wildlife. To them it was just a huge mosquito pool, and a place to eventually dock their boats. I could do nothing.

I sat down, shaken and unable to think. All of this beautiful estuary would someday be destroyed, as had so many others. Rick, Grandfather, and I would have to find another place, another estuary farther south to visit later on in the summer. We now would be pushed farther into the bay before we could find the purity and magic that was once so close. I knew not far to the north of where I sat was our camp from last year, and judging from the surveyors' stakes it was probably right in the middle of it all. All I could do was to gaze in horror at the whole thing. Though the area was still so pristine and beautiful the stakes marked the beginning of the end. Never again would I be able to play in this part of the wilderness. I thought if I only had one more season in this place, I could honor the land for the last time. I could fuse my spirit with this land so it would forever be part of me, thus always alive within my mind and heart.

I began to whisper to myself, asking some unseen force when it was all going to happen. When will it all disappear, I thought, and with that thought, the landscape seemed to surge again in response to my question. I was taken aback by the feeling at first but then became fascinated by the subtle changes I saw unfolding right in front of me. It was as if time was speeding up, days flicking past like the pages of a book. I could see this early summer day where I sat move into the wavering heat of midsummer, then quickly change into late summer and early fall. The vegetation slowly turned brown, then wilted. Winds began to blow and snows covered the Earth. The little waterways went through a series of freezing and thaws. Snows came and went, until the landscape slowly began to turn the green of early summer again. This was so fascinating, yet confusing, for I did not know what was really happening.

Suddenly I heard the same sucking sound I had heard during my dream. The late spring landscape had now turned into a turmoil of activity. Dredges, bulldozers, trucks, hammering, all in a frenzy of quick activity. Then, as suddenly as it all began, the landscape surged and returned to this time and place. I was so taken aback by the experience and its reality that I could not think at first. All I could do was to marvel at all that had happened. I don't know how, but I got an answer to my question of when it was all going to happen. The answer was also right with my Inner Vision, and I knew it to be truth. Despite the fact that I was sick over the eventual destruction of the estuary, I knew without a doubt I would have at least one year left before I would have to give it all up. I could at least honor the area one last time.

I began to walk out into the exterior, picking my way from island to island, and trying to make it to the camp we had used the previous summer. It wasn't hard to find the camp area, but to anyone else the area would have looked as everything else. No signs that anyone had ever been there, that's always the way we would leave a camp. As I suspected, there was the surveyor's stake right in the center of our old camp, and judging from the color of the flag, it would soon become a road. I knew now the day was growing late and I would have to begin my journey back to Grandfather's camp. But I decided I would sit in this old camp for a few minutes and ponder the outcome of the impending construction. I hoped it would not overwhelm the estuary, and would leave the outer banks alone, but I knew there would be little chance of that.

I began to daydream about what this place would eventually look like in a few years. As soon as the question was made manifest in my mind, I heard the sound of a car and found myself sitting at the side of a roadway. The car sped past as I crawled off the roadway and next to a small tree. As I stood and looked around, I was surrounded by a sea of houses, roadways, and lagoons. I was spellbound by it all, unable to move. It all happened so fast that I lost my bearings. I had no idea of where I was. One moment I was in an old camp area and the next I was in the center of a development. I began to wander in a daze, unable to assimilate all that had happened. Nothing made sense. I began to run, trying to find a patch of woods, like some animal caught out in a parking lot. Finally I found a safe haven of forest behind one of the houses and ran right into its depths. Again the landscape surged, but I hardly took notice.

I continued running, but I had sensed something had changed. I stopped, looked back, and all the images of the development were gone. I decided I had enough and began to hike back to Grandfather's camp, moving quickly and through a different route. I knew it would be faster if I followed the old migration trail through the Pine Barrens, the same trail we always used to get to the estuary. The bad thing about taking this route would be the fact that I would have to cross both the roadways, but at least I would be back before full dark. I had so many questions to ask Grandfather before the day was over. Tomorrow there would be no chance because I had to be back home before my dad went to work. My mind swooned from lack of sleep, fear, and an ocean of questions I didn't know how to ask. I also wondered to myself how I ever got locked into the image of a development. Certainly I had asked to see what the area would look like in years to come, but I could see no clear purpose in the asking.

As I began to cross the first roadway I noticed a huge billboard. Across the top were written the words, "COMING SOON," and underneath was an artist's rendition of a bay development. There was no doubt in my mind that the picture was of the same development I had just emerged from. The houses were the same, the roadways were the same, and the lagoons were the same. The lower map showed all would be destroyed, in that the outer edges of the development reached right to the edge of the bay. There would be no estuary left after next spring. All I knew now was that I had to get to Grandfather and tell him we would have to go to the estuary soon, for it would soon be lost forever. The sign confirmed in my mind and, more importantly, in my heart, that all I had seen had been true. I had asked for the future, dictating time and date, and I had received an answer.

I had traveled fast and arrived at Grandfather's camp just as the last light was passing from the sky. I knew even before I got into his camp he would be waiting for me in his sacred area. I didn't have to wait, for he immediately told me to sit down. I did not have to ask a question for he immediately began to speak, saying, "Yes, Grandson, I know about the estuary. I had been given the same vision of the possible future many years ago. Now, you have seen that it will become the probable future, and there is nothing we can do about it, at least not yet. We will go to the estuary when you return next week from your home. We will honor the land and hold it in our hearts so we can pass down the beauty to our grandchildren. These lands will forever remain alive within us."

"But why was I given the vision of the probable future? I had no purpose other than curiosity," I said. Grandfather answered, saying, "You may have thought you did not have a pure purpose, but the voice of your Inner Vision did. You were

given the first vision of possible future so you could know that
you had but one season left to honor the land before it was put
to death. The second vision of things that would come many
years from now also had a purpose. Knowing what will happen
to this land will fuel the fires within you. This land's eventual
death has taught you that you must prevent this kind of destruction from happening to other areas in the future. You must help
man to understand the delicate balance of these places for they
are the lifeblood of the bays and oceans. The world of spirit
allowed you to see into the future, so you can change things in
the future. This land's sacrifice has become your lesson, a lesson for the future. That is its purpose, that is your purpose."

"How can I ever prevent things like this from happening
in the future? These people who destroy the land are very
powerful and I am a kid," I said.

Grandfather replied, "There are many ways to make changes
and to change the possible futures. It is the same power we
use when we heal others, only now we heal ignorance. You
can change things through the physical realities, which is very
difficult and very limited. You can also change things through
the spirit which is all power and knows no limitations. It is in
the spiritual power that we make change. But, Grandson, you
must rest now. Take the week and understand all that you have
learned. When you return and we visit the dying estuary, I will
teach you the wisdom of spiritual power, which is the greatest
force on earth." Without another word or question I slipped
into my shelter and fell into a deep and dreamless sleep.

8

Power of the Spirit

The week at the house was uneventful at best. Rick and I got to go out and explore the woods immediately adjacent to where we lived, but those forests were far too close to civilization to be pure. There too was an alteration in the flow of nature, but that was better than nothing as far as we were concerned. All week long I had constantly thought about the many lessons I learned about Inner Vision, the world of spirit, the possible futures, and so much else. I so often got wrapped up in thought that I daydreamed constantly to a point where my folks thought I might be sick. However, I was determined to do a great job with the chores, because I didn't want anything to stand in the way of my going back into the woods for a full week with Grandfather and Rick. Not only did I want to live at the estuary for the week, but I still had so many unanswered questions. Though Grandfather had been by to see us several times during the week, we knew better than to ask him any questions, especially spiritual questions.

During that week at home, Rick and I did a lot of talking, especially about the spiritual experiences of the week before. Ironically, Rick and I had similar experiences concerning the

time of the possible future. Like my vision, Rick too had a
vision of a forest being destroyed by a landfill company. He
had wandered upstream on the same day I had followed the
stream to the estuary, and there at the upper reaches of the
stream saw a landfill, where acres of forest had been cut.
Though in the reality of now, the forest remained uncut, Rick
had found out in the local newspaper that indeed the land had
been purchased by a landfill company and was slated to be
destroyed later this same year. Rick's vision of the probable
future had been correct.

So too had Rick wondered to Grandfather what the purpose in it all had been, as I had, and Grandfather told him
essentially the same as he had told me. Rick would use the
landfill as a fuel to fire his memory, so he could protect
other lands from falling prey to the landfills. The impending death of the forest, like my estuary, was a valuable lesson that showed us man's stupidity and intolerable, mindless
destruction. I also found out that Grandfather had mentioned
to Rick about the power of the spirit world: how things in
our flesh reality could be changed through the world of spirit,
for the spirit world was all-powerful and knew no limitations, as did the flesh. This fired our imaginations and was
a great source of speculation throughout the week we were
home.

As the end of the week drew near the excitement became
almost overwhelming. The expected trip to the estuary became
a dream that was about to be fulfilled, and the possibility of
deeper spiritual lessons seemed like the greatest gift of all. We
could not believe all that we had learned in such a short period
of time, yet as we looked back we could see it had taken Grandfather years to get us to that point of understanding. There was
so much that we had learned, we had trouble sorting it all out.
We had spent a good many hours going over all the things we
knew in a sort of list form. We found, however, the overall
wisdom was not just the sum of all its parts, but rather a greater
and more powerful philosophy than we could ever realize fully
at the moment.

There had been one incident during my week at home that really bothered me deeply. I had to ask Grandfather about it, for I was afraid that I had broken a spiritual law and I would lose my ability to use my Inner Vision. I had been riding with my mother in our old car heading into town when the incident occurred. The traffic light up ahead was turning green, when suddenly I got the overwhelming feeling that we had to immediately stop the car. But I did not know why. All I knew was that my Inner Vision was screaming at me to have my mother stop the car. I did not know what to say and in desperation I told my mother I was going to be sick to my stomach. I began to gag and she hit the brakes and pulled off the road, not fifty yards from the traffic light which now had just turned green. A moment later a huge tractor trailer, which had been coming up to the light fast, came to a screeching stop, jackknifing in the center of the intersection.

Fortunately, no one was injured and the truck drove off. If we had not stopped when we did we would have been in the center of the intersection when the truck had run the red light. My mother looked at me and said, "Thank God you got sick or we would have been dead!" She also looked at me with a wry expression on her face and said, "Or did you know it was coming?" I had let little things of the spirit slip before accidently, but my parents were growing suspicious as to how I could know things before they happened. This concerned me quite a bit because I might have broken some spiritual law, not only in letting my ability slip out, but also in using the Inner Vision to save myself and my mother. I felt, in some strange way, that to use the Inner Vision to help yourself was using it for purposes of the ego, thus evil in some way. That question I could only ask Grandfather.

Finally the end of the week arrived and we were on our way to Grandfather's camp. The past week had felt like a month, even though it had barely been six days. The excitement of going to the estuary was powerful, and the closer we got to Grandfather's camp, the more overwhelming it became. Just as we hit the trail leading out of the estuary camp, we saw Grandfather sitting by the edge of the small freshwater pond. He had made camp, not in the original site, but nearer to the pond.

We joined Grandfather and almost immediately he began speaking. Grandfather said, "Grandson, you did not make bad medicine by using the power of the Inner Vision to save yourself and your mother. What comes to us through Inner Vision, especially those things that come without asking, can only be of pure purpose. It is the way in which the spirit world and the Creator warn us of danger or of things to come that will concern us. However, you must take greater care in hiding that which you know. You must always be on guard and be humble.—Now, we must get to work," Grandfather said. I felt the relief sway over me and we busily worked well into the night preparing camp and finally collapsing to sleep in our shelters, thoroughly exhausted from the day. It felt good to escape into the mindless abyss of sleep.

For the next two days, Rick, Grandfather, and I explored the estuary areas. It was a grand time, the estuary was teeming with life and the warm summer days lavished us with their life-giving forces. We swam in the bay every day, digging clams and collecting all manner of shells and odd pieces of driftwood. It was a naturalist's paradise, where there was never a moment without an adventure or something new and wondrous to be discovered. We even made friends with the local duck population. At first we wrapped reeds around our heads and covered our faces with mud, then drifted up to them like some floating island. Eventually we didn't need the camouflage and could swim with them at will. We could even walk right up to where they were resting on the bank and they would rarely even lift their heads. By the end of the second day we could even touch their backs without even a slow hesitation as we reached for them. As far as we were concerned we had been adopted by the duck people.

Not only were we accepted by the local duck population, but became part of everything else. We swam with turtles, fed muskrats, and tickled the bellies of innumerable fish. It was

certainly a paradise, teeming with the lifeblood of the bays and
oceans. Here the small fish would feed and grow into young
adults, then eventually make their way into the oceans. Here,
all things depended on everything else—a chain, where no link
could be broken without causing a lasting disaster. Playing in
the sun and swimming endlessly in the bay took my mind
from the impending disaster that would soon strike this center
of life. Days seemed so endless, and I became time-rich. All
of us were transformed by becoming part of the estuary, and by
becoming part of the estuary we became part of all the oceans
and all the fishes of the world. We were here, where so much
life began—a vibrant nursery of life, and we were accepted
and whole.

On the morning of the third day, as I sat at the far end of
the estuary, watching the sun rise from the bay, I was startled
by the sound of an oncoming vehicle. Like the very animals
of the area, I ran and took refuge in a large stand of cattail
reed, positioning myself so as to see what was coming. I had
become so much a part of this natural world that for a time
I forgot I was human at all, and became an animal. In fact,
I was as frightened as the animals were by the approach of
the roaring engine. It all seemed so alien in this cradle of
purity and life. As I crouched listening, and a little frightened,
I watched animals fleeing. Birds took to the air, muskrats dove
down their underwater tunnels, turtles slid from the banks, and
all manner of things hid. It was as if a hideous poison had taken
hold of the land and I imagined even the vegetation cringed at
its approach. At this point I felt more a part of this estuary than
I ever had before, because I was now one of the inhabitants,
hiding from the roar of civilization and progress.

The sound of the engine was coming from the distant tree
line that marked the edge of the estuary. The sound would stop
for a few minutes, then continue again. With each stopping
sequence, I could hear a chainsaw start, a tree creak, crack,
and then fall to the earth with a crash. Each time I grew more
angry and upset, for it seemed like the very forest was being
raped and killed. Each time a tree would fall, the local animals

would go into a frenzy of activity, as if the tree were part of their own flesh. I too was caught up in this terror. The forest was a barricade to the estuary, and now the wall was slowly falling, allowing the cancer of society to ooze in and destroy the area. I grew sick to my stomach, for the paradise I had known over the last few days was now defiled. The sanctuary was being destroyed as I watched, and I could do nothing.

I watched as a man cut the last few trees at the edge of the estuary, and as soon as they fell and cleared, a huge truck pushed its way to the edge of the grasses. Several men and a woman jumped out of the truck and began to set up some sort of table. Taking what appeared to be maps and other equipment from the truck, they began to gather around the table and look out across the land. I could barely make out their body language as they pointed to the bay and to various parts of the grasslands. I could tell they were talking about the main channel of water coming in from the bay and probably deciding where things should be placed. Subsequently, surveying equipment was brought out and two of the men and the woman walked out across the estuary, stopping periodically to set up their equipment and do whatever surveyors do with that equipment.

The whole procedure made me very angry. Nature did not lay down imaginary lines that divided the Earth. Only man and his greed had to separate things, marking parcels of land he could call his own. In nature, the only lines were natural, like the line between bay and ocean, between estuary and forest, between forest, mountain, and desert. No one could really own the land, I thought, for only the Creator can own the land. Man can only own the land in his heart and only then when he gives up all things for the land and becomes part of the land. Only when man can live with the land completely will he ever come close to owning the land. These surveyors, or builders, or whatever they were, did not know the land, for if they knew it, they could not destroy it. Their presence brought me back to the harsh reality of the ultimate destruction of the estuary.

I watched them work for the better part of the morning. A duck that we called "Gimpy" had waddled up near me and now sat next to my leg, testing me with his beak every so often for assurance. I felt that he was trying to coax me into stopping the slaughter that was going on at the far end of the estuary. In a half whisper, talking more for my benefit than for his, I told Gimpy that I could do nothing about what was going on. Even though I was human, I was not powerful. After all, I told him, these people had the permits, owned the land, and had the money. That was all it would take to make it legal for them to kill the land, and people like me are powerless to do anything about it at all. Land didn't matter to these people, for they saw the land only as profits and money, not as the mother of all things. Their ignorance would not only kill the land but reach far into the oceans.

The surveyors, or builders, began to set up some equipment I had never seen before. It looked more of a scientific nature than of something used for construction. This really grabbed my curiosity and I began to move across the estuary to get a closer look. At first I had plenty of cover so that my progress was rather quick, but as I neared their location the vegetation grew thin and I had to belly-down to get closer. Sometimes I had to swim directly through the muck to get to the next island of vegetation, and it wasn't long before I was completely covered by all manner of dirt and vegetation. The last fifty yards to the work crew took nearly two hours to complete but I finally got to a distance where I could not only hear their words, but almost touch them.

Stalking humans was always so easy, for they were so unaware in the wilderness. Even those who were hunters or naturalists, though better than the typical masses, were inept at understanding the flow of the forest. To me it appeared that most people lived in a vacuum, unaware of anything around them. When Rick and I had first learned to stalk, we practiced on humans all the time, but it wasn't long before we realized that the general human race was no challenge at all. Most of the time I could walk right up to people and they would never see me, but here in the estuary I wasn't going to take any chances. As I said, I felt more of an animal at this point than a human, and these beings were not only alien to the estuary but to me also. I thought this would have been a good time to turn in my membership in the human race, and forever be an animal. I just didn't want to be associated with these beings at all. They might as well have been from another planet as far as I was concerned.

I did not know it at the time but Gimpy had quietly followed me all the way to where I now lay. I almost jumped out of my skin when I felt his beak nibble at my thigh. I am glad I had such control and figured out what it was that nibbled at me, for if I had moved at all the work crew would certainly have noticed me. The duck did not hesitate in climbing onto my back and squatting down to rest. I tried to shoo him away, but he was persistent and settled in for what appeared to be a long nap. I figured that I would just let him stay, not only was he so naturally camouflaged, but I was covered with mud and appeared as just another part of the landscape. I decided we were both very safe right where we were and went back to listening and watching as the work crew set up their equipment.

It wasn't long before I realized that two members of the work gang were having a heated argument. The lady who stood holding a map was arguing with one of the men of the work crew. I suspect this man was the boss of some sort because he was very well dressed and did not help with any of the menial tasks of setting up equipment. Also, he spoke with an air of authority and easily ordered around the other workers, who seemed to obey without question. The lady kept looking at the map and telling the boss-like man that the construction should stop here, pointing to mid-estuary. The boss-like man kept shaking his head and talking about something not being cost-effective. He said he wanted to get everything he could out of the area, and the little strip of land that she wanted to leave really didn't matter at all.

The argument between them seemed to fluctuate between highs and lows. At times they seemed to agree about something but most of the time they disagreed. Through it all, the boss man, like everyone else in the crew, sprayed on insect repellent and complained profusely about the smell of the muck, the green-head flies, and the mosquitoes. Every time the woman talked of saving the outer edge of the estuary, the boss man said it was nothing but the breeding ground of mosquitoes and the smell of the muck would not be appreciated by his clients. She argued that saving the outer edge of the estuary would add a certain aesthetic and pristine value to the ground, making the clients feel as if they really lived on the bay. The argument grew more heated and the stalemate more apparent, continuing well over the next hour.

Finally, the woman got angry, threw down the map, and stomped off directly towards me. My heart leaped into my throat. I felt Gimpy look up and around in her direction, also startled by her fast approach. There was no escape for me, I had to stay put, hoping that she would pass me by and not step on me. Unfortunately, she spotted Gimpy sitting on my back. I could tell by her voice as she began to approach the duck that she hadn't spotted me underneath. As far as she was concerned, I was nothing more than part of the mudscape. She began to approach Gimpy very slowly, speaking to him in a very slow voice. I was surprised that Gimpy hadn't moved away; instead, he just sat there, apparently listening, soothed by her voice in some way. She moved within inches of me, still talking to the duck, and unknowingly standing on my fingers. I slipped into the place of silence to still my breathing and set aside the pain of her shoe on my hand.

She continued to talk to Gimpy, who now stood directly on my buttocks. Still she hadn't suspected that the mound the duck stood on was actually a person. She said, "Hey, little fellow, I know you are upset that we are going to steal your estuary, but I'm working hard to try and save the outer portion by the bay. Trouble is, the owner and builder want all the land. The only reason they even want the outer edge is to get rid of the smell of the mud during low tide, and keep the mosquitoes down to a minimum. Their clients don't understand this place is a very important home for a lot of things. I'm trying my best, but I'm just a hired planner and they don't have to listen to me. I'll still see what I can do for you." Without thinking, and catching myself only after it was too late I said, "Thank you!"

The lady fell back into the muck and let out a bloodcurdling scream that echoed across the entire estuary. Gimpy exploded into flight and, without thinking, I stood. This panicked the woman even more and she screamed again, then began begging me not to hurt her. I must have looked like some strange swamp beast, because no parts of my flesh were visible and the outer covering of debris made me look even more fearsome. I tried to calm her, but the more I spoke the louder she screamed, back-crawling through the mud as she tried to get away from me. After a lot of quick talking on my part, she began to calm down, then finally broke into a hysterical laugh. I laughed too, and in a playful way she picked up a handful of muck and hit me square in the face. She was now laughing so hard she was nearly in tears.

I sat down near her and told her what I was doing in the estuary, and that the duck was actually one of my friends that lived here. She listened, showing great interest in all I was telling her. She told me about how she wanted to save the edge of the estuary, just as she had told the duck. I found out that her name was Nancy and she had been actually brought up on the bay by her grandfather. Though she had been away at college she was planning to move back into the area. She took the job as a planner for the secret reason of saving part of the land, but she admitted that the owners would not hear of it. She was at a point now were she would lose her job if she persisted. She also said that she had tried all manner of other means to stop the construction, but people just did not understand why this place was so important. They only saw money and development.

The men that were part of the work crew had heard her screams from the far end of the estuary and finally arrived in a panic, fearing she had been hurt. As soon as the two workers saw me they stopped running. They were so startled that one slipped and went down into the mud, cussing as he fell. The boss man finally arrived and, after scrutinizing me in a panicked way, began yelling at me. He told me to get off his land and that I should be beaten for scaring the lady. With that he picked up a piece of driftwood and began to come at me, swinging it over his head. The lady tried to stop him, grabbing his arm as he moved by her. He pushed her aside and she fell back into the mud, hard. The man kept coming at me, angry and more aggressive than before, a string of curse words flowing from his mouth.

When I saw Nancy fall back into the mud, I got angry. Though I was only a young boy and half the size of the boss man, I stood my ground. Grandfather had taught me long ago the way of scout wolverine fighting, and I could easily take on this man. He was overweight and out of shape, gasping for air as he ran to me. He was shaken for a moment when I stood my ground, but after hearing his men laughing at him, he took a swing at my upper body. I easily ducked the swing and the follow-through nearly cast him off balance. He swung again, now at my body, infuriated by missing me the first time. Again I easily slipped the blow, and this time the aggressive follow-through sent him to his knees. His fury boiled and he tried to hit me in the head, but that was all I could take, for he was really trying to hurt me now.

The animal within surged inside me and I blocked the stick, grabbed his arm, and threw him over my shoulder and into the slough of deep muck directly behind me. We had practiced that disarming move so many times I didn't have to think. The boss man went in headfirst and buried up to his waist. I now held the stick and, as one of his men began to run at me, I hurled the stick and caught him below the knees, sending him facedown into the mud. The other man backed away with his hands out in front of him in a gesture that he wanted nothing to do with the fight. Nancy just sat in the mud, smiling. By this time the boss man was cursing and ordering his men to get me. I just slipped into the mud and vanished into the estuary. My quick and easy disappearance seemed to infuriate the boss even more.

As I slipped further away I could hear Nancy's giggle.

The boss and his two workers must have searched for me for the better part of an hour before they gave up and went back to their truck. As I watched them drive off I knew the boss was really infuriated and embarrassed by being beaten by a mere boy. Even more so because I had escaped so easily. I knew now that Nancy's job would be nearly impossible because of what happened. There was no way she could ever save the outer edge of the estuary. This boss man was not about to lose another battle. As I watched the sun setting I began to hate this man and all that he stood for. I hated his greed, his ignorance, and his attitude. He represented everything that I hated in society, and the more I thought about it, the more my anger grew. I had won this small battle, but he was going to win the larger and more important one. He would destroy the whole place because of his ignorant greed.

At the same time I was feeling such a hatred for this man, I was also feeling very guilty. So guilty I grew intensely upset. Grandfather, in teaching the wolverine fighting of a warrior, had warned us that a true warrior was always the last to pick up the lance. He had told us that a warrior would first try everything possible to stay out of battle, and only as a last resort would he ever unleash the wolverine. I had not tried to negotiate, I had not dealt from the heart, but through the bad medicine of hatred. I had beaten and humiliated a man through anger and hatred. These were not the virtues of a warrior and I knew I had probably done more harm than good. I had met anger and aggression with anger and aggression, and then no one wins. In a way I felt I had failed Grandfather, violating his trust by abusing the skill of a warrior. So many times I backed away from a fight in school just to follow the way of the warrior, but now I had violated that sacred law. I had to find Grandfather and tell him what happened.

Grandfather lay on the outer edge of his camp, staring up into the intensity of the starry skies. He did not wait for me to say a word but immediately said, "I watched the whole thing happen." Then he fell silent and my stomach became so upset I wanted to vomit. Though the tone of his voice was not accusatory or angry, I still worried about what he might have been thinking about what he had seen. Finally he said, "You made no mistake, Grandson, for you could have been badly injured. The man would not have listened even if you had tried to reason with him. His ability to reason was overruled by his anger. So too did you make the mistake of allowing your anger to overrule your heart. You were not wrong to take his weapon away, but the hatred that followed was very wrong. How many times have I told you that you must love all things, even those situations and people who you would otherwise hate?"

Grandfather paused again and I fell into the silence of my mind. It was so hard to love someone that stood for all the evil things I despised, but to meet hatred with hatred would only compound the power of the hatred. When love replaced hatred, then there was hope. That was easier said than done, especially dealing with such a powerful emotion as hatred. Grandfather spoke again, saying, "I know that at times it becomes so difficult to love, Grandson. This man deals in greed and will soon destroy this place that we love so much. But it is not he that is really at fault. You must see his side of the story to understand him and to finally love him in your heart. He is governed by the values of this society and knows nothing of what he is really doing to the land. It is his ignorance that drives him and causes him to be hated. Do not hate the man, but correct the ignorance."

Again there was a pause as Grandfather allowed me to digest all that he told me. I could see now that it probably was not entirely this man's fault. He was nothing more than a product of a society that looked at land only as a source of income. Even society was not entirely at fault, for no one has tried to teach the masses the truth. But, I thought, modern society is a very strong animal and it would take a very powerful person and finances to reach everyone. It would be too late to save the estuary, and judging from the boss man's attitude, impossible to change his beliefs. As far as I was concerned, there was no hope of saving even a small part of the area. After all, Nancy had tried and failed, and she was college-educated about these things. The more I thought about it, the more hopeless the whole thing seemed.

Grandfather's voice again broke into my thoughts, saying, "Nothing is hopeless, Grandson. You wonder how we could ever change the attitudes and beliefs of this man who would destroy this land. You are right, we are not powerful in the ways of society, and he will never change through just flesh and logic. However, Grandson, there is another way, a way that is powerful and knows no limitations. It is the power of the spirit. If he cannot be reached through the flesh, then possibly he can be reached through the spirit. It is much like a spiritual healing through the power of the spirit, only we try to heal the ignorance and not the body. Until then, until we are directed to use the power of the spirit, we can do nothing. Now, Grandson, you must get some sleep, for at the sunrise of the morning we must honor the estuary as we have promised the spirit of the land we would do.

I could not sleep at first. All that Grandfather had just told me raced through my mind. I could not, to this point, believe this boss man could be reached in any way. Now Grandfather was telling me that there was a way even greater than that of the flesh. I knew the spirit world knew no limitations, but I could not understand how its power could be used to reach someone, or heal someone, who did not even understand the earth, far less the world of spirit. It baffled me, but the prospect also excited me. Where I thought could be no hope, Grandfather had given me hope. As the thoughts of the man were set aside in my mind, I now gave my attention to honoring the estuary, for what would be probably the last time. It was going to be a great loss. Tears filled my eyes as I finally drifted off to sleep.

It was still dark when Grandfather woke Rick and me. We walked immediately to the center of the estuary area, picking our way across the labyrinth of waterways and around mud pits. Finally, by the time we reached the center of the area, the distant horizon was just beginning to lighten with the nearing of dawn. We all stood, awaiting the rising sun. Grandfather, standing as if before God, began to deliver up prayers, while Rick and I bowed our heads in reverence. I knew, though there was much I did not understand of Grandfather's language, he was thanking the Creator for the land, for the waters, and for the rising sun. As the sun began to rise, we all prayed silently to ourselves. Grandfather began a soft drumming on his little drum. Songs of praise were then sung, followed by chants of thanksgiving. The whole honoring ceremony was so beautiful, but so tearful. It was like saying good-bye to an old and trusted friend, a friend that was about to take his final walk to death. I cried like a baby, Rick cried, and Grandfather's eyes were swollen with tears. With difficulty I fought back hard the hatred I felt for those who would kill this place.

Finally, when the prayers were finished and the sun was well above the horizon, Grandfather stopped the drumming and the ceremony was finished. We knew then that this land would forever be part of our hearts, and always in our thoughts. I just felt so bad for the children yet to come, who would never know the power of this place. I vowed then that someday, somehow, I would tell the story of this estuary, this temple. Slowly, Grandfather turned and looked toward the distant edge of the estuary, by the tree line. He then smiled and made a gesture, as if to acknowledge someone's presence. Perplexed by his actions, I turned to see what he was looking at, feeling at first that it might have been a spiritual presence. To my utter surprise, in the distance I could clearly see the boss man watching us. He too waved back toward Grandfather and then walked off into the forest. Grandfather then turned to us and said with a voice exuding complete faith, "The outer edge of the estuary will now be saved." With that he just turned and walked off to camp.

I sat for a long time in absolute silence. Rick had wandered off and I was alone for the first time all morning. I could not believe what Grandfather had said. How could he know, especially with such confidence, that the estuary edges would be saved? He had never met the boss man face-to-face and he

could not have known much about him. Yet he intimated in
his few words a certain familiarity with the boss man, as if
indeed he had met him, but it baffled me as to how. What
also perplexed me was why that man had come to the edge of
the estuary so early in the morning. I was not surprised that
Grandfather had known he was there, but what did surprise
me was the recognition between Grandfather and the man. I
decided to go to the area of the tree line to see what I could
find out about the boss man's presence there.

I reached the area where the man had stood earlier that
morning. It was now approaching high sun, but no one was
around. There was no evidence of the crew or the man. I began
to think that it was not the man I had seen this morning, but his
spirit. But I did not know how. After a good deal of searching,
I finally found the man's tracks, tracks of the flesh reality, and
not the spirit, as I had begun to suspect. Ironically, the tracks
were made before first light, probably at the same time we had
reached the center of the estuary to pray for the land. Following
the tracks back to the area where his truck had been parked that
morning, I found that he had sped to that location, left the truck
in a hurry, and ended up on the edge of the tree line where he
had stood for over two hours. The whole scenario of the tracks
told of a man who had been almost driven to this area at that
time, in a very rushed way. He certainly was not out for an
idle stroll but appeared to have had a mission.

I began to think about the time the man had originally
arrived, how he had rushed to the place, and yet, when he
had gotten to the edge of the tree line, all the rushing stopped
and he just stood there. There was no evidence that he had
done anything else but come here, watch, and then leave.
I could not understand why it had seemed that he had some
sort of urgency, when he did nothing at all when he got here.
So too had he shown none of the anger he had possessed on
the previous day, but instead seemed rather cordial when he
waved back at Grandfather. I was beginning to suspect that
Grandfather had something to do with all of it, but I did not
know how or why. All I knew was that the man had acted out

of character by coming to the estuary so early, and there had to be a reason for it, a reason that was beyond any reason.

I spent a good part of the day wandering and exploring the estuary, especially the section that ran along the bay. It was this section that the argument had been over, this section Grandfather said would be saved. I could see now why it was so important to Nancy to save even a part of this outer area, for it was here in the lush outer reaches that life really abounded. Here were the largest schools of small fish, huge populations of shore-birds, and all manner of other life. If this part of the land was saved, then so too would be a lot of life, and the destruction of the inner estuary would not be so devastating. Of all the estuary areas I traveled, this fringe area was the most exciting, affording all manner of adventures and possibilities for exploration. It became my favorite place.

I lay down on the bank for a while, closing my eyes and relaxing. The thick aroma of the estuary, the sound of lapping waves and singing birds, and the intensity of the midafternoon sun became almost intoxicating. I felt so primal just being near the place, even the horseshoe crabs reached far back in time and were part of the misty dawn of Creation. Here is where truly all life must have begun, here at the shores of the bays and oceans, the Grandmother of all things. My mind felt cleansed and at peace, as if the intensity of the moment washed all my cares away. I was still concerned for the area, but I no longer hated the boss man, especially after this morning's encounter. Something had changed inside me and it felt good. I thought it just enough if all I could ever do was to lie here for just one afternoon. Then the estuary would seep into my very soul and would forever be part of me.

My daydreaming was abruptly broken when I heard voices. I carefully rolled to my belly and looked out across the estuary, toward the direction of the sound. Again there was the work crew, Nancy, and the boss man, doing the same as they had done the day before. This time I could see no argument, but Nancy and the man seemed to be working together. Laughter now replaced the incessant bickering of yesterday. I was amazed, but I was also frightened because I did not want a repeat of the battle that I had faced. I was still leery of the man's temper; after all, nothing really had changed. I decided to stay put, and not move until they went away or, if need be, to the cover of darkness. Then I would slip away without being noticed. It was better, especially in the true mind of a warrior, not to seek out a battle but to walk away from it.

The afternoon wore on and the heat intensified, but the crew continued to work. They tended to stay together, moving from one small area to another, but never moving very far from where I lay. Finally, in the late afternoon, they began to come toward the place where I lay, appearing to want to go right to the bay's edge. I would surely be seen, so I slipped out into the water, followed the edge to a small slough, and began to silently swim back toward my camp area. I felt like an animal again as I easily eluded the work party. Grandfather always said the hunted man always had the advantage, and at times like these it was always so easy to see why. I just kept moving up the slough, being careful not to make a sound or ripple. At one point I must have come within five feet of their position but, judging from their voices, no one noticed me. So too did I pass by many birds and animals along the bank without even alarming them.

As I slid onward, not unlike an alligator, I began to hear the voices farther and farther behind me. Feeling safe now, I crawled up onto the bank, and slid right to a set of human feet. I jumped back and into the slough, taking up a defensive position, only to hear Nancy laughing at me. "Well, I finally paid you back," she said. "Now it's your turn to take a fall in the mud and have the hell scared out of you." I could not believe I had missed her sitting on the bank by the slough. That was stupid of me, for that lack of awareness in another place and time could have gotten me hurt. I had assumed all of them were back by the bay, but that assumption, without evidence, had made a real fool out of me. I felt very embarrassed, especially by being spotted by a human. That was as humiliating as things could ever get. I know Grandfather and Rick would probably have a good laugh if I ever told them.

I rinsed myself off, checked the distant position of the work crew, and crawled up on the bank again. I sat down beside Nancy, still feeling a little embarrassed, then we both began to laugh. It wasn't long before she began to speak about the estuary, but this time with tremendous hope in her voice. She told me that the boss, whose name was Bill, had decided not to destroy the outer estuary. In fact, she told me he was going to save more than half of what she had asked him to, and that the untouched land would be deeded in such a way that no one could ever build on its edge. It would be forever preserved. Then she said, "I don't know what happened to him. It was like a transformation, a miracle. One day he wanted it all, and the next, especially after his trip to the estuary early this morning, he wanted to preserve much of the land. The only thing he said was that he had a dream last night, where an old 'Indian Man' came to him and asked him to save the land."

I was struck speechless, not only because it was some of the best news I had heard in days, but I also knew damn well who the "Indian Man" of his dreams had been. The outer edge would be saved and that's what mattered most—I didn't care how it happened, but it happened. It was a miracle! I was so happy and excited that I jumped up and let out a scream of joy. The next thing I knew, Nancy and I were having a mud fight. Both of us were laughing to a point of tears. Suddenly we heard Bill's voice, and looking up, startled, I saw him standing just a few inches from where we were. I was stunned and immediately frightened as I could feel the animal well up within me. In a flash Bill jumped in, rolling around in the mud like a child at play.

After we were all thoroughly exhausted and covered in mud, I showed them both how to wash it off without getting muddy again when exiting the water. While sitting on the bank, warming in the late-day sun, I was amazed to see Gimpy the duck swimming up the slough and right to us. He waddled up the bank, walked over to me, and lay down at my feet. I picked him up and held him on my lap, and as I looked at

Bill his face looked utterly amazed. Even though we had not talked about the saving of the estuary at all, nor had either of us apologized for the fight of yesterday, there was a certain understanding between us. I looked at him for a long time, then finally picked up Gimpy and placed him on Bill's lap. Bill stroked the duck in amazement. I looked at him as I stood, and said, "This is one of the people you will have saved," pointing to the duck, and I began to walk away. "Tell the old 'Indian Man' that I said hello," Bill said, and I disappeared back into the trough and slipped away.

As I traveled back to Grandfather's camp, my mind was not only swimming with questions, but amazed that Bill had known I had something to do with the old "Indian Man." I knew now, beyond all doubt, that Grandfather had played a big part in this miracle. What I didn't know was how he could have done it, especially with such an instant and miraculous change in the man. Essentially, somehow, Grandfather had reached the man's heart and subsequently saved the estuary. Grandfather not only accomplished all of that, but drew him to the edge of the estuary on the same morning. I was so overjoyed with the saving of the outer estuary and the miracle that happened to Bill, I was crying with joy when I reached Grandfather's camp. It had all touched me so deeply. A hopeless situation was now full of hope.

Grandfather appeared to pay no attention to me as I walked into camp and sat down. Without looking up, he said, "I had already told you that the outer land would be saved. Why is it now such a shock to you? Or was it that you did not really believe me when I spoke that truth?" Now I felt a little embarrassed because at first I really didn't believe Grandfather. Even after I saw the tracks of Bill, there was still doubt. Without waiting for a reply, Grandfather said, "You wonder now how all of this could have happened, and happened so quickly. You know the answer already, for I have told you before. As I have said, there are many ways to reach a person, and many ways to heal a person. We can do these things through the flesh, but the flesh is weak and is at best powerless. But through the power of the spirit, which knows no limitation, everything is possible. When the ways of the flesh have been exhausted, we then approach the power of the spirit."

Grandfather paused and slipped into himself, closing his eyes as if to end the conversation. I knew very well he had said that a healing and so much else could be accomplished through the power of the spirit, but I did not know how. Grandfather spoke again, without opening his eyes, saying, "As I have told you long ago, Grandson, whatever occurs in the physical world—whether actions, thoughts, words, or dreams—also occurs and is preserved for all time in the world of spirit. Our actions here affect the actions in the world of spirit; every action thus changes the world of spirit. So too have I told you that actions and powers in the world of spirit can and will affect and change the actions of the physical realities. What is true for one must also be true for the other.

"You see, Grandson," Grandfather continued, "We can make a change in the physical world which will change the same reality in the spirit realms. If we had confronted this man, Bill, on a physical level, then so too would we have affected him on a spiritual level. But with this man, we could not approach on a physical plane, instead we had to approach his spirit. If we can thus create a change in his spirit first, then that change will make itself manifest in his physical self. If we want change of any kind in anything, and we cannot accomplish this change from the physical and logical level, we can effect this change by using the power to change the spiritual reality. The results will be more powerful, lasting, and absolute. But, as with all things of the spirit, it must be guided by the voice of Inner Vision, otherwise there is no power."

"But how do you go about creating that change in the spiritual reality, and know it will become physically manifest? How did you reach Bill, and draw him to the estuary this morning?" I then asked. Grandfather answered, saying, "Last night, when you slept, I took a spirit journey to find the spirit of Bill. I then took him on a journey through the estuary, showing him how important the land was to all things. It was then that I sat down with his spirit and spoke to him about all the things in life he was missing. How he was trapped by the society, and how he no longer knew life because he was so imprisoned by his flesh and the shackles of success. I told him, his spirit, how he should visit us in the estuary this morning, so he could see how the people who love the land treat the land. Then he would know his dream was reality. This is the way I approached him, it was through the spirit."

"But," I said, "Bill does not appear to be a very spiritual man, and I am sure he has no conception of the way of the spirit you speak of. How then can you reach a man that knows nothing of spiritual things?"

Grandfather then said, "No one, no thing, is without a spirit. The spirit of a man who knows no spiritual things still exists, but is only resting in the reality of spirit, waiting to be awakened and used. All we have to do is to find that spirit through the guidance of Inner Vision and then awaken that spirit. Even those who once showed no spiritual knowledge know their spirit has been touched. If you can then heal the spirit, and heal that spirit with enough belief and power, then the power transcends the spirit and makes itself manifest in the flesh. But remember, we are just a bridge, a vessel, to be used by the Creator, and it is not us who decide to use the power."

To say the least, I only vaguely understood what Grandfather was talking about, but it was enough to help me to understand many of the workings of the spirit consciousness. As far as I was concerned, I still had too many questions. All that I had learned over the past several weeks still lacked power, and I was still but a spiritual child. There was still something missing, still some piece of the puzzle left out, but I did not know what it was. I felt that I was still living too much in my physical and logical consciousness and not enough in the realms of spirit. Journeys to the spirit worlds were still infrequent for me, and still obscure and mostly powerless. Grandfather's voice broke into my thoughts, saying, "To understand all that you have been taught, you must now understand and begin to live the duality of flesh and spirit, where both worlds fuse as 'one.' For the last days in this place, you must learn to walk the duality." With those words, Grandfather wandered off to pray, as did I, awaiting the dawn of duality.

9

Duality

I awoke to the first fissures of morning light that enhanced the deep mists of the estuary, turning the landscape into a wonderland of soft colors and shadow. I had fallen asleep sometime during the middle of the night, in the same place I had gone to pray and meditate. It was a weird feeling, for I could barely remember the prayer time, and now it took me a while to get back in touch with my reality. All I could remember was Grandfather's conversation of the night before, all else seeming so dim and vague. There was far too much for my mind to handle, so too was there still a lot of work that I had to do. The most pressing of which was to try and understand, and more important, to live the duality that Grandfather had so often spoken of. Again, like all the other times, I had no idea where to start.

I began to think back about this duality of flesh and spirit. Grandfather had mentioned it so often, from as far back as I can remember. I suspect this duality was some sort of doorway, and when one finally passed through that doorway, it was much like a rite of passage. However, duality, where one walks in flesh and spirit simultaneously, is easier said than done. For

me, up until this point, the passage into the spiritual realities
had been difficult at best. I had to first enter the place of
silence, where all waters were stilled, and the physical mind
and body were transcended. It was only after this point could
I enter that world, and then not with much power and not very
effectively. So too did I have to go through the silence any
time I wanted to purify my Inner Vision or, for that matter,
any communication. It was so infrequent and quite by accident
any time I even came close to that duality, and with that came
difficulty in separating flesh from spirit.

I could very easily see the importance of walking the duality,
for it put one in constant touch with the world of spirit, while
still existing in the world of flesh. So often I would miss very
important spiritual communications because I was too wrapped
up in the flesh. Then, only the stronger voices of spirit would
hammer through into physical consciousness. When the duality
was reached, that perfect equilibrium, then nothing would be
missed. I knew very well that Grandfather lived the duality
at all times, for he missed nothing in flesh and spirit, he was
constantly and fully connected to the worlds beyond flesh. He
had said so often that we should live equally in both worlds,
but I suspect that Grandfather lived more in the spirit than in
the flesh. In fact, most of what he did was through the spirit
realms.

In my perceptions, right or wrong, I could see there was a
barrier between the flesh and spirit much like a thick veil. In
fact, I was sure now that it was a veil, because upon my own
passage to the spirit world I could see and feel myself pass
through its power. Grandfather had always referred to this first
doorway as the veil, so I suspected, to live simultaneously in
flesh and spirit, one had to exist within this veil, and become
part of its power. Even if my suppositions were true, I did
not know how to become that veil and dwell within its power.
Every time I experienced the veil, or doorway, I passed right
through without any control. I knew that, in any case, I had
to begin my searching within the confines of the veil. At least
the assumption felt good to my Inner Vision.

Somehow, I had to find a way to get into that veil. This way I would still hold onto the physical self, but also live in my spiritual self. By way of shifting my consciousness I could look at something in the physical, then, in an instant, experience the same thing on a spiritual level. I thought also that if this could happen, there would be no need to go through all the silencing techniques that had been needed before to transcend the body and physical mind. Up until now it had to be either full physical living, or full spiritual living, with nothing in between.

Essentially, I thought, this is the living example of what Grandfather called the "bridge." He said that all healers, shamans, spiritual leaders, and visionaries, were bridges between flesh and spirit, and it was through this bridge all power flowed. I could also now understand that it was not the power of the spiritualist, but the power of Creation and the spirit that created this bridge.

I wasted the better part of the morning living in my head. All I had accomplished was to make clear in my mind things that I already knew. At best I had a possible direction, but it was only a vague possibility, nothing substantial or provable. I was working on pure physical mind, and I knew the mind could not understand any of this fully. As I sat, still wrapped in contemplation, a distant movement caught my eye, but when I looked it was gone. It had appeared to be the movement of a person, a presence that I could feel but not see. Then I suddenly realized what it was I had seen or, rather, been given an answer to. Since I could not figure out how to obtain the duality on a physical level, then possibly I should go back and ask the guides of the spirit world. They would surely be a help, and possibly they were already trying to reach me with the movement I had just felt.

I knew, more by instinct than by Inner Vision, I had to move from the area I was now sitting before I could do anything further. I began to wander into the estuary, exploring areas I had not yet been, while allowing my Inner Vision to unconsciously guide me to where I should be. It was a strange feeling, doing one thing and knowing full well on a deeper level you were doing something else, yet not fully apparent to the physical mind. It was like knowing that everything I was doing on a physical level was also happening in the spiritual realms, but not being conscious of it happening on that spiritual level. After all of my excursions into the spiritual realms, there was no question in my mind it was true, for I had so often seen the evidence. Certainly, a strange but very beautiful feeling, but still confusing.

Ironically, after wandering aimlessly for an hour, I arrived at the same place in the estuary where the camp stream entered the bay. It was the same stream I had wandered the week before: the stream that led me to the vision of the future of the estuary. There was no doubt in my mind I had to be here. I sat down in the same place I had the week before, and relaxed for a while, going within to make sure this was where my Inner Vision wanted me to be, so there was no doubt. There was already so much confusion and so many questions of duality that still lingered in my mind, I wanted to make sure I didn't begin this whole quest in a place I shouldn't really be.

As I sat and looked out across the estuary, I slipped into the place of silence, stilling my mind and transcending my body. I could feel the misty veil slip by me, almost unnoticed, and I knew that now I was wholly dwelling in the spiritual realities. Ironically, and quite by accident, another veil of some sort passed by, and the estuary changed completely. When I passed through the first veil the estuary hadn't changed, except for the fact that I could feel a multitude of spiritual presences that could not be defined. As the second veil passed, quite by accident and not knowing how or why, everything had changed. The estuary in this new place was different, it was sunset, and I could actually see many spiritual manifestations where before there had been none. It was a bizarre feeling of having moved from one room to another, and then to another, but not knowing how.

At first I was frightened, for I had only had this happen but a few times before and both of them were by accident. This was the most dramatic change I had yet experienced, and that was the frightening part. The unknown in the spirit world can be frightening and dangerous if you don't know what you are doing. I sat in spiritual awe, gazing off across this vast spiritual landscape, where various forms and entities moved about. These entities and manifestations were not of people, animal, or anything recognizable to me, but more like sensations of misty energy I could feel more than I could see. I had no idea what to do next. I tried to communicate, but to no avail. All I could do was to sit, watch, and marvel at all that was going on before me. I could not understand what was happening or really where I was.

Then suddenly and without any warning, another misty veil slipped by me. The forms of spirit that I could only feel before now seemed to become more visible. It was like seeing things moving in a thick mist where all features were blocked out and all that could be seen was a vague gray outline. This frightened me immensely, but I would not yield to that fear. Again I tried to communicate, but it was met with silence from the entities that passed me. Finally, in the mist I could see a form moving toward me and I could sense that it knew I was there. I could not tell whether this form was a man or woman, but definitely a human form. Still in the thickness of the misty outline I could clearly see that it beckoned me in the old way, Grandfather's way, and I knew the entity was of a Native American spirit.

Without questioning his action, I got up and moved toward his misty image. All fear had passed and somehow I knew this entity was not going to harm me. As I moved nearer to him I again felt another veil slip past me and suddenly I walked into brilliant sunlight. It was much like opening the door of a darkened room and walking into a brilliant day. I was almost blinded at first, but soon I regained my full vision. There, standing right in front of me, was the image that beckoned me. He was no longer just a misty image now, but a young Native American man, dressed in the clothing of a warrior. He gave me the hand gesture of welcome and motioned me to sit down. At first not a word was exchanged between us, for he only scrutinized me, and I was so amazed that I could not even speak.

Finally, after a long moment, he said, "Welcome, you have come a long way, Grandson, and you have only just begun your journey." He paused for a moment, possibly to allow me to get my composure, then he spoke again, awaiting no reply, and said, "Your journey will last your entire physical lifetime, but now you have taken the first step. All that you have learned in the past weeks and months has brought you to this starting point, and now you must begin the journey. It is only the beginning of a long and difficult path, for there are few in the flesh that truly understand. You must learn as the first step to live the 'duality' and become the 'bridge,' as Grandfather so instructed. It is then, when you learn to live the duality that your journey really begins. It is few indeed who make it to this first step, for the masses seem to be just satisfied with the silence and nothing more. You have seen beyond that silence and know in your heart there is more."

Again there was a moment of silence, and I still said nothing. I also suddenly had realized that the spirit spoke in a language that I could clearly understand, with only a hint of an accent. To say the least, I was at once mystified, terrified, and in awe. I felt a little overwhelmed by hearing him say this was only the beginning of a very long journey. So too was I amazed at how much he knew about me. He spoke again, saying, "You must journey to the inner places of the veils, and seek out the old woman who weaves baskets. This Grandmother that you seek will teach you the wisdom of the veils, all that you have passed through to get here." With that, he stood, looked out across the ancient estuary, turned back to me, and said, "I must go now, you have much work to do." Then he disappeared, the whole of Creation surged, and I was back in my flesh reality, sitting quietly in the flesh.

I had no idea of whether I had dreamed it all, or if the vision was of spiritual reality. The whole thing seemed so real, but I had no idea of what the spirit had meant when it said I had to go visit the Grandmother who weaves baskets. I knew of no one, except for Grandfather, who wove baskets and the spirit had left me no direction to go. The spitit hadn't even given me a hint of where I could find this Grandmother. All he said was that I had to journey to the inner places of the veils, and I did not understand what he meant. Anyway, I thought that there was only one veil to the world of spirit, not many of them. I was confused also by the fact that when I had taken my journey I had somehow passed through several things that felt like veils, though I still did not know how or why. I had to find Grandfather, for my confusion was both frightening and I knew it would hold back any further progress. I did not know where to go next to find answers, other than through Grandfather.

I finally arrived at Grandfather's camp in the late afternoon. I was really confused now, because the entire way back my mind had tried to sort out all that happened so I could figure out some answers. The more I pondered, the more confused I had become. Grandfather sat by the edge of the estuary, and as I drew near, and without looking up, he said, "I talked to the young warrior spirit." Those words hammered at my mind. How could he have known that I had met a spirit, I wondered? Could it have been that his spiritual presence was also there when I was there and, if so, then why did Grandfather not try to help me when I was there in the spirit? Grandfather again spoke, saying, "You come here to find out what the spirit meant about finding the Grandmother that weaves baskets in the outer veils," and he motioned me to sit down by him.

Grandfather said, "The reason that the spirit did not give you further details of your journey was that he sensed in you a certain confusion and fear. He knew that you would come back to me so there would be no more fear or confusion. You should have understood by now that your Inner Vision was telling you this spirit would not harm you. If your Inner Vision gave you the feeling of bad medicine, then you would know that what you spoke to had evil purposes, but this was not the case. So too do you know what the spirit spoke of when he told you of the outer veils. When you began to move through many veils to get to the spirit, you should have seen then, and known in your heart that there is not one veil, but many."

Many veils, I thought; I was having enough trouble trying to understand one veil, and now Grandfather and the spirit were saying that there were many. This seemed to really complicate things greatly, so much so that I did not even know where to begin to ask questions. Grandfather spoke again, saying, "The world of the spirit is at once one place, but also many places. It is a land of many dimensions, each separated by a veil. With the first veils passed, you enter the world of the spiritual reality of its physical counterpart. Then more veils are passed as you go to the veils of the past, and future, and beyond are vast domains of very powerful places and spirits. In these domains are both good and evil. The farther out into these veils that you travel the more powerful the spirits and places become."

Grandfather continued, "When you begin your spiritual path in life, it is these places and veils that will become your teachers. You will make long and short journeys into these veils, learning of what the spirits have to teach you. They become your guides and teachers, and will direct you to other guides and teachers, as the young warrior spirit has just done for you. As always, your journeys there must be guided by your Inner Vision, for it is not a place for random exploration. To go there without pure purpose would subject your spirit to all manner of attacks. There are not places to play in, for a spirit that goes into these veils without direction is in danger of being lost in the abyss forever. There is no play, only wisdom, and the path is very long and difficult. So too can the battles there leave lasting physical manifestations in your life. So take care in your quests of the spirit, that you always follow your heart."

With those words, Grandfather vanished, and I found myself back in the place where I had encountered the young warrior spirit. Even with all that I had lived through thus far in my short life, I was not ready for such a quick change in consciousness as I had just gone through. It was so astounding I literally shook. It took me a long time to get back my composure, and even to fully realize where I was. It took me longer still to get rid of the fear that was inside me, causing the paralysis that I felt. Grandfather's warnings about the power of the veils really scared me and I wanted to make sure my Inner Vision was working well before I ventured any further. As I looked around, the young warrior spirit was nowhere in sight. I could sense things moving across this ancient estuary, but nothing made itself manifest. Suddenly, I spotted the young warrior spirit far up ahead, and partially hidden again by a misty veil. He beckoned, and I moved toward him without hesitation, trying to smother my fear.

As I drew near to him and passed into the mist, I heard him say, "Begin your journey to the Grandmother now, she is just beyond this place," and his voice was gone. Immediately upon passing through the veil I was moved into a different dimension. Again the estuary appeared in its ancient state, but now I could hear the voices of people, though they did not speak English. I looked behind me, from where the voices came, back toward the direction of the veil that I just passed through. To my amazement there was a full village of Native Peoples. Within the village there was a tremendous amount of activity as people worked and children played. I began to unconsciously walk toward the village but, to my amazement, no one took notice of me, but went about their business. I knew, especially because of the location on the estuary's edge, that it had to be a Lenni-Lenape village.

As I looked around, learning first hand their skills and life-styles, I noticed at the far end of the village sat an old woman, weaving a basket. Without a doubt, I knew this was the Grandmother I was supposed to see. She looked up at me and smiled, but I was puzzled why she could see me and no one else in the village could. Without hesitation, she said, "Do not worry about the village, for I am the one you have come to see, and it does not concern them. I am the basket weaver and herbalist of these people, it is my medicine and purpose that allows me to see you. Though you will encounter many spirits in your journeys through the veils, not all will be able to see you. Only those spirits that have led very spiritual lives when in the flesh will be able to communicate, the remainder will remain unconscious of your presence."

She paused and then continued, saying, "You see, Grandson, it is in the world of spirit as it is in the world of flesh. There are those who remain asleep still, going about spiritual life as they went about life when they were in the flesh. Their existence here is benign, and does not affect things either way. As for the rest of us who sought in life only the things of the spirit, our existence here is powerful, but that power varies greatly. We now seek the purity of the 'void,' as surely as we sought the purity of the spirit when we were of flesh. Though our world has changed from flesh to spirit, the quest remains the same. True enlightenment for us only comes when we touch the void, that which stands before the Creator can be touched. You pass from physical life to spiritual life, but the battle rages on, there is no rest, Grandson, so prepare for a long and difficult path, the path that leads to God."

My mind, or my spiritual mind, I do not know which at this point, raced, and was overwhelmed by what she had said. I could not believe the battle could go beyond that of the physical battles. What she had just told me was that when we pass to the "other side," the battles would continue. The wars in the physical world also take place in the spiritual world and the battles do not end until we touch God. It seemed to me to be one endless trail of tears, as I heard Grandfather so often speak of: one long and hard path that never seemed to end. But, to give up one's life for the saving of the Earth, for the countless grandchildren, that is enough reward, if we love enough. It seemed to me that it was well worth the sacrifice of self, and the self, the ego, had to be sacrificed if we were to reach the spiritual limits, which knew no limits.

The old woman continued, saying, "As you begin your journey, you will perceive this spiritual world as having many veils, many lands and spiritual entities. But as you grow old and wise in the ways of the spirit, these veils will fuse and the spiritual world will no longer be defined by the veils. This then will happen only when you no longer need the veils as signposts that mark the various dimensions of the spirit world. Use then the veils in your spiritual travels, for they help you to know where you are going, like landmarks in the wilderness. For the moment, you must only understand what they are, and nothing more. However, and I warn you, some veils cannot be entered at first, not until you understand the powers and wisdom needed to penetrate them and to understand what is on the other side."

The Grandmother-who-weaves-baskets continued, "Your quest right now, Grandson, is to understand what is truly meant by the duality. Once understood, then you must live that duality, for it is in the duality that we really begin our spiritual journey through life. If one does not constantly live the duality, then he will receive only incomplete messages, and then only part of the time. Life is not just one dimension, but two, and both dimensions must be lived. This dimension will become like a doorway to you and mastery must be the foremost quest on your mind at this moment. To find that duality you must start with a Vision Quest. It must be here in the edge of the estuary, where I now sit." She stood and motioned at the ground where she had sat. I moved into her original position and sat down without saying a word. I did not know if I was to take this quest in the spiritual dimension or the physical. I just obeyed without question.

As soon as I looked out onto the land, she was gone, the daylight was gone, and I found myself sitting in my flesh reality at night, by the edge of the estuary. At first I was not shocked by the speed of the change, but at my new location. It certainly was not the same place at the stream where I had started earlier that day. It was all so baffling, for all I could clearly remember of a journey was my travel from the stream area, where I originally met the young warrior spirit, to Grandfather's camp. From Grandfather's camp, to the place of the old woman, and then to this time, place, and new location, I remembered nothing. All I knew was that right now my physical body and consciousness were here and now, but in an entirely new location, with no recollection of how I got here.

I began to wonder if I had somehow unconsciously wandered to this place while I was in my spirit mind, thus having no memory of the spiritual journey. Even though it was still full dark, I began to crawl from the area on my hands and knees, searching for footprints of mine that would have led into the area. That would confirm my suspicion of the unconscious wandering. Normally, I could pick a fox track from the leaves and follow his trail while blindfolded, but this night I could find no tracks at all. Animal tracks, yes, but certainly no human tracks. This really perplexed me, because it defied any logical explanation, but I suspected that I was just tired and out of touch with tracking. After all, there was a lot else now going on in my mind and I was exhausted at all levels of my existence. I lay down to try to think more clearly, but quickly fell into a much needed sleep.

I awoke to a most beautiful sunrise, thoroughly refreshed and at peace. It wasn't long before my curiosity got the better of me, however, especially when I could not find my tracks leading to the area where I sat. I wandered away from the area, searching for evidence of my approach, but there was nothing to be found. I really began to grow confused and in desperation headed over to my original sit area by the stream. There were my tracks, but only my tracks leading into the area from the day before and no others. There were no tracks leading out, no tracks leading back to Grandfather's camp, either. I had no idea what was going on, but all I knew was that I had gone to Grandfather's camp and ended up in the new sit area. I could explain the trip to Grandfather's camp possibly as a spirit journey, but I could not explain how my body got to the area where the old woman had directed me to sit.

My mind was very troubled for answers, but there were none. The assumption that I had walked over to the new area in an unconscious state was dashed, for there was no evidence at all. I began to wander in huge circles around my original sit area by the stream, the same way I would have done if searching for tracks of a lost hunter or child. Still there was nothing, and the more of nothing I found the more confused I became. Suddenly

I sensed something watching me as I circled my sit area, and to my amazement there stood the Grandmother-who-weaves-the-baskets, looking at me sternly, but she was not in her time and place, but mine. She said, "Grandson, I told you that you have work to do. You are supposed to be where I told you to sit and seek a vision. Why are you wasting your time on things you will learn later, but cannot be explained now? Go back to your Vision Quest. Answers to these questions will be given only when you can understand them." With that she was gone.

I felt ashamed, for in a way I had let her down and subsequently let myself down. I had allowed my mind to lust after answers, effectively removing me from the spiritual task at hand. I should have realized last night, when I could not find my tracks, that I was placed here for a reason. Not to figure out how I got to this place in the first place. I wandered back, feeling a little depressed over the whole thing, but decided to let all the questioning go until I finished my quest and saw Grandfather again. Right now I had to get back to where the old woman had directed me and undertake the task of understanding the duality. I had a feeling the answer to the missing tracks would also be found when I finally understood duality. Everything else I had questions about would probably be found there too.

I settled back down in the area for a long stay. I had only five days left until I had to return home and four of those days would be needed for a traditional Vision Quest. I had already wasted a lot of time sleeping and subsequently searching for tracks and answers, and now I could waste no more. As is the custom before all Vision Quests, I prayed to the Creator, asking for blessing and enlightenment. I also felt a little guilty, because for the past days and weeks my concentration had been on the spirit world and removed a bit from the Creator. I knew that this was very wrong, for it is only through the Creator's love that we have the world of nature and the world of spirit. It is our birthright, given only by the Creator, that lets us even come close to these gifts and not by the doings of nature or spirit alone.

After a long meditation and prayer, I gazed out across the estuary, thanking the Creator for such beauty and all of the things I was given the privilege to learn. The sheer beauty of the area, coupled by the intense vibration of its life, seemed to cast my mind into a state of euphoria. All seemed so perfect, a perfect gift of life on a perfect day. I could not ask for more. In this state, I let go all of my thoughts and questions, satisfied to just sit and relax as my quest began. It felt good to get away for a while, a short excursion from living in my head as I focused my attention back to nature. After all, wilderness was what this was all about, this is what I was trying to save, and it was just so good to get lost in its beauty once again. It was the best reality the flesh had to offer.

It was not long until the state of peace and euphoria vanished and I was back into my mind, concentrating on what I was trying to understand. The duality seemed difficult, yet I had learned so much over the past few days. I tried all manner of things to find the answers. I tried to clear my mind to the point of quiet waters, where there was nothing but pure thought which produced nothing. I then tried for several hours to use my Inner Vision to direct me, but there was nothing clear as to the way I had to go to find answers. I tried penetrating the silence of the veils, and though I could easily slip through the deeper veils, nothing communicated with me. I hoped I had purpose enough in trying to seek answers so I would stay safe while wandering these spiritual realms, but still the fear at times became overwhelming.

As I often felt, especially during the Vision Quests of the past, nothing of Earth or spirit really wanted to communicate with me. I felt this lack of contact was due to my unworthiness, or for something I had done wrong and was ultimately being punished for. Again, as always, I felt as if I was being carefully scrutinized and tested, but I did not know how. All I could sense was an intense vulnerability, at times bordering on unreasonable panic. It seemed that the more I tried to find answers or direction to the wisdom of duality, the more resistance I met, the more I felt like I was being watched. Still, for all my intense trying, I was getting nowhere, except for being very frustrated and a little angry. Yet the anger was not toward anything outside myself, but for myself. I was failing in my quest and I did not know why.

There came a point, late that night, that I was so upset and mentally exhausted that I just let go of my search for duality. It was not that I didn't care anymore, but more of a feeling of being unworthy, thus giving up the battle for answers. Up to this point in my life I had never used so many spiritual techniques on any Vision Quest, and never before had I received so little in the way of knowledge. To me it had all been a failure, and now the first full day of the Vision Quest had been wasted. As I began to slip off to sleep, I thought that it was enough for me if all I ever learned about the world of spirit was what knowledge I already possessed. After all, most people would never come close to the things I now knew. I thought that possibly my spiritual education was now finished and that was all there was ever going to be for me. Or, possibly, there would be many years before I could ever take the next critical step to duality. What I had learned in the past few weeks had been learned fast enough, now the spirit world seemed as if it were pausing for a while, or abandoning me. I fell into a deep sleep.

That night my dreams were many, bordering on nightmares that at times would rocket me out of my sleep in a cold sweat. I dreamed of landfills and developments, the cutting of forests, and the waters of the earth being defiled and poisoned. I dreamed of hideous beings, half human and half spirit, biting at my back and tearing apart my body. Most of all I dreamed of the veils which turned into walls of brush and rock, becoming impenetrable, or getting stuck in those walls, imprisoned and smothered, where I could not get out. I cried to the spirits for help, but they turned their backs on me, sometimes ridiculing me to the point of tears. At times several dreams would fuse together creating even more hideous and tormenting images. Finally, somewhere before dawn I dreamed I had crawled to Grandfather for help. He saw me and said, "Give me a reason to help," and with that he turned his back to me and walked away.

I awoke in a panic, pouring in sweat, and crying like a baby. The whole night had been one long struggle, but as I looked out to the dawn sky I felt a sigh of relief sweep over me. I worried for a while that my dreams were a result of not being in touch with my Inner Vision enough during the day, and that they really contained a deep message. What message I did not know, only that I had been tormented and everything seemed to be turning its back on me or attacking me. Even the things I trusted, including Grandfather, had turned their backs on me and I felt so alone, so unworthy still. It was at this point that I prayed, and prayed in earnest. I called out to the Creator, and said out loud, "Please, I have to find the wisdom of the duality. I have to know what it is to be that 'bridge.' I cannot go on without knowing. I cannot help anyone, anything, or the Earth, without being able to live that duality. Please, I want to be that bridge. Show me the way."

I looked up from the intensity of my prayers, my heart aching, and my eyes still filled with tears of despair. As I looked out across the estuary, I was startled to see Nancy and some older man walking along the outer edge, near the bay. I became curious because I had never seen this man before and I wondered to myself if he had something to do with the construction. I also grew worried because I thought he was going to talk Nancy out of saving the outer estuary. Without thinking and working more on instinct than anything else, I decided to go down to see them, forgetting I was supposed to be in the midst of a Vision Quest. As I got closer to them I could see that the man was a little older than Nancy, but not by much, and assumed at this point that possibly he was her boyfriend. He seemed to be talking to her, but she was paying no attention, almost as if she was purposely ignoring him out of anger.

As I stood, I waved, and they waved back, and Nancy motioned me over. I began to talk to Nancy, asking her how the saving of the estuary was going and waiting for her to introduce me to her friend. She looked a little upset and preoccupied and I again assumed they had a fight. I found out from Nancy that the outer edge of the estuary was already written into the outer plan and approved and things were going well. I then asked her why she looked so depressed.

Before she could speak, her friend said, "Because she is having an affair with Bill, who is too old for her, and she does not want to leave him to go back to college and get her master's. She doesn't really love him either, but she won't admit it to herself." Nancy just ignored him and said to me that she was just feeling a little sick. I replied, "Well, that's a lot to consider, no wonder you feel troubled." By her startled reaction, I could tell she had no idea what I was talking about. Nancy looked bewildered. The man then said, "How did you know what was upsetting her? Can you see me?" At that moment, I realized this was not a man at all, but a spirit. I instinctively was directed by my Inner Vision not to reveal his presence, so I quickly tried to recover my statement with Nancy by saying she just looked very frustrated about something, and shrugged the rest of it off. I secretly hoped I didn't reveal too much. At the same time I was dumbfounded for a moment, for I was seeing both flesh and spirit. That realization struck me and I was overjoyed, almost animated, because I now stood on the bridge between flesh and spirit. The spirit was also overjoyed, to say the least. Nancy just stepped back with a dazed look on her face.

The spirit then introduced himself as her father, and his name was Mike. He explained to me that he had been desperately trying to contact Nancy ever since he and his wife died several years ago in a car crash. He was overwhelmed with the idea that he finally could speak to Nancy. That is, through me. While we were talking, Nancy suddenly sighed and started to share her problems with me. Mike gave her fatherly advice which I translated as best I could. After about an hour of talking, Nancy finally said, "All right, all right, I don't know why, but I'll take your advice. I'm going to finish college and get my degree. Gosh, you're not my father, you know." At that point she turned to me as if she just heard the answer to a question she never asked. She continued, "There's something familiar about you, but I can't put my finger on it." She then gave me a quick hug and thanked me for the advice and walked out of my life. Mike also thanked me, and turned, continuing to walk beside her.

As I sat back down I began to think about Nancy, and how happy she had been when she left. When I first met her she seemed so strong and together, only to find that she had been tormented deeply. I felt, if even for a moment, that I'd been a bridge for her.

I realized I had to get back to my Vision Quest and start my search for answers. My biggest problem right now was that I did not know how I got into the consciousness of duality in the first place. One moment I was sitting in my quest area, and the next moment I was watching Nancy walking with a spirit. The only thing I was absolutely sure of was that before I saw them, I had been deeply in prayer about the duality, and that could have been the catalyst. Still, I was not sure as to how or why.

I decided then the answer must lie somewhere in the prayer, or at least in the circumstances surrounding the prayer. I went into a state of prayer again, saying almost the same thing as before, only this time with much more earnestness. I opened my eyes as before, but unlike before the estuary remained silent and unchanged. Nothing was about, nor did anything try to make its presence known to me. I tried again and again, but was met with failure. Frustrated, I attempted to enter the veil, going through silence very slowly and carefully but, to my anguish, nothing happened, there was not even a veil. I had to leave and tell Grandfather, as if he didn't know what had happened already.

I walked out of the quest area and directly to Grandfather's camp. The whole trip was agonizing, in that I did not want to face Grandfather, but I knew I had no other alternative. Still, the one thing I felt good about was being able to help Nancy with her problem. It was one of the best feelings I had in a long time and, in a way, I was proud of myself. I was also humbled by the power that flowed across my "bridge," especially honored to be used by the spirit world. I desperately wanted to be able to do that again, to help more people.

I reached Grandfather's camp at dusk and found him sitting by a cold fire. He looked up at me and smiled, then said, "The duty of a true healer is to be a 'bridge' for those who cannot see. You become a light in the dark, used by the Creator and the world of spirit to help others." Grandfather paused for a moment, and I felt a smile creep over my face. He then continued, "However, Grandson, you almost revealed your power without your Inner Vision telling you to do so. Great care must be used to hide the ability, and each situation will dictate what you must do. But I feel in your heart you will know what to say, because your inner voice has become stronger and purer. You should have known before you came back to me that your Inner Vision was telling you what you did was right, and that you broke no rules. So too did your heart tell you what you did was good, and you enjoyed the feeling of being able to help someone. A feeling that is one of the most satisfying you have ever had. In a way this is a reward to Nancy, from Creation, for helping to save the estuary."

He continued, saying, "Now you must go back and finish your quest, and find the rest of the answers that you seek. You did not lose anything that you have gained thus far. The reason you feel the duality has left you is because you are not needed right now by the spirit or the Creator. There is nothing to be done at this moment, but you still live the duality. Though the duality is not yet strong within you, you are still able to see both worlds when the spirit so directs. Your Inner Vision will call to you when you must shift worlds, or see those worlds at the same time. It is only when we make the last commitment that we are permitted to live these worlds of flesh and spirit at once. You have already called out to the Creator and the spirits, but you must, someday, seek a full commitment." With that, Grandfather motioned me back to my quest area, and I left immediately, not even thinking to ask more questions.

By the time I got back to my quest area it was full dark. Now all I had left of the quest was a little more than a day, and still so much work left to do. At this point I could barely stay awake, not only because of the extreme fatigue I felt, but because of the relief I felt from finding out I did not lose the duality. It was like getting a new lease on life. I do not know what I would have done if these gifts had been removed from me, for I was still very young, and I could not conceive of the rest of my life being little more than wandering in flesh reality. That would be like not living at all as far as I was concerned. I could not understand how most people in the world were so satisfied living only in the flesh. Spirituality to most was worshiping one day of the week for no more than an hour. Spirituality was constant worship.

It wasn't long before I fell into a deep and much needed sleep. Unlike the night before, there were no tormenting dreams or thoughts that awakened me. Instead, I awoke at dawn in the exact position I had fallen asleep. I felt so awake, ready to face the last day of my quest with a clear mind and a rested body. As I looked out across the estuary, getting ready for my morning prayers, I noticed a man coming directly toward me. As he drew closer, I was amazed to see that it was Mike.

Finally reaching my quest area, he sat down at the edge and smiled at me lovingly. I looked quickly around the area and found, to my delight, I was also seeing the physical world. I was back into the duality and I almost cried. He smiled at me again, and said, "I want to thank you for what you did for me and my daughter. I have tried so long to contact her, but she could not hear, nor did she know how to listen. If it was not for you, then she would have made a terrible mistake. I cannot thank you enough." With that, he put out his hand and touched my arm, then cried.

At this point I did not know what to say to him. I hadn't realized not only did I help Nancy but also her father. It was a good lesson, for I thought I could only help someone in the physical world and not the spirit world. I did not know the power of the bridge could flow both ways, at least not until this moment. The spirit finally spoke again and said, "Since you have helped me so much, I would like to return the favor and help you. But you must understand I do not have much power here, because while of the flesh I did not lead a very spiritual life, and here I struggle." I told him I was not looking for a reward or for any help. That was not the reason I helped Nancy or him. I wasn't into all of this just for rewards.

Finally he said, "Grandfather has told you there must be more commitment to the world of spirit and the Creator, before the duality can grown stronger, before you can live both worlds at once. What he meant by that was very simple, yet at the same time, very profound. The commitment means simply that you must give up your life for the Creator. All your hopes and dreams, your ego, and all else must be dedicated. Total commitment of all that you are, even to laying down your life. But you are too young yet to make that commitment and there is still much that you must learn. I only wish that I could have made that same commitment when I was young, for now I could do more good. No matter what philosophy, doctrine, or religion one follows, we can only become tools of the Creator when we make that total commitment. Until then, the power and purity of duality can not be realized."

He thanked me again and walked off into the estuary, then disappeared in the morning mists. I had been too shocked to say good-bye. Total commitment, I thought, the absolute sacrifice of one's life to serve the Creator. That would be a hard one to make right now, for I loved the wilderness too much, and I didn't want to lose it and have to go back to society. My Inner Vision hammered at my heart that I was right, but only for now.

I sat for much of the day, pondering the things the spirit had told me. I was not tormented by what he said, but rather awed. The final and absolute commitment would be the supreme test of faith, and an awesome responsibility to live that commitment for the rest of one's life. I decided, on a logical and spiritual level, that the spirit of Mike had been right, in that I was not ready to make that kind of commitment now. Not

because I couldn't, but because I did not know enough. That
at least gave me some peace of mind and uplifted my spirit.
I knew also that Grandfather must have been faced with the
same commitment and that now he lived it fully. I understood
why he did the things he did, so many times without logical
explanation. It was because his life was not his own, but guided
by the Creator. I cried for him, long and hard.

I stood for a while, trying to shake the last of my tears
and anguish away. I spent the last remaining night in prayer,
thanking the Creator and the spirit world for all of the wondrous gifts. By the first hint of the rising sun, I was headed
back to Grandfather's camp. Even though I knew I would have
to return home the next morning it didn't bother me. I had too
much to digest in my mind and I would need a mindless break
from all of the searching. The past month had been a powerful
lesson in spirit, now it was my turn to run a little wild and free
for a while. I finally reached Grandfather's camp shortly after
the sun came full into the skies.

I told Grandfather all that had happened to me, leaving out
the part where I had cried for him. After a long moment,
and with a smile on his face, he said, "Do not cry for me,
Grandson, for I have made my commitment long ago and I
would not live life any other way. I do as the Creator asks,
and it makes me soar to the skies. There is no greater feeling
of satisfaction in life than to work outside oneself, especially
for healing the Earth and the people of the Earth. I do as my
vision and my heart tells me to do, for a man not living his
vision is living death. For me, Grandson, there is no other
way to live. Everything else is but flesh and there is no middle
ground. Either you are committed or not, for no one can be
half committed. You too, someday, will know and will have
to face the ultimate decision."

Grandfather continued, "Questions also abound in your mind
as to how you were able to move from my camp to that of the
old woman, the basket weaver, so quickly and easily. When
you walk the duality there is no effort in changing worlds, for
your Inner Vision empowers you to move to where you have

to be or to where you are needed. So too do you wonder how it was that you journeyed from the place of the stream to the place of the quest, yet leave no tracks. It is because, Grandson, your spirit was so strong in the place of the quest that it brought your body to it through the veil. There was no need for the body to travel, but just reappear where needed. These things are not to be understood by you now, for you have much to learn. The time will come, the time will come soon enough."

There was no other conversation about spiritual concerns for the rest of the time at the estuary. Instead Rick, Grandfather, and I just explored and played for the rest of the day. It felt so good to be set free of my constant searching for a while and revel in the splendor of this place. At sunrise I left camp and headed home. I turned one last time to look at the estuary, and there, standing in the rising sun, was Mike, waving at me. To my shock, standing beside him was Grandfather, and they both waved. Finally, I was beginning to understand, but without really understanding what I understood. That was good enough for me.

I had touched what was and what could be. I finally entered a world that few people of the flesh would ever know or even understand. I was satisfied, however, that no matter how wrapped up in the flesh society was, they could all sense there was a greater world that lay just outside their comprehension. No matter how much they denied the existence of this world, no matter how much they tried to rationalize with their overbearing rational skepticism, there remains deep within each of them a sleeping spirit. A sleeping spirit that now I so desperately wanted to awaken. As I walked up the dirt driveway to my home, I could feel myself slipping toward the point of total commitment, and now I understood Grandfather.

10

Water

It was mid-August: hot, dusty, and still. There was not a breath
of wind to stir the choking air. The high humidity acted like a
magnifying glass that caused the sun to sear the flesh with such
intensity that even the shady areas afforded no relief. I pressed
on along the trail called Drudgery that led through an area of
the Pine Barrens we called Hell. Hell was a good description
of this particular land for there were no streams or springs for
many miles, and this part of the forest was always so dry. We
always avoided cutting directly through Hell, especially in the
hot summer, for it could become torturous. Many times we
would go out of our way for several extra miles just to avoid
the heart of this land. Although it would take us hours longer
to circumvent, the extra miles were well worth the water along
the way.

I had no choice but to cut through the center of this area,
for I was seeking an area called the Cauldron, where I was
told to stay for several days. The Cauldron was located almost
directly in the center of Hell, and there was no other way to get
there but by Drudgery Trail. The Cauldron was a place always
avoided in summer. Simply, it was an old gravel pit, no larger

than 100 feet across, but so deep that when sitting in its center, one could not see the trees. Nothing grew in this pit, for there was no water or seeps, and the soil was little more than stones and hard sand. In the summer it was like a furnace, with intense searing heat, magnified further by the white sands and opaque stones.

I had been walking the trail nonstop since first light, and now the high sun burned my flesh and cracked my lips. I had no water, nor would I drink it if I had. In a way I was being punished, punished by my own complacency and for taking the gift of water for granted. Grandfather had sent me here, or rather requested that I come to this place, but his requests were more like law than choice. If I wanted to learn, I had to push beyond my limits and at least attempt every request he made, otherwise my knowledge and understanding would stagnate. Each lesson, each request, became like a rung on a ladder, bringing me closer to the ultimate "oneness" with each step climbed. To Grandfather, this was to be one of the most important lessons of my life.

As I walked along Drudgery Trail my mind began to wander back to the events of the previous day, a day that now, in the choking heat, seemed so long ago. That day, yesterday, seemed to start out like any other day, but as the August heat turned oppressive, events and moods seemed to grow sullen, where everything seemed in slow motion. Every chore became difficult, and thinking became a distortion of reality. The camp chores, coupled with the heat of the afternoon, became a real test of endurance. However, I knew I had to work up to full capacity, even in the heat, because that would eventually build the body and mind to be able to function in all weather conditions. It was our practice to do our daily workout routine in the harshest weather conditions we could find. This way, we would not succumb to adverse conditions when a survival situation demanded the most from us.

It was during mid-afternoon when my troubles began. We had just returned from a long and waterless hike that took us from our camp area to the sandstone pit, then back to camp. Not only was the heat violent, but there was no shade along the trails. To make matters worse, I had carried two huge sandstone blocks all the way back to camp from the sandstone pit. We needed the sandstone blocks as our sandpaper to smooth our arrows which we had been making for the past few days. To say that I was exhausted when I reached camp would have been an understatement. I was so tired, hot, and thirsty by the time I reached camp and put down the heavy blocks of sandstone, my head swam at the edge of blacking out. As usual, Grandfather looked totally unaffected by the whole ordeal, even though he had carried double the number of blocks back with him.

As soon as I dropped the blocks I ran straight to the swim area, plunging in without hesitation. I swam and drank at the same time, as I imagined my flesh making a hissing sound much like water hitting the hot sweat-lodge rocks. I drank so quickly that I almost choked myself in the process. Slowly, I could feel my strength and energy returning and my mind cleared as the waters worked their magic. The waters washed away all the fatigue of body and mind and I felt whole again, refreshed and invigorated. It was then that I noticed Grandfather sitting by the water's edge staring into its surface, unmoving and solemn as he gazed.

I knew he must have been as parched and thirsty as I was, yet he would not enter. Instead, as always, he prayed as he touched the surface of the water. Slowly, his body trembling in the rapture of it all; he then entered the water in a slow and elegant way, much like the ritual of baptism. It was a long time before I saw him drink. At first he only touched the water with his finger, then moved that single drop to his parched lips. He held a handful aloft as an offering to the Creator. He gazed again into the waters, cupped his hands and held it up to the light, and breathed in deeply its fragrance. Then and only then would he drink. First a long and thoughtful sip, like a wine taster testing a rare vintage. Then again a prayer, and finally a long awaited drink.

I looked at him, as always, in utter amazement. He did this every time he entered water or took a drink, but why, I thought, when he was so damn thirsty and hot. He had always honored water, but surely there were times when he could have just plunged right in as I had, especially on such a hot day. I'm sure the Creator and the spirit of the waters would understand that he still honored the gift. Without looking at me, Grandfather spoke. "No matter how burning the thirst, we must always take the time to honor the gift of water, for it is sacred. It is a gift of life. It is in the times of dire thirst, when the body craves the water most, we should especially take the time for prayer and thanksgiving. By doing so, in a small way, we sacrifice part of ourselves to the waters and hold our thirst until all is honored. This way the Creator knows the appreciation of the water is more important than our thirst, more important than our physical relief."

It no longer shocked me that Grandfather knew exactly what I was thinking, for it was something he always seemed to know. Over the years, I began to accept this without question. I told him I couldn't see why the Creator or the spirit of the waters could not understand we still honored their gifts, even when we did not go through the actions of prayer and thanksgiving. I also told him I felt the time to honor the waters was during times that we were not trying to quench our burning thirst and that we always honored the water during the sweat-lodge ceremonies. "Is this not enough?" I asked. Grandfather looked directly at me and said, "It will never be enough. The masses no longer honor the water at all, nor do they talk to the water, for they just use it and infect it with their complacency. They take the water, this blood of our Mother, for granted. So we must take care to honor the gift so we do not take the gift for granted. We must realize the blood of the Earth is also our blood, and the blood of all our ancestors."

"So what you're saying is we must honor the water all the time with each use or we may grow to think as the masses," I said. "But I don't think I will ever grow that way. I always appreciate the gift of water." I replied. "No, you don't,"

Grandfather said, "you have already grown complacent and unappreciative, otherwise you would have honored the water before quenching your thirsty body."

I thought hard, trying to find words to defend myself, "But why couldn't I honor the water after my thirst was quenched and my body restored?" I asked. "Because," Grandfather said, "then there is no sacrifice of self. Even to stand for a moment of thanksgiving before drinking symbolizes to the water and the Creator that you would sacrifice yourself for your Mother's blood."

I thought again about what Grandfather was saying, searching desperately now to defend my actions. Even though Grandfather's voice held no accusation or berating, somewhere deep inside I had to find answers. "I still do not see why we have to honor the water every time," I said in desperation.

Grandfather answered, saying, "You cannot understand, Grandson, because you do not know the spirit of the waters. You think it is too much to set aside your thirst for even a moment, to honor the waters. You do not know the waters, so how can I expect you to die for the waters. Until you know the waters and the destiny of our Mother's blood, you will see no need to honor the waters each time the gift is taken. Until you live the wisdom of the waters, I cannot make you understand about which I speak."

I was hurt in a way, but I knew what Grandfather was telling me was right. I could not understand the waters as he did, and I did not know where to begin to find the answers, nor the wisdom. How could I ever learn the wisdom of the waters, and what I was missing? My thoughts were broken by his voice: "If you want to learn of the waters, then you must take a physical and spiritual journey to the waters. A journey of duality, where you will at once know the waters on both the physical and spiritual plane. You know something of the waters on the physical level of thirst and necessity, but your lessons are not complete. You must also know the blood of our Mother on a spiritual level, before you can fully understand and become one with the wisdom and spirit of the waters.

"And how do I take this journey?" I asked. Grandfather answered, "Journey to this place called the Cauldron and take no water with you. Enter that place as you would sacrifice yourself to the Vision Quest, and await your answers. Make no preparation, nor give the quest of water any thought along the way. Just go purely and sacrifice yourself to the wisdom of the waters." Sacrifice yourself to the wisdom of the waters. Those words echoed through my head as I continued along the long trail that now felt like a hot anvil under my feet. But, I thought, how can I sacrifice myself to the waters when I will be in an area where there is no water? My thirst burned holes in my mind as the plumes of dust continued to rise in soft puffs behind me.

I arrived at the lip of the pit by mid-afternoon, the sun burning down hotter than it had all day. As I looked into the pit it was plain to see and feel why we called it the Cauldron. Heat boiled from its depths. It was featureless and barren, nothing more than a cup-shaped depression in the Earth. Most of its banks were very steep and scarred by deep, eroded gullies. No trails led in or out of the pit, for they had long since collapsed and given way to the deepest of the eroded gullies. Even the trail that led from Drudgery Trail to the lip of the Cauldron had overgrown and now virtually disappeared into the landscape.

I jumped from the edge and worked my way down the steep, rocky banks and into the center of the pit. At best this quest would lack comfort, for the ground was strewn with rocks mixed with white sands baked hard as concrete. There were hardly any tracks, except for a few birds that searched the sands for insects or small grains of sand to aid in their digestion. From the center of the pit there was no view except for the burning sky. The trees around the pit were far from the edge and out of sight. Here, in the center of this hot pit seemed to be a world of hot barren Earth and featureless skies. It was the apex of where Earth and sky fused and became one, and their fusion created a place of fire.

Sitting in the center of the pit became a chore in itself. All I had on was a loincloth, which barely covered my bottom.

The Earth burned my feet, seared my buttocks, and scalded my hands. It seemed to take forever just to sit down and relieve myself of the exhaustion of the journey. I sat for hours, until my body cast a shadow that cooled the ground. Finally I could lie back without getting my back burned. It felt so good to stretch out and just relax. The sun disappeared over the lip of the pit and the day was finally getting cooler. I quickly fell into a deep and much needed sleep. My body ached with exhaustion and thirst, and sleep was a momentary relief from my torment.

I awoke to the blackness of full night, shivering out of control. The burning fire of my sunburn caused the night air to feel even colder against the skin. It was hard to believe that I would have gotten sunburned through my dark tan. I couldn't swallow because my mouth was so dry, and salivating would have been a luxury. On and off, for the rest of the night, I slept fitfully, waking at times to shivering and at other times to extreme thirst. My dreams were tortured and disoriented, always of water. There was no relief from the pain of the mind or the body. So many times I awoke not knowing where I was and it took me longer each time to orient myself as to my whereabouts and the reason for it all.

I awoke in a panic, feeling the sun baking my flesh and not knowing where I was. I had slept through dawn, right to mid-morning when the sun began its scorching path across the pit. I couldn't think clearly nor stand without falling for a long time. Each time I tried to get up a whirling blackness swooned through my consciousness and I quickly had to sit back down to prevent a full blackout. Finally, in desperation, I got on my hands and knees, trying to gain my equilibrium, before slowly standing up and trying to walk. Each step only burned my feet badly and I was again forced to slowly sit back down.

The day was long and torturous. Not a cloud broke the monotony of the hazy sky, nor breath of wind below to cool my burning flesh. My thirst intensified to such a degree that I wanted to escape the fires of the pit and get back to camp. My shoulders, back, and thighs were blistering and I could feel the deep cracks in my lips. My forehead, nose, cheeks, and chin were covered with watery blisters that oozed when touched. My eyes burned from relentless squinting to a point where when viewing the pit it shifted in and out of focus with the wavering heat. Most of all, my head pounded with a violent headache and I began to drift into periods of shivering and overheating, despite the pounding sun. Thirst overwhelmed all of my thought.

To this day I can barely remember the afternoon and night of the second day. All I remember is the pounding heat and the violent thirst. There seemed to be nothing else in my life than that constant thirst and the images of water dancing on the wavering lines of heat. My body constantly faltered every time I tried to stand and I could not think clearly. There was nothing to break the monotony of the torture, for in this fiery apex of sky and Earth, there could be no thought. At least not on the logical plane.

It was on the afternoon of the third day, when I could no longer function, that I tried repeatedly to climb from the Cauldron and head back to camp. I was out of my mind with worry, for I knew that I could not go for much longer without any water. The many long and waterless miles back to camp would have been impossible, but getting back to camp was my only hope. I tried to stand and walk repeatedly, but I kept passing out. My body had no strength, my skin was cracked in places and bleeding, and my lips were torn with deep fissures, plugged with dried blood. I was losing the battle, in fact, losing my life. I needed water and needed it soon, or I would die. I realized at that moment unless I got help, I would die of thirst.

In a blind panic, mustering all the strength I had left in my body, I tried to climb to the lip of the pit. A few feeble and panicked steps, then I would collapse. As I lay in the dust, I tried to pray, but nothing but weak fragile words could be heard but barely understood. I thought of water, heard water, and could actually smell and taste water. I saw images of water in front of me, around me, but when I put my lips to the water to drink, the taste of the dust jolted me back to reality. I must have lain there for hours, somewhere in a place between pain and sleep, hallucinating in a deathlike stupor.

Again I heard the water, this time falling from a high place. I shook my head repeatedly, but the image of the waterfall would not go away. It was then that I heard a faint voice coming from the waterfall. An obscure and misty image of something seemed to be moving in the sprays. "Save me, save me," it begged. In amazement I lifted my head and said, "Save you, how can I save you, I am dying of thirst. You must save me before I can help you." There was a long moment of silence, punctuated only by the background of rushing water. The voice came again, saying. "The time to have saved me is long ago, now yours is the plight of the grandchildren yet to come. You are too late." The voice vanished into the rush of water, silent to my beckoning calls.

The water surged on, swirling with a mass of disassociated scud and spray, billowing and roaring like a thousand screaming voices, begging me again to do something, anything, to prevent the slaughter of the grandchildren. Out of the searing spray walked the spirit of a woman, clothed in the whiteness of the snowy froth. She stood in the most violent torrents, unaffected by the power of the fall. Beckoning, I drew closer to her beauty. I touched her hand and for a brief moment my thirst vanished to distant memories. For a moment I felt a sense of peace and my strength began to return. Now, I thought, I can really help save her, this spirit of the waters.

Suddenly her beauty surged into a defiled and ugly image of a demon. Her once beautiful flesh melted away, only to be replaced by scars and lesions, oozing pus and blood. Infected and retching, great volumes of fumes and human waste, she fell before me, begging me for relief, begging again for me to do something, anything to ease her pain. I stood horrified, helpless to do much of anything. In a flash of agony, she was gone, the waterfall was gone, and I was returned to the fires of the furnace, my thirst intensified and I could feel my own death pulling at my mind. I should have done something sooner, my mind burned with regret and thought, and I collapsed into the dusty dead flesh of the Earth.

My mind reeled; for a moment there had been relief, but now all was gone. I cried, cried out loud, yet my wails were devoid of tears, for now my body desperately tried to hold all its water. What could I have done, I thought. In my state of weakness and thirst, I was powerless to help. I didn't know what to do to save the water and, even if I did know, the spirit of the water said I was too late. I wailed again, screaming out loud, "If only I had been warned, if only I had been warned sooner. Then when I had my strength, I could have done something." I collapsed again into the dust, my head swirling with thirst and anguish. If only I had known.

I awoke again to the sound and smell of water, some kind of Pine Barrens stream. I looked up and saw a tiny ribbon of water cutting through a cathedral-like cedar swamp. Shafts of brilliant sunlight cut through the mists of the temples of cedars and splashed onto the soft carpet of sphagnum moss that lit up like pools of emerald green. Waters danced and sang over logs as they wound their way through the swamp. The place seemed so lush, so pure, so holy, a place where the Great Spirit could surely be touched. It was then I noticed Grandfather sitting on the bank of the stream, gazing into the waters, and my heart leapt for joy. I was saved.

I ran to the water, falling just before the edge. I could feel the cool carpet of sphagnum moss beneath me and see the purity of the waters dancing before my eyes. At that moment I heard Grandfather crying and looked toward him. His eyes were full of tears as he gazed to the waters, his lips moving in prayer. I asked him what was wrong, forgetting my thirst, more concerned with his anguish. He looked at me, directly in the eyes, and said, "The water here is dying, and it is poison to drink. The spirit of the water has called to me and told me of its pain, and it is near death." "But the water looks clear and pure," I said, staring now into its surface in disbelief.

"You cannot see what is killing the spirit of the water," Grandfather said. "It is the invisible killer of society that seeps into these waters. Soon, all will be dead. This temple will die and the cedar giants will become bleached white skeletons, a monument to man's greed and complacency." I stared again at the water in absolute disbelief, my thirst now returning like fire in my soul. "You see, Grandson, the fish and turtles are dying, some have already perished." Grandfather continued, "Even the little plants and mosses of the bank are seared and discolored." It was then that I looked beneath the surface of the water and saw the limp white remains of fish. Turtles floated by, feeble, discolored, and riddled with oozing lesions. "Do not drink, Grandson," Grandfather said, "you have been warned, and the waters will bring your death. You have been warned."

I cried out in anguish, my thirst now so intense. Suddenly it was all gone and I was returned to the Cauldron, my grave. I remembered, this was not a dream. It had happened to me a few years before, when he had warned me not to drink the waters of a stream that was several miles south of camp. He had been right, for today, as I lay in the dust, I knew that the stream had long since died and the cedars too were dying. I knew that now there were no fish or turtles left, and few animals ever came to drink from that stream anymore. I truly had been warned, but I had done nothing. Just as the spirit of the waterfall had told me. I had been warned.

I awoke with chills to a starry night. I knew that now would be a good time to try and get out of the pit and back to camp. This way, by walking in the night, I would not have to fight the heat and sun. I could then conserve what little moisture my body had left. I also knew that the nearest water was a little over eight miles from the pit and I could reach that little lake by dawn. There on the banks I could recuperate for a day before heading back to the camp. However, I knew that the waters of the lake were not that good to drink, but if I didn't drink much, it wouldn't hurt me. I planned to drink just enough when I got there to get back to camp. So if I made it to the lake, I could swim and relieve my burning flesh.

Getting up the bank of the Cauldron seemed to take me forever. By the time I had climbed up and over, I barely had any strength left. I had to lie down and rest for a long time before attempting to travel the trail. I realized now that the trip was going to be a lot slower and more painful than I anticipated. Looking at the position of the stars I felt that I still had several hours of darkness, which would keep me out of the sun and heat until I was almost to the lake. There was no doubt in my mind that I had to go, for to stay in the Cauldron would mean I would surely die.

I walked off into the night, feeling the pain of my flesh and the intensity of my thirst. Each step was hard work, for I stumbled and fell frequently. At times I became disoriented and could not stay on the trail that connected the Cauldron to that of Drudgery Trail. It took more time than I could ever imagine to finally get to Drudgery Trail, and within the first mile the skies were turning light. As I walked, a horrible feeling hit me. I had got nothing from my stay in the pit. Yes, I appreciated water now more than ever, but the lessons learned were nothing of the intensity that Grandfather had foretold. There was something missing, but I was too close to dying of thirst to turn back now.

I pressed on, ignoring the oncoming light. My thoughts, enhanced by the surrealistic landscape of the night, were bizarre and frequently interrupted by periods of disorientation or panic. I felt so defeated, for I had failed in my vision to seek the spirit of the water. I really did not know that spirit, and except for a deeper sense of appreciation of water, my perception of it remained the same as it had always been. I had certainly learned the lessons of the body and the mind but I had not entered the realm of water on a spiritual level. For a long time I was torn between going back to the pit and pushing forward to the lake. It was my ever burning thirst that pushed me on to the awaited relief of the lake.

I walked through the morning, my walk hindered now by the burning sun and oppressive heat. Normally there should have been so many animals along the way, but now all were hidden from the sun. It seemed that I was the only creature, the only fool, walking in the direct sun. The only fool dying of thirst. I felt so contrary to the flow of life and of nature's laws. I could also feel my vulnerability, as nature once again began to break me down, dispelling my arrogance and humbling me with its heat. Still hammering at my mind was the fact that I had gained nothing substantial spiritually in the pit. I had failed, and now lacked the resolve to turn back.

Finally, just past the point of high sun, I could see the distant shores of the lake. I could not run to it, for most of my energy had been thoroughly drained. A tremendous sense of relief washed over me as I drew close and I stood for a long moment gazing at the waters. Waters that would bring me back to full life. What bothered me, though, was a thick mist that shrouded the lake. A mist at this time of day is contrary to what should normally be, but I passed it off without a second thought and waded right into the mist-shrouded water. All I could think about was the relief that a swim and a good long drink would bring.

No sooner had I entered the water than my eyes and throat began to burn violently. It was a caustic burning, much like breathing in some vile household cleaner. I could barely breathe or see, and I began to feel sick to my stomach. So too did my feet and legs begin to burn. Any part of my body that came in contact with the water began to burn. At first I thought it was just my sunburned skin's reaction to the water and without hesitation I dove in all the way. At this point my body felt like it was on fire and I could not breathe. The water that did make it into my mouth tasted like turpentine and I began to wretch uncontrollably as I raced out of the water. I had no idea what was going on. My mind seemed affected by some hazy chemical blur.

As I reached shore and dove onto the beach, out of the water and mist, I began to breathe normally again. I looked down at my body only to be horrified by the seared flesh and oozing burns from the water. I looked about in disbelief only to see that on the far edge of the lake were strewn dozens of steel drums, many broken and oozing chemicals. The contents of the drums had spread out and covered the whole surface of the lake. Decaying and bloated fish floated on the surface and the vegetation along the banks looked dead or wilted. The lake was dead, my body, seared and burned by the chemicals, was in severe pain, and my throat began to restrict to a point where I could no longer breathe. I began to gasp violently for air, and I awoke on the fiery floor of the Cauldron.

It had all been a dream. A horrible dream, and I had to slowly sit up and think for a while to shake my mind free from its grasp. Thirst came pounding back into my consciousness in a whirling daze as I tried to sit up. It took me a while to realize the glowing horizon was not the end of the day, but the beginning of a new one. I had lost time and place and my mind tried desperately to get back to some sort of physical reality. All seemed a blur of dream and reality, so that the separation of the two entities became nearly impossible. Suddenly, as I looked across the Cauldron in the soft morning light, I had the feeling that someone or something was watching me.

I searched the lip of the pit with my eyes, but there was nothing to the dawn side of its edge. The western side of the pit was still cast against the darkness of the night sky. A few stars still shone through the deep and dark blue of the sky. It was then that I caught his silhouette. At first I thought it was Grandfather, but soon saw that it was too gaunt and frail to be Grandfather. I realized that it was the old man of my vision, my grandson, haunting me again with his presence. Reminding me of that vision, reminding me that I still had done nothing.

I waited, gazing toward the darkened silhouette, waiting for those words that would twist my soul. He said nothing, but shook his head and walked away. A wave of loneliness and longing swept over me. Even my intense thirst could not distract me from the thought or image of that old man, and the searing message he always brought. I still had done nothing. I still was leaving a legacy of destruction and pain for my children and grandchildren. I lay my head back on the dusty flesh of the Earth and cried without tears. I had done nothing, and the slaughter of the Earth continued all around me. I had no idea what to do. Surely my voice would never be heard above the headlong rush and din of society's destruction.

As I lay flat and close against the Earth, I once again could hear water running, dripping, and seeping. At first I did not know where it was coming from and as I raised my head to look around, it was gone. Baffled, I lay my head back down on the ground and the sound of water returned. It dawned on me that the sound of the water was coming from deep inside the Earth. I knew that beneath me lay a huge reservoir of water. The Pine Barrens was little more than a huge sand lake of pure water, this I knew very well, but to hear the water was odd. I remember Grandfather saying if you listen close to the ground, you could hear the blood of Earth Mother surging and pumping beneath. I listened for a long time, somewhere in a state between dream and imagination, and finally fell into a deep sleep.

At some point I began to dream about sinking into the Earth. I could feel the ground all around me, as if I were floating in a liquid soil, much like the feeling of lying in deep mud. I sank deeper until I fell through the ground and into a huge underground cavern. All around me was damp rock, dripping with water. Sounds of running water splashed and echoed through the huge caverns as I stood trembling at the images of it all. In the center of the cavern, and disappearing underneath a huge rock wall, flowed a deep and crystal clear stream, of a purity the likes of which I had never seen. It was at this point I realized that I was having a dream, but I could not wake. The images were so real and intense. I could feel my body shivering in the cold dampness and purity.

Whether in some spiritual reality or imaginative dream, I began to wander through the caverns, following the stream. At the point where the stream met the solid wall of rock, I jumped in and floated with it on its journey. It seemed to take me many miles from the initial cavern, intensifying and throbbing as it went. I felt like I was in some huge bloodstream of the Earth as I floated without resisting, giving my body and mind completely over to the course of the stream. Never before had I swum in such purity. In the soothing healing waters, my body felt whole and healed.

At times, on my journey I could look up and see the trees above me, through the sand and rocks. It was much like a fish would see when looking through the surface of a quiet pond. I could feel the deep roots of trees reaching down to the water. I saw springs bubbling to the surface above me as animals drank from the quiet pools. I was floating through the lifeblood of the planet, watching all living things nurtured by the water. I could, all at once, view the purity of the underground water while also seeing everything it touched and nurtured.

Suddenly the pristine beauty of the tangled root systems and quiet pools above gave way to a labyrinth of pipes. Some were old and rusted, others were new and deeper than all the others. Pipes now replaced all the roots and I could feel the volume of the water dropping as the pipes sucked in great volumes. No longer could I see the trees, for these were replaced by solid foundations of buildings and houses. The water began to cloud and take on an odd odor of sewer and chemical. I could see huge septic tanks dripping and oozing into the water, surrounding me in filth.

As I floated on, the water grew dark and very discolored. No longer was it transparent, but filled with a murky slur of suspended bits of feces. The stench and turbidity intensified and grew more vile. Suddenly above me was a constant drip of searing chemicals that burned the waters and filled the caverns with a caustic chemical smell. Looking up I could see buried barrels, split and dripping their vile contents into the water. The oozing and dripping continued and then violently intensified as I passed beneath a huge landfill. I could not awaken, I could not get out of my dream. My skin burned with the chemical sting and the caustic air and water gagged me.

Suddenly I was sucked up into a huge pipe, and the world of vision and dream went black. I could feel my body flowing in the caustic mix of vile water, feces, and chemicals. Now back to light I could see many pipes dumping even more vile slurries into the water, as I floated on the surface, carried by a huge river of sludge. I passed by huge factories and moored ships, all leaking their death into the water. The farther along the river carried me, the more the water burned the flesh and throat. I could not swim or move. I was helpless, just like the water. "Helpless, like the water," a feeble voice called, and I looked to the distant shores to see the old one standing there watching me again.

A blur of images and feelings now surged through me. I could feel my body lift up, then crash back down, surging in rhythmic undulations. The caustic smell dissipated slightly, replaced now with a rich saline pungence, and I knew I had been carried into Grandmother Ocean's arms. Here the waters did not feel so helpless as the old man had said. I could feel the power of the surging surf and see the waves pounding at man's jetties and the bulkheads of many shores. A sense of power welled up inside me as I watched the awesome power of the oceans bring man to his knees. I felt hope, hope that the sins of man would be washed away by the power of the oceans, the waters purified once again.

Something crashed into my body, something big and heavy. In horror I turned and looked upon the carcass of a huge dead and bloated whale. The stench of rotted flesh was overwhelming and I tried desperately to swim away. I churned the water furiously, but to no avail; I could not get away. The surface of the ocean was covered by floating garbage, mixed with dead and bloated fish. Their skin was burned and discolored, huge oozing sores covered their carcasses. Dead sea gulls and all manner of other birds lay drifting on the surface. The saline pungence was replaced again by the smell of chemical rich sewage. The feeling of helplessness returned, the power of the ocean diminished, and I drifted with the flotsam, only to be cast up onshore.

I lay on the sands for a long time before I could move. My body was covered in seaweed, old netting, and dead fish. As I stood, I saw the beach was covered with all manner of decaying garbage and rotted fish. The ocean's waves were black with oil, and hundreds of dead dolphins lay across the sands in various stages of rot. I ran from the beach, from the burning waters, trying desperately to get away. Stumbling, falling, I raced to the sanctuary of the dunes and fell at the base. There above me stood the old man of my vision. "This will come, Grandfather, this will someday come, because you have done nothing," and I buried my face in the sands to escape the words.

Again I awoke in the Cauldron, screaming, as I tried to push my face deep into the hot sands, his words still echoing through my mind as I came back to this reality. I sat up, startled and shaken by the dream or vision I had just lived. It was all too horrible to even imagine, but it was happening, I knew it was happening even as I sat in this pit of hell. The old one was right, the waters were helpless and all of this could come, but I still had done nothing. If the vision or dream was right, I would never have to live this nightmare in reality, but my children and grandchildren would. All because I had done nothing and I was still using the excuse that I did not know what to do. I felt as helpless as the waters. I knew that the waters were helpless, but I wasn't. Possibly I could protect them in some way, but how?

I grappled for answers, but nothing real came into my mind. I lost track of time and place again, unconscious of the advancing storm above me. Surely, I thought, in the final analysis, the evaporation process and the rains would purify the infections of the waters. Possibly our children would live life fully and with plenty of water, water from the purification of the rains. My thoughts were punctuated by a clap of thunder which echoed through the Cauldron, sounding louder in the pit, which magnified sound like some big ear to the universe. Rain, I thought, finally a break from the sun's intensity, the ultimate quenching of my thirst. Again, more thunder rolled across the skies, the still air now moving, and the first few drops of rain hit with a puff of dusty grit.

The air chilled, and I could feel the moisture surge and build to a relief greater than the humidity that had tormented me.

There was movement in the skies as the clouds boiled and the winds intensified. Dust swirled in the pit, heralding the oncoming savior. Water, falling, would soon quench the fires of my thirst, and I could feel the trembling excitement erupt within the consciousness of my body and soul. More rains pelted the parched and dried earth, stinging my burned and blistered body with new life. Painful but soothing, my mouth now opened wide to gather any drop of relief, as I lusted for the moisture.

As the rains began to fall and the thunder rolled across the skies, the landscape surged, and suddenly I was no longer in the pit. Desperately I tried to hold onto the reality of the rain, fighting to hold onto my consciousness. If I lost and lapsed into a dream, I could not collect the rains, my thirst would then carry me to death. I rolled onto my back, holding my mouth open to the sky, praying that even if I did lose consciousness I could collect enough in my mouth to buy me more time, more life. I could feel the rains stinging my body and filling my mouth. I gobbled the water, forgetting to breathe, then choking, vomiting the precious water, then the chalky bile of a dry stomach.

I raised my head again, trying to catch more water, but it burned my mouth. It felt more like an acid than a rain. Shaking my head, I trembled to a sitting position and looked across the pit, but it had vanished. Instead, now I sat staring across an evergreen forest, bathed in misty sheets of rain. The mists cast the forest into a surrealistic haze, making the foremost trees stand out in bold relief against their neighbors now fused with the mist into an opaque blur. The rains continued their drenching and relentless cascade, bathing the land and my body in their life-giving forces. I could feel my thirst vanish as I began to get caught in the power of it all.

The rains now fell harder, hurting my eyes with the power of the drops' speed. At first it turned very cold, then, like a rain of fire, it began to scald the landscape. Trees began to wilt and turn brown. Branches were torn away by the fiery sheets of rain. Lakes, swollen and overflowing, seemed to boil, driving the fish, turtles, and frogs to the banks, where they lay dying, unable to escape the corrosive power of the rain on their flesh. So too did my flesh begin to burn again, and there was no escaping the liquid fires of the skies. The sanctuary of the trees overhanging branches was now stripped away, and I huddled close to the trunks of the barren skeletons. The forest now appeared burned and barren of all life—burning not from the fires of Creation, but from the acid fires of man.

My pain surged beyond all my limits and I rolled on the hot Earth, trying desperately to put out the burning lesions on my flesh. There was no relief, only the tormenting anguish of fiery pain, the likes of no Hell ever imagined. The rain seemed to burn past the flesh and into my aching viscera, scorching even the soul. I yelled and screamed, slapping my flesh, as if to put out some unseen fire. In my torture I looked around me for a place to hide, but all was a nightmare. Dead animals and plants lay about the Earth, flesh still bubbling with the gas and fumes of the burning. There was nowhere to run or hide, nothing but pain and torture, and I crumbled to the ground, unable to fight anymore.

In a flash of consciousness the rains stopped and the landscape lay cloaked in an acid mist. Nothing moved, there was no sound, except for the incessant hiss of acidic puddles burning holes in the Earth, trees, and flesh. I pulled myself up on a burned sapling, my flesh blistered and festering, and I called to the Creator to end my life. Nothing answered, my words fell onto the silence of deaf ears. All had vanished, both flesh and spirit, and I was alone to face my misery. The loneliness of it all became like salt on a wound, intensifying my pain. I felt like the last living thing on the face of the Earth. Man, with his fiery chemicals, had finally destroyed the Earth. I had destroyed the Earth because of my complacency, my excuses, and my ignorance, as surely as anyone else had. I tried to cry, but there were no tears, just a burning in my eyes, as the acids of man replaced even my own tears.

I heard a voice call my name and, looking up, I could see something moving in the acid mists of man's destruction.

It was the image of something or someone moving in the shadows of the burned forest. I was not frightened, but there was a sense of apprehension that stirred deep within my soul. Something I could not quite put a finger on, though it was not fear, I still felt a certain uneasiness. The voice came again, saying in a hoarse whisper, "Even the rains cannot purify the sins of man, Grandfather," and I knew in an instant that it was the old man of my vision, haunting me again.

I could take no more of his accusations, no more of the pain I had caused him. I ran blindly through the charred remains of the misty forest, then stumbled and fell into a pool of the caustic rain. Vile chemicals choking me, gagging me, I lost my breath, and I began to drown in the putrid sting of defiled water. Gasping, I lifted my head and I awoke in the center of the Cauldron. Beneath my face lay a puddle of pure water and I began to drink without hesitation. My stomach could barely hold the water down, but I forced it to, as the thunder rolled across the sky and the rains fell harder. I lay for a long time, trying to keep from vomiting the precious water, trying to orient myself to the reality of the Cauldron.

Eventually, as I felt my full consciousness return, I feebly pulled myself into a sitting position. My head swirled with dizziness and I grew sick again, vomiting the water all over my chest and legs. Time and place seemed to spin far out of reach of my comprehension, and the thirst again burned within me. I had to drink and keep the water inside of me. Thunder again rolled across the darkened sky and the rain intensified to a point where the edges of the pit could not be seen. I looked toward the skies, trying again to catch the water in my mouth, hoping that the storm would last long enough for me to get some water, some life back into my body. The rains suddenly stopped as quickly as they had begun and the thunder trembled on the distant horizon. I watched in horror as the puddles began to seep into the porous surface of the pit.

I sat in the misty aftermath of the rain, my mind wheeling in a frenzy of emotion and fear. Surely, I thought, I am going to die. I lost the water, lost my chance. I lunged desperately at the last remaining puddle, sucking the sands for some precious moisture, but the sands choked me as I sucked them into my throat. All was gone, all hope was gone, and I could take no more. I just gave up, reconciling myself to a prolonged death, for I had not the strength to even walk. The old man of my vision was right, I had done nothing, and now I could do nothing. The waters had been taken from me, as surely as they would have been denied to my children and grandchildren.

There was a stirring in the misty horizons of the pit's edge and the old man of my vision spoke to me again, this time asking me a piercing question. His voice, older and weaker, said, "It is not what you have done to me, Grandfather, but what have you done to yourself? Do you not understand that you cannot drink the waters that you do not honor, each time no matter how much your thirst burns? If you do not honor and cherish the waters, then how can you ever expect others to? How can you ever hope to save something you take for granted, something you do not honor and cherish, and something you do not really know? How could you ever hope to teach others when you yourself do not set the example, the same example that your spiritual grandfather has set for you?"

I sat as still as stone, listening to the words that poured from the old man, my grandson's lips. "You do not think it is necessary to honor the water each time," he continued, "because you do not know the spirit of the water. But now, as you have seen the possible future of man, you understand how precious and how frail the spirit of the water, our Mother's blood, is. You see how easily it is destroyed by those who do not know or honor the waters. The waters are the fluids of life, they are the fluids of your ancestors and of all living, growing things. They are the fluids of your life and your soul. Thus, the spirit of the water also flows in you. Honor it then, no matter the burning thirst, then and only then will you know this spirit," and he vanished into the mists.

The mists thickened and a light rain again began to fall. I gazed at the skies, but not with mouth gaping. Instead I prayed, prayed to the Creator and desperately honored the water. I could feel the drops of rain seeping between my lips and rushing to my parched throat, reaching deep into my dying body. I could feel the rush of relief sweep over me, humbling me, enlightening me. It was then, in this moment of ecstasy, rapture, and wisdom, I heard another voice, but this one was different and not the old man. Vaguely I recognized it, for I had heard it before many times. It was the woman of the waterfall. In a kind and loving voice of liquid she simply said, "Save me as I have saved you," and the rains fell harder. I was saved.

As my strength returned, I began to walk the long road back to camp. The clouds never cleared the next day, but sent forth periodic refreshing showers borne on cool winds. Each time the rains fell, every time I passed the waters of the trail, I prayed in the deepest form of thanksgiving. I finally knew the spirit of the water, understanding fully that precious but frail gift of life. Reaching camp, I never really had to discuss my journey with Grandfather, for he knew. I simply sat down beside him by the waters and prayed.

11

Four Visions

In my life there have been four visions that have been the strongest guiding force along the path I now walk. Certainly there have been many visions which teach, guide, and empower, but these four are of the probable futures of man. They are sometimes frightening and overwhelming, driving me to work as hard as I can to save what we have left of the Earth. Two of the visions were my own, and two were visions that Grandfather had been given and ultimately shared with me. It is known that when a vision is shared it also becomes part of your vision. What was the most frightening thing about all of this, was Grandfather's uncanny ability to foretell the future. In all the prophecies he shared with me, he was never wrong. His prophecies have always come true, not only in the exact time and place, but also exactly as they were predicted to happen.

The first prophecy he related to me about the destruction of man's world was what he called the Four Prophecies of Destruction. Certainly he had foretold the future many times before he related this prophecy to me, and that is what made it so frightening. He had never been wrong. Thus the Four Prophecies of Destruction had a haunting impact on my life. There

215

was no doubt that they would come true unless something was done to change the possible futures. As I see it now, that was my first step in bringing Grandfather's message to society. Even though, at the time, the last thing that I wanted to do was to leave the wilderness, his vision was clear. I simply could not run away and hide. For to hide is to be responsible for the destruction of the Earth. Complacency makes one as guilty as those who destroy the Earth.

Rick and I had been with Grandfather for five years when the vision of the Four Prophecies of Destruction was given to us. All that day, Grandfather had been explaining to us the necessity of getting the message out to people, the message that man had to live closer to the Earth in balance and harmony. He believed, as I now believe, that the only way to truly save the Earth is through reeducation. Legislation and petitioning have never seemed to work that well in the past. What was needed was a change in the global consciousness, and no one could afford now to run and hide in the wilderness. We were a little argumentative at the time, because neither Rick nor I cared to ever leave the woods. We felt that society had nothing to offer, and it did not seem fair to us to have to return there. We told him we could see no need, and that's when he hammered us with the tormenting vision that forever changed my life.

Grandfather was well into his forties when he had the vision of the Four Prophecies. He had been questing at the entrance to what he called the Eternal Cave. It was in this cave, he told us, that those who seek visions are led to foresee the future. It is the cave of all pasts and all possible futures. It was at the mouth of this cave that the spirit of a warrior appeared to him and revealed the possible futures of man's ultimate destruction. The spirit told Grandfather he would be given four visions of man's destruction. If, after the first two became reality, man did not hear the warnings, then the Earth could no longer be healed physically. After the second vision passed, the Earth could only be healed spiritually. The spirit then warned that after the third vision became man's reality, then there was no longer any hope. Only the children of the Earth would survive.

What Grandfather had told me about the definition of the children of the Earth was very simple. It was only those who could live in perfect balance and harmony with the Earth, and need nothing manufactured or produced by society. So too was there not only a physical ability of survival needed, but also a deep spiritual commitment to the Earth and the things of the spirit. All others, no matter how much they thought they knew wilderness, would perish in the wilderness and in the cities. They would long ago have been given the choice, and now the wilderness would not accept them. The children of the Earth would need nothing, for the wilderness would be their home and the Earth would provide all things. All others would perish.

The spirit of the warrior revealed the first vision of destruction to Grandfather by leading him to an African village. Here Grandfather saw mass starvation, children suffering, and a world with no hope. He was met by an elder there who told him that the world would see this first sign, this starvation, like nothing before it. But the world would not realize that it was to blame. The warrior also returned to tell Grandfather that a disease would infect the land. The disease would turn common illness into a killing disease, and there would be no hope or cure for a long time. And the warrior foretold of wars in the streets, where drugs were the lords and law of the lands.

Then came the second sign, the holes in the skies. This was revealed to Grandfather when the skies above tore open and oozed with a vile stench. He saw piles of garbage reaching to the skies, floating waste and the bodies of dolphins. There were tremendous storms and the Earth shook with violent tremors. The land turned brown and barren, the animals of man began to die, and all around were changes in the Earth and sky. The Earth was in a fever, fighting to throw off the disease of man's greed. Again it was told to Grandfather that after this second sign the Earth could no longer be healed physically. There must be a change in the consciousness of man, and society must reach for the riches of the spirit and abandon the false gods of the flesh.

Many days passed before Grandfather received the violence of the third sign. That sign meant the societies of the world would no longer have hope, and that man would perish. At this point it was revealed that there could be no turning back and only the children of the Earth would survive. The third sign thundered through the skies and suddenly all skies were bloodred. Even the stars of night shone red, and all of Creation seemed to be in limbo, awaiting some unseen command. Grandfather said the stars and the skies remained red for the next seven days. And it was during this time the warrior spirit told Grandfather that the children of the Earth would have but one year to escape. They would have to seek the wild places and hide from the final winter of man.

It was then that a child's voice spoke to Grandfather, telling him of the fourth and final sign, the sign which would mark the final winter. The child foretold of the crops of man and his animals dying, of waters becoming poison, even those waters deep within the Earth. The child told Grandfather of diseases and wars that would sweep the Earth. He spoke of wars, starvation, and brutality. The child spoke of roving gangs of people that would hunt down and kill other people for food. And the child told of the grandchildren feeding on the decaying remains of the grandchildren. The only hope the child gave was to tell Grandfather that there would become a new society, born from the children of the Earth. And the society would flourish in the old way, living close to the reality of the Earth and spirit.

When I heard of this vision of prophecies it frightened me, but I could not believe that things such as this could happen. I remember laughing to myself about the holes in the skies. No one would believe me if I told them that, I scoffed. How could anyone see holes in the air? The whole thing seemed so impossible That same night that I was given the Four Prophecies, I too had a vision, or a dream, I don't know which. In the dream I saw the skies torn with huge holes and the stars turned red. A spirit spoke to me and asked me why I did not believe these prophecies. He told me that I had borne witness so many times to miracles, yet I denied these visions. Grandfather's vision of the Four Prophecies of Destruction was, at that very moment, passed on to me and it forever became part of my vision.

It was not long after I heard the four prophecies that I received one of the most powerful visions of my life. It was during my first forty-day Vision Quest when it was revealed to me, and it remains one of the most powerful driving forces in my life. Certainly before this and many times after I had many visions of man's destruction, but this remained one of the most violent, the most powerful, and the most moving. I had been directed to take this forty-day Vision Quest during another quest. Throughout that first quest I felt I was being watched and tested, yet nothing spoke to me. It was then, during the final day of the quest, that I was commanded to take the forty-day quest, and take it soon. Once that quest was over, I felt like I had passed some sort of test, yet I did not know why.

The forty-day Vision Quest took place at the edge of an old sand-pit. At first I did not want to quest there because I could not bear to look at the scars of man for forty days. But the area kept calling me back to it as I searched for other quest areas, and I gave in to this place. I was well into the latter part of the forty-day quest when the most hideous vision was revealed to me. I looked over the edge of the pit only to find it strewn with random piles of bodies—people that looked as if they had died of starvation. A small group of children fed on these bodies, much as a pack of wild dogs feeds in a dump. These children were eventually hunted and killed, gutted and eaten, like a hunter would treat a deer. Nothing more than meat, an animal that had to be hunted for food. It made little difference to those who hunted that they were eating children, and it made little difference to the children that they were eating decaying human bodies.

Still in my vision, I followed one of the hunters into what remained of a city. The city looked as if it had been bombed out and burned. People lay dead or dying in gutters. Starvation was everywhere, legs and arms of humans were being sold in makeshift meat markets, and roving violent bands of people seemed to be the only rulers. In this land I could sense no hope. All things which were pure and natural were dead, and it seemed as if the spirit world had turned its back on this place. An old man approached me from the ruins of the city. He was gaunt, starving, and diseased. He looked at me and asked, "Why have you done nothing? Why have you sentenced me to this living hell? Is this the legacy you have left for me, Grandfather?" His words shook my very soul, for I realized at that moment this old man could have been my grandson, and I had done nothing. I had no answers for him.

It was not long after the spirit of my grandson appeared to me that another spirit appeared. As he spoke, the distant skies rolled with thunder and the Earth trembled. He gave me no chance to speak, but said, "You have seen the stars that bleed and witnessed the destruction of the possible futures. You have seen the sick and barren Earth, the hatred, the destruction, and the vision of your grandchildren dying. You have seen the children feed upon the remains of the children, and you have seen an Earth of no spirit or hope. This is not the possible future, but the probable future, and all that you have seen will come to pass. You are responsible for this future, so too are all the rest. All those who have run to the mountains and wilderness to hide are responsible, like all those who chased the false gods of the flesh. There are none innocent, except for those children who die in this place for the sins of their grandfathers and grandmothers."

The spirit continued, "The old man asked what you had done to prevent this, and you had no answer. Nor have you even thought to answer, for you have done nothing. You who have borne witness to this land of death, there can be no answers, for there can be but one question. When will you do something to stop this death? Only when you have worked to save the Earth and the grandchildren can you have any answers. Only when you no longer run away and hide can there be hope. To run and hide in wilderness is to be responsible for the death of the world. There can be no running away for those who love."

I asked the spirit what I could possibly do, using the excuse that I was just a child and no one would listen to me. The spirit answered, saying, "You cannot change things by thinking about changing things. You must do something, not talk or dream. The only answers lie in teaching the people and leading them back to the Earth and spirit. All other methods of change are but temporary and ineffective. You can only change things by changing the hearts of men. Each person must change before society changes, for it is the individual who contributes to the society, the wars, the hatred, and the destruction of the Earth. So then, if enough people are reached, the course and destiny of the flock will change. To teach and to lead, is to love."

The old man, the one who called me Grandfather in that vision, now haunts my every dream and vision. At first he appeared only infrequently, watching me, as it were, as I grew and learned. But now he is there all the time, watching and waiting. Though unspoken, the question remains the same, "What have I done?" He is a constant reminder that I cannot rest, for his future and the future of so many other children is in our hands. He lives in the probable future, our legacy, our greed and our hatred. He suffers for the sins of his grandfathers and grandmothers who live now. He will become our legacy and our sacrifice, unless we can change the possible futures.

It was during the ninth year that Grandfather and I were together that he revealed a second vision to me about the oncoming destruction of man. Like the vision of the Four Prophecies of Destruction, this vision also hammered at my heart and fired my spirit. Its lasting impact still haunts me to this very day, and there are still parts I do not fully understand. It was also during this time that Grandfather told me he would soon have to return to his people and that I must wander then on my own. He said that his path here had almost been completed and the vision of the white coyote was coming into its own. He also foretold of Rick's death, and said again that I would someday teach. All of this tore me apart inside, but the vision that followed was like none I had ever heard.

Grandfather said there would come a time, after the prophecy of the holes in the sky were reality but before the skies would bleed, that there would be other warnings. He said there would be a time of peace and of hope, though this would be but temporary and shallow, for the peace and hope would be born of the false gods of the flesh. He said that nations would come together in peace, barriers would be broken down, and a new tomorrow would appear. But he said that this era of peace would be founded on economics and political gain, rather than on the hopes of saving the Earth, and the hope and peace would eventually perish. He warned that the nations of the world could not base anything lasting on the false gods of the flesh. In order for this prophecy not to become reality, it was here at this time that the nations of the world would have to seek the things of the spirit.

Grandfather then told me that his vision foretold that many people in this country would search for a new definition of life. He said that many would grow tired of the emptiness found in the false gods of the flesh. There would be many that would seek new spiritual truths, and many that would seek to return to the philosophy of the Earth. Grandfather said the vision revealed to him that there would be those who would protect the Earth, and the consciousness of society would begin to change. But he also warned that the people who would seek the Earth would remain alien and not know how to return to it. They could only fully return when they became children of the Earth. He also worried that those who would seek the spiritual paths would only complicate things with useless crutches of the spirit, thus tainting the purity. He also worried that the movement to save the Earth would not be deep enough or understood, more of a fad than of reality.

After the spirit that bore this message appeared to Grandfather in his vision, the vision became unreal and difficult to understand. Grandfather foretold of the black blood of the Earth, inflamed and running unchecked on the face of Grandmother Ocean. He spoke of huge fish vomiting fire and men. He spoke of white snakes in the skies, and of invisible death.

The violence would become so intense that the very flesh of men would melt from their bones. The explosions would be so powerful that the Earth would be returned to the days before life. Nothing would be safe from the white snakes in the sky, for their poisons would reach all parts of the Earth and sky. He spoke too of an endless winter, where not even the children of the Earth would survive. This, he said, would become the other probable future.

At this point in relating his vision to me Grandfather made it clear again that there were many possible futures. The strongest, he emphasized, was the future of the bleeding skies and man feeding on man. But the possible future of the white snakes in the skies, though not as powerful, was also a strong possibility. He warned that if the battles grew so powerful in the world of spirit that the physical battles were forgotten, the white snakes would appear. That is when the Creator will turn his back on man and nature. That is when the battles of the spirit world will be lost also. Earth and spirit would be destroyed through man's greed, his evil, and nothing would again exist. All that would be is a nothingness.

This vision of Grandfather's really frightened me. The vision of the Four Prophecies of Destruction was bad enough, but at least they left some sort of hope. The vision of the white snakes in the sky left absolutely no hope. Grandfather had also warned that the two visions could combine and become an even more violent reality. Grandfather had told me that this vision had come to him only a short while after the Four Prophecies of Destruction and, in fact, had been carried to him on the voice of a white snake. So too did he speak of stars falling from the skies, trailing showers of sparks, of waters boiling, and of burning rains. No one could hide, no one could run, for there would be no hope anywhere. All peoples of all nations would perish and the world of spirit would be held accountable to the Creator. This would become man's legacy, his hell.

To me, this became one of the more powerful visions, because if there remained any doubt in my mind that I should leave the woods and teach, this vision said that there would be no place to hide. I could not become complacent, nor could I hide anymore. I had no choice but to work in any way I could to prevent these visions of the future from happening. Still, at this time I had no idea of what I could do. I had tried to teach those I came in contact with, but with not much success. Sometimes when I taught, people mocked me. At other times they just would listen and then go right out and do the opposite. The problems of the global societies seemed so impossible to correct. I still could not see what one person could do. I could not see what an army of people could do. People just did not understand, and my small voice would not make much of an impact, if any at all.

I remember being very frustrated with the question of what I could possibly do. Grandfather knew that this vision of the white snakes in the skies had really shaken me up. He also knew that I wanted to do something, anything, but I was doubting my impact. He sat me down and said, "So many times, Grandson, you have been told in vision and in reality that everything you do will affect the spirit-that-moves-through-all-things. Your trouble comes from not seeing the impact that one small voice, one idea or belief, can have on a world that is out of control. If that is so, then tell me of this man they call Hitler. He was one man, his voice was weak at one time, but did not it infect the thinking of many? Did he not try to conquer and destroy? Was he not followed blindly by the masses? So you see, what was done with one small evil voice, can so be done with one small good voice. However, evil always seems to prosper in men's hearts, while the good needs constant cultivation."

The Eternal Cave is also part of these four visions which have had such a profound effect on my life. I had been wandering out West, in a way searching for this Eternal Cave that I heard Grandfather so often speak about. He said I would some-day find that cave, yet gave me no real directions to it. When I finally did find it, I knew it well, not only from Grandfather's descriptions, but also because I could feel it within me. The Eternal Cave was always a place where one could seek the vision of the future and a place of guidance. Visions there are sometimes so hard to understand. Time and place do not really exist and at times one feels disoriented, where it is difficult to separate reality from vision. Yet the visions received from the Eternal Cave become reality no matter how obscure they may seem at first. It is a powerful place, frightening, draining, and at times enthralling.

The cave is a series of caves within caves. The design of the cave is much like the designs of the possible and probable futures. All those who visit this cave on a physical level are met only with rock, tunnels, and chambers. But for those who spiritually seek its wisdom and who have been led to its secrets, it is a labyrinth of mystery. It contains all past history, the chamber of the present, and all of the possible and probable futures. The chambers and tunnels of this cave system are also rich with the possible futures that have long passed but have never been lived. It is much like taking a trip through the spiritual veils that house all the possibilities that ever were. It was here in this Eternal Cave that I saw again the agony of the probable future, and again it changed my life.

The probable future of man revealed to me the destruction that would become man's reality. I saw the piles of garbage that reached to the skies, I breathed the air that burned the lungs and made my eyes tear, and I walked on soils that burned the soles of my feet. I witnessed the cities of destruction, the roving gangs that were the law, and I saw the people of this land of no hope, feeding on the remains of the dead. I saw the waters that burned the skin, the skies of red, and the wilderness that now lay in blackened ruin. It was a world of no hope and no spirit. A world that I had seen so many times before in many visions, and a world that Grandfather said would surely come if man did not change his ways. It was a horrible reminder of what I had to do, the path I had to walk.

Yes, this cave revealed to me the horror of the probable future, but it also gave me hope. In one of the tunnels, leading off the chamber of our nows, was a future of hope. Though it was small and insignificant compared to the tunnel of the probable future, it was still there, and that meant there was still hope. In the massive tunnel of the probable future, I saw again the world of destruction, of war, of famine, and of the children eating the children. I tasted the foul air and my feet burned upon the infected soils. But in the other tunnel, the tunnel of hope, I saw a different world, a better world, and a purer world. That little tunnel of possibilities gave me such hope. Something to fight for and something to live for. It was the one vision I had which gave me such hope.

In that tunnel, there was a world where the Creator and the spirit were the rulers. The wilderness were the temples, and the peoples of the Earth followed their spiritual paths, not the false gods of the flesh. It was a world where people and nature lived in perfect balance and harmony. A place where there was no hatred, no wars, no greed, prejudice, or malice. There people worked for peace. A man's riches were inside himself, no longer based on gaudiness and excess. Everything in this place lives in harmony with each other, where nothing is killed, envied, stolen, or coveted. The Earth belongs to everything and to nothing. Life is sacred there and no one is lost or searching for himself. It is a world of peace for all things.

In this world of the small possible future there was no fear. Mankind lived out his days singing praises to the Creator and Creation instead of cursing his existence. Everything is valued in this place, for the smallest creature is as important to the whole as is man. Each entity in this world has its purpose and is respected for that purpose. The water in this world runs pure and clear, the oceans are alive with fish, and the trails are covered only with the tracks of life. Trees in this place grow uncut, untrimmed, and the wilderness becomes the utopia, the Garden of Eden. It becomes the home for all forms of life, a perfect home, free of fear and destruction.

This small place of possible future had only the sounds of Nature as music. The forms of communication transcend all language and action, and are from the heart. Here all things speak to each other, and there is no separation between flesh and spirit. The worlds fuse and become as one. Man in this place is naked, yet unashamed. The elements and storms are viewed as friends, natural and real, something to give energy and life. Man in this place belongs to the Earth and the Earth belongs to all things. Man is whole again. Man in this place becomes a tool of the Creator. It is a world of perfection, of hope, and of love. Though I only got a brief glance of what could be, I knew it to be the perfect place, and it gave me hope. Something to live for, something to work for.

These were the four visions that have so changed my life and directed my path. Grandfather's vision of the Four Prophecies of Destruction, my vision of the old man and the pit of bodies, Grandfather's vision of the white snakes in the sky, and my vision in the Eternal Cave are those visions that fire my soul to action. They are the visions that prevent me from running to the wilderness and hiding from that destruction. I know that I cannot run. For, as the spirit said, "To run away is to be responsible, for to run is not to know love. To not know love is to not know the spirit-that-moves-through-all-things. When one part of that spirit is lost, hurt, sick, or searching, the whole is affected." These visions could become the legacy of man's greed, hatred, and the results of chasing the false gods of the flesh, and I had to at least try to show a different way.

Yes, there were many visions before and after these visions. Many showed how the destruction would begin. Some visions clarified these four visions, and some of the visions spoke to me of the way that I could lead people back to the Earth. Even with all of the hideous destruction I have witnessed, both in reality and in vision, I still have hope. I have to believe that man can and will change things around. But the old man of my vision persists. He is always there, watching, waiting, and pushing me onward. What frightens me is that the old man is there more frequently. He is forever in my dreams, always there when I teach classes, and especially present when I try to take a break for myself. There can be no rest now for anyone who loves the Earth and believes that there is more to life than the gods of the flesh.

12

Searing Air and Infected Soils

It had been a long time since I was last in the Pine Barrens. My wanderings had taken me far across country and up into Canada over the past year, and it felt good to be back into the place of my spiritual birth. I set up camp in one of our old camp areas and prepared to spend at least the entire summer there. It was so difficult building camp in the same area where Rick, Grandfather, and I had camped so often. This area was so special to me for many reasons. As I built my shelter and collected firewood, I became overwhelmed with all manner of memories. Grandfather used to say that being alone and loneliness were two different worlds, but I still missed him terribly.

Certainly I cherished my aloneness, but at times like these, especially living in areas that had been such a part of my early life, it became unbearable. Fortunately, the loneliness would not last long. I could always feel Grandfather's presence, no matter where I was or what I was doing. After all, there was no death, and as long as I was guided by Inner Vision and had a pure purpose, a purpose beyond self, I could go and visit Grandfather in the spirit world. Other times he would come to me, though in spirit, his visits were always a treat, and we would spend hours talking and reminiscing. I got the feeling that he missed me as much as I missed him and that made me feel good. But it still was not like having him around all the time in the flesh. We both had work to do—he in the spirit worlds, and I in the interface between flesh and spirit; thus our visits never lasted as long as I would have liked.

It was at this time, when I was engrossed in thought about Grandfather and our sacred area, that the wind shifted slightly. My eyes began to burn and water with the sharp odor of harsh chemicals. The air, though moving, seemed caustic, thick, and choking. I had no idea where it was coming from, but its origin must have been relatively close to where I sat. However, the winds fluctuated quite a bit, and it was hard to decide a general direction. I wondered to myself if someone now was in the process of dumping chemicals illegally, or if it was from some distant factory, spewing pollutants into the area. I began to search the skies, looking for some smoke or other indicators of the origin of the caustic fumes, but except for the monotony of the overcast skies, there was nothing else.

The wind shifted again and the chemical smell vanished, though my eyes still burned for a while afterwards. I listened hard, cupping my ears to the direction that the smells had come, but I heard nothing out of the ordinary. The smells didn't return for the remainder of the day, and since nothing was revealed to me as to where it was coming from, I was happy just to relax again and think of Grandfather, this area, and all of the things that I had learned here. As the sun began to creep low in the sky, the slight shift in the late day breezes brought back the caustic smells of the chemicals again. This time they seemed more fierce and burning, almost searing to the flesh. At this point I was both concerned and perplexed, in that I did not know whether to leave my quest area and investigate, or to stay put. The major concern was that someone might have been in the process of actually dumping the chemicals, though I still could not hear anything out of the ordinary. The concentric rings of wildlife activity foretold of a normal day in the woods. What bothered me was that there was hardly any sound of bird or animal coming from the direction of the chemical smells. I spent the better part of sunset and into the night torn between going to investigate and staying in the area until my quest was finished.

Throughout the night I was awakened time after time by the searing smell of chemical. Every time the wind shifted and blew in my direction I began to gag and my eyes began to water. With the heaviness of the night air, it made the smells even worse, to a point where I could barely tolerate staying in the quest area. I grew very angry, almost out of control. I was certain now that the smells were coming from some kind of toxic dump, an illegal dump, and it had to be close. I shuddered to think of where it might be. Any part of this area was sacred to me, and had been to Grandfather. If I could smell the chemicals so strongly, then it had to be somewhere in the areas around camp. What also began to bother me was that it was coming from the direction of Grandfather's old camp. That made me even more concerned and angry.

Sleep that night was tormented. No sooner would I get over to sleep than the night breeze would shift and fill my quest area with the stench of chemicals. I dreamed again of people killing the Earth and mocking me. Anger seemed to fester deep within me all night, until finally I could take no more. I left the quest area in search of the origins of the chemical smells. Traveling at night made the search harder and the constant ebb and flow of the shifting air made it difficult to follow the vapors for very long. After a few hours of fruitless searching I decided to head right to Grandfather's old camp. That was the last direction I remembered the fumes coming from and now that seemed the most logical choice. I prayed the whole way there that Grandfather's camp had not turned into an illegal dump site.

The skies were just turning light when I finally reached Grandfather's old camp. To my relief, the camp remained as I always remembered it to be. Though the vegetation had grown deeper into the clearing, the little area was as beautiful and tranquil as ever. I could close my eyes and feel Grandfather's presence there so easily. I also felt lonely and depressed and had to sit down and try to fight the tears back. I really didn't want to visit this old place because, out of all the camps, this one I knew from the beginning would stir up all the old memories. As I looked around the area I could picture where his shelter had been, where he had built his fires, and exactly the place he so often sat. I slipped over to this area and sat in his place, somehow feeling unworthy of even being there. Here I could sense him even more, and the loneliness hammered my very soul.

The dawn breeze began to stir. I watched its advance in the trembling of the upper oak leaves. Holding my head up and awaiting the air, I was suddenly struck by the harsh sting of the chemicals. My eyes began to tear again and I gagged. This time the smells were even more violent and penetrating than they had been before. I looked to the direction of the breeze and, to my horror, I found that it was close to where Grandfather's old quest area had been. I ran out of camp in a frenzy, determined to get to his quest area, and fearing the worst. My pace was slowed to a walk, however, by the thick brush and the ever-increasing smell of chemical waste. It was hard to breathe and my eyes watered so badly I could barely see. I had to squint and cover my mouth with my hand.

I blundered right into Grandfather's old quest area, not realizing at first that I was there. I was horrified. All around the area, the trees were dead, nothing grew from the ground, and no tracks could be found. The bases of the smaller trees looked as if they had been deeply burned by some sort of acid. In various parts of the area, trails of vapors could be seen seeping from the pores of the badly stained Earth. I could clearly see the tracks of a huge truck, but not a tractor-trailer type truck. Apparently the truck had backed deep into this woods and dumped its entire load. Knowing the sands of the Pine Barrens, it would not take long before the chemicals would seep into the aquifer. Looking up into the trees to try and get my bearings, it suddenly dawned on me that this was Grandfather's quest area, or what was left of it. It was at this time too that I realized that my feet were burning and stinging as the soil ate at my flesh.

I backed out of the area and dragged my feet in sand, but the stinging and burning sensation would not go away, but worsened. I ran back to the stream in a blind panic, fearing that the chemicals would burn my feet so badly I might not be able to walk. I had to get to the stream and soak my feet to try to get rid of whatever was on them. It felt like the chemicals were eating through my calloused feet, callouses that were so thick that I could easily crush campfire coals with them without feeling it at all. Now the burning and pain was so intense that it was like walking on coals. Finally reaching the stream I plunged in and began rubbing my feet with the sphagnum moss. It took nearly an hour before my feet stopped burning and upon inspection I found that the callouses were nearly burned from my soles. I had never seen anything like it in my life.

Frightened and angry, I cautiously walked back to Grandfather's old quest area carrying a bowl of water. I wanted to see what would happen if I dumped the water on the Earth, hoping that it would give me some kind of clue as to what the chemical had been. As I poured the water onto the infected soil, there was a slight sound of hissing and then a column of noxious vapor rose from the sands. It was clear that whatever had been dumped here, it had to have some sort of acid base, such was the smell of the vapor. In a way, it was a relief that it wasn't something more dangerous, since now my feet were burned to the pink flesh. I could have really been hurt, so too would any animal that walked across the area. No wonder all the trees in the area had looked badly burned at the bases.

I backed away from the area, fearing that any shift in the breeze would again blow the vapors toward me. I could only imagine what this stuff would do to my lungs, especially after seeing what it had done to my feet. My anger again flared into a rage and I began to search the outer edges of the dump area, looking for clues as to who had done this. It had been dumped after the last rains and it was still so concentrated since no more rain had fallen. I located again the truck's tire marks and began to follow them out to the main trail. By the look of the evidence, whoever drove the truck knew exactly what he was doing and where he was going to dump the load. Just as I reached the main trail, I noticed another area that had been badly chemically burned. This one was fresh, and the same tire tracks also led up to this one.

As I searched this area I found again the footprints of the man that had dumped the chemicals. These prints led away from his truck and out into another area of the landscape. It wasn't difficult to follow, even in full dark, for the land had been so badly damaged by the weight of the truck. Small saplings had been crushed and the wheels had left a huge trough in the ground I could easily feel with my feet. I grew careless as I tracked, mumbling to myself and allowing my anger to take over again. Fortunately, the lack of animals' sounds caught my ear and I sensed something moving up ahead of me, but I could not see what it was. Then, like a loose coal from a campfire, I could see the flare of someone's cigarette in the night and my senses came alive. Possibly it was the man, I thought, searching out a new area to dump. That would be a deadly mistake for him. I could feel the raging animal stirring deep within me, almost out of control.

I had to stalk to get close, taking care not to make even a hint of sound. I also had to keep from stirring up any animals that would alert the guy to my presence. As I got closer, I could see the faint outline of his truck against the sky. It was as I had suspected. The truck was a small tank truck which looked as if it had been converted to do its illegal dumping. I could clearly see the white lettering on the side of the truck which spelled out diesel fuel. I could also see that the license plates had been obscured carefully with mud. As far as I could tell, there was no other lettering on the truck. I quietly slipped up behind the truck to the passenger side and slid under. I deftly took the spark wire from the distributor cap, thus disabling any possible escape. The man moved through the woods far up ahead, paying no attention to the truck at all.

I slipped back out from under the truck and began to peer through the windows, trying to see if there were any guns. It was difficult to tell, but there was an empty shotgun rack in the back window. I had to assume the man might be carrying a gun with him now. I could also see the glove compartment was open and there were several shotgun shells lying inside. Now I could not take any chances, for it could mean death. He could easily shoot me and drag my body into the bush. I would never be found. I began to move closer to the man, calculating my every move, searching for an opportunity to jump him and take his shotgun away, that is, still assuming he carried the gun with him. As the match flared to light up another cigarette, I could clearly see he was carrying a shotgun. I could feel the trembling deep inside of me as my body geared up for the challenge. I had to fight back the rage, for the rage would create mistakes I could not afford to make.

Finally, I began to work my way to within a few feet of him. I moved when he moved and froze whenever he paused. He had no idea I was around at all, though from his actions he seemed a little above average as a woodsman. I almost laughed to myself that he didn't know I was so close to him and I could have reached out with a stick and easily tapped him. Any Apache scout would have sensed my approach long ago. This man appeared to me to be living in a vacuum, insulated from anything that moved outside his world. At this point, I began to grow a little cocky and accidently snapped a twig. He spun around and I sank to the earth without a sound. He moved toward me in his search to find the origin of the sound but stopped within a few inches of my head. I could see the barrel of the shotgun not three inches away.

It seemed an eternity had passed before he moved again. He was very jumpy and likely to react by pulling the trigger of the shotgun before thinking. I began to follow him again as he continued to search for another dump site. I could not let anything so stupid as a snapped twig put my life on the line again. I knew I would have to remove the shotgun from him, but I was hoping that he would put it down. If I jumped out at him and tried to grab it from him it would only put my life in danger and I could not take the chance of missing the grab. All I could do was to continue to follow him close, hoping that he would make a mistake. It wasn't long before the man stopped for a moment, tossed down his cigarette, and leaned his shotgun against a tree. He then moved off a few steps and I could hear his zipper coming down and I knew he was going to urinate.

As soon as I heard his urine hit the ground, I slipped up behind the tree and quietly took the gun. I knew the sound of the urine would cover a faster-than-stalking move. I then slipped quite a distance from the man. I knew that when he found his gun missing he would begin to search the area. As I thought, I could hear the man move to the tree, then curse under his breath. From his cursing and words, it was clear he did not suspect anyone took the gun. Instead he kept telling himself that he had to be more careful where he laid his gun down at night. The longer he searched for the gun, the angrier he got, and the more difficult it became to keep from laughing. The man kicked at the ground a few times and headed back to his truck. I assumed he would return with a flashlight, so I took that opportunity to slip deeper into the woods and work my way to the far side of the truck.

I could see the flash and flare of his flashlight moving in the distance as he now frantically searched for his gun. I placed the gun well back into the woods and returned to his truck. He had left the door open in his haste to get his flashlight. I searched the inside of the truck hoping to find some document that contained information about him or the origin of the chemicals, but the truck was clean. It was clean of papers and documentation, but it was otherwise littered with old beer bottles and innumerable other kinds of trash. The flashlight flared dangerously close to the cab and I again sank to the ground and disappeared under the truck. The man arrived back at the truck cursing his head off, left his flashlight on the passenger seat, slammed the door, and walked around the other side. As soon as he was at the back of the truck, I slipped out, grabbed the flashlight through the open window, and disappeared into the bush.

The man jumped into the truck, shoved the key in the ignition, and tried to start the truck. He took no notice that his flashlight had now disappeared. He began to grow violently angry when the truck refused to start. While opening his door and cursing the truck, he reached for his flashlight only to discover that it was gone. He stormed out of the truck and rushed around to the passenger side, searching the floor of the truck and the ground by the door. It suddenly dawned on him then that the disappearance of his gun and flashlight and his truck not starting were not by accident. I could almost sense the change in his violent attitude when these coincidences began to hit home. He walked to the front of the truck, looking around nervously as he opened the hood. I could see the match flare as he looked inside and I clearly heard him gasp in disbelief.

He ran to the door of the truck, becoming violently angry at all that had happened. He was like a cornered animal, an animal that was totally out of his element. Without the security of his truck, his gun, and his flashlight, he knew he was in trouble. The only way he knew how to react to this trouble was through violence. He grabbed a large pipe wrench from under his seat and began to challenge the night woods. He called out in every direction but mine, menacing the unknown with his wrench, and threatening the "chicken-liver S.O.B. that stole his gun to show himself." It was difficult at first to swallow my laughter, then suddenly something seemed to snap inside of me. Rage began to fill my consciousness as I watched him standing there in such a defiant way. He should be humbled, I thought; how dare he challenge me after what he did to my woods and to Grandfather's quest area? I quietly stood, grabbing my stick as I began to slip forward into the night and toward him.

I could feel my hand tighten around the stick and my arms and chest harden with the rage of the animal. I could feel my rational mind slipping away, giving over to an uncontrollable violence. I approached him deftly from behind and swung my stick with such a surge of energy the woods echoed with its whipping sound. I caught his wrench just above his hand and sent it flying through the air. He stood before me dumbfounded and trembling. My stick was up and ready like a baseball bat, ready to be powered down onto his body. I could feel the raging animal inside of me going out of control. He pleaded with me not to hurt him and fell to his knees trembling and protecting his head. I could only answer his plea with a deep growl and a violent pounding of the Earth with my stick as the animal within flew out of control. All I could say was that he was going to pay dearly for destroying my woods.

I saw a movement behind the man and at first thought that it might be his accomplice, but then realized that this movement was too precise to be anything but a spirit. Another movement caught my eye, and there by the edge of the clearing stood an old man. It was Grandfather. Ignoring the man trembling at my feet and still partially controlled by the raging animal, I asked Grandfather in an unkind way what the hell he wanted. He said, "It is not you talking, Grandson, it is the violence. What do you think you will accomplish by hurting this man? You try all too often to defend our Mother through violence and rage, and so many times you have seen this does not work. Our numbers will not increase if you keep beating those who would otherwise become our allies. Why don't you ask this man why he does these things? If you had, you would find he is not fully to blame." As I held this conversation with Grandfather's spirit, the man looked at me as if I was insane. He looked around him to see who I was talking to, and when he saw no one, he began to go out of control with fear.

He begged me, sobbing, not to kill him. Now that the animal within had subsided, I demanded to know why he was dumping the chemicals. He sobbed that he had no choice. He said that his boss had threatened his family and his friend had been killed because he had not followed orders.

By this time I had completely calmed down and threw away my stick in a gesture of peace. Finally he introduced himself as David, and started to explain that he had been recruited by a firm in the northern part of the state to do some odd jobs. As he got involved, they began asking him to do things which he knew were against the law, but the money was good and he could finally support his family. It wasn't long before his boss began asking him to run the chemicals into the Pine Barrens, and he had been dumping for over two months. He told me he had tried to get out of this organization but that they had threatened him and his family, and now he had to do what he was told. He said he was chosen because he knew these woods so well. He had moved here with his parents when he was eleven years old and had always hunted around here, and he hated what the chemicals were doing to the area. He also said that he had no other choice.

I really felt sorry for this poor man, for he indeed had no choice other then to obey his boss. I then told him he must really feel bad that his children and grandchildren could never come back here, since the land was now poisoned and infected. I then showed him my feet, and he grew very upset. Not to press the issue, for I knew that he more than understood, I reiterated that I could try and help him out of his dilemma. I retreated into the woods behind his truck, handed him his flashlight and distributor wire and told him to get his truck started. I then handed him his fully loaded gun, without even wondering whether he was going to use it on me. As he took the gun we looked each other directly in the eye, and we both understood.

Dave drove me out of the Pine Barrens and directly to Joe's house. I told him I knew this old State Trooper who would help us out, as he had helped me so many times before. Though it was just coming into the edge of dawn, I knew Joe would more than welcome hearing Dave's story. It didn't take me long to explain the situation, and I left Dave and Joe alone to work things out. I knew if there was anyone who could help Dave, it was Joe. I told them both that they would know where to find me if they needed any further help, and I wandered back into the Pine Barrens. When I arrived, I quickly fell into a deep and much needed sleep. At the same time it began to rain, and as I drifted off to sleep, I imagined all the chemicals being washed into the Earth. Eventually Dave's children and grandchildren would have to drink them.

I awoke just before dawn to the sound of Grandfather's voice. He said, "If you had met ignorance and fear with violence, you would have hurt an innocent man. The plight of man's greed sometimes far exceeds those who are caught in the act of destroying the Earth. You have done more with your compassion than you could have done with any violent act. Now, you see, if only you would reach out to another and try to understand their ignorance, you can create miracles. Nothing is solved through violence and aggression. I know your pain, Grandson, for they have defiled that which is sacred to you, but what you have done for this man and his family is far more sacred. You have given up a part of yourself for him." With that, Grandfather's voice disappeared into the dawn mist.

I stayed in the area for a full day, but I knew that my reason for being here was now over. I had learned many lessons from it. Finally, I had learned what it was to be a true warrior. A warrior was not an animal that dealt in violence, but a passionate and loving person.

I knew now, beyond any doubt, that the problems with society could not be solved with violence and rage. People had to be led back to the Earth in kindness and with love. Most of them did not know better and should not be punished for their ignorance or fear. But for those who knew better, for those who refused to be taught, there remained the violent rage. At least now I was certain of the difference, and I knew where the line was drawn, however small and obscure. The line between passion and rage was clear to me. At least now I could go on understanding people a little better and loving people a little more, despite their ignorance and fear. I had to teach people Grandfather's way.

13

Return to the Eternal Cave

I was wandering aimlessly through the Southwest when I again visited the Eternal Cave. I was not consciously planning to go to the cave, nor had my Inner Vision directed me to take a Vision Quest of any sort. I was more involved then with exploring and finding adventure in the same places that Grandfather had probably once wandered. I had been so out of touch with time and place that I didn't even realize I was anywhere near the cave. As I rounded a ridge, there it was, right in front of me, its entrance high up on a cliff. It hadn't changed at all over the years, and I was amazed and shocked to see it there. I had never approached it from that direction before and that must have been why I was so surprised to see it again.

Almost at the same time I was gazing up at it, I was hit with the overwhelming feeling that I had to go to it again. Though the feeling was not from my Inner Vision, or that I had to take some sort of quest, I just felt like I had to go to it and find out how much it might have changed over the years. I think that a good part of the feeling came from the fact that the cave had been and still was such a big part of my life and my vision. So too was the cave a big part of Grandfather's life. It was something we both had shared, and though it was not at the same time, the cave still spoke to me in the same way it must have spoken to Grandfather. It was the visions of the probable and possible futures there that had guided us both along our paths.

It took me the better part of the morning just to reach the base of the cliff. It then took me several hours to climb up the cliff and to the entrance of the cave. At times I could feel Grandfather's presence, climbing along with me, for the way I took was one of the only ways to get to it. I could only imagine how many people of the past had climbed that wall, and I wondered if anyone in the future would seek the wisdom of the cave. Certainly, if people explored and searched this area they would eventually find the cave, but the cave would not speak to those who were not drawn to it spiritually. For all of those, it would be nothing more than just a small cave. But for those who were compelled to it by the spirit, it held the wisdom of the past and all the possible futures.

The cave was one of the most powerful places in this part of the country. Even in the flesh it seemed to call to the surrounding wilderness. Its voice would change with the winds and weather. At times it would be a haunting howl, at other times it would be a quiet whisper, and still other times it would growl deeply. So too could singing and chanting be heard. It became so hard to separate real sound from the countless spirit voices that came from its depths. At night, the sounds of the cave would change again; at these times it would sound as if the cave was whispering so close that I could feel it more than hear it. I could also feel the world of spirit fuse with the world of flesh, especially as I walked through the door. I could not stand before it without feeling a deep spiritual trembling that would manifest in the flesh like an uncontrollable shivering.

This time, as I reached the lip of the cave, there was no exception to its power. I trembled so badly that it became almost impossible to drag myself over the lip that sat in front of its entrance. I gazed again into its dark depths, as I had done so many years before. The voices of the cave seemed now so powerful and beckoning, compelling me to step into the darkness. I still had no idea as to why I had been called to it, for my Inner Vision would not communicate clearly. All I knew was that I had to be there. I also realized that it was not by chance that I had wandered upon it in the first place. As I thought back over the past several days, I realized that what I had thought were undirected meanderings had actually led me in a straight line to the cave. I knew now that the cave had been calling me the whole time, but still I did not know why. I still did not feel that I had to take a Vision Quest there.

As I drew closer to the entrance, the intensity of anticipation almost overwhelmed me to a point where I could barely walk. I then remembered that Grandfather had once told me that when the cave calls, Vision Quest or not, one would learn. The cave had such power that the act of questing, except for those who were unworthy of its power, became a secondary act. There was no doubt in my mind now that the cave had called me here to teach me again. I had no choice anymore, for the sense of urgency and anticipation prevented me from even moving. In a way, I was frightened by the feeling, especially having the unexplained feeling of urgency. I wondered, as I stood frozen in my tracks, if the message it would reveal was one of disaster. After all, the cave spoke of possible futures, and possibly the future that it held was ugly.

I began to grow even more frightened, for up until this point I had still not lived my vision. I had just wandered for years in the wilderness and had done little in the way of teaching people. Certainly I had taught a few, but our encounters were short-lived and people seemed to be easily distracted by the false gods of the flesh. The cave might be calling me here to tell me that my vision was all but dead, and the Earth would be facing the final winter of man. Guilt rushed over me in a big way, because I had not really attempted to teach or do anything. I had been selfish in my wanderings, telling myself that I had still too much to learn before I ever came out of the wilderness to try and teach. I so often imagined myself to be

Grandfather's age before I could have enough knowledge to do anything beneficial.

I also knew that the vision in the cave was the one vision I had that gave me hope for the future. I had seen that beautiful possibility, that tunnel of peace, and though it was not very large or powerful, it still held hope. I wondered now if that possible future was still there. Maybe the cave was calling me there to show me that future was lost forever and there was no longer any hope. That thought really sickened me because it was that hope that kept me going for so long. It was that hope that helped me through the most disastrous times of my life. Now I faced the possibility that it would be gone, gone possibly because I had really done nothing. Yet I took some satisfaction in the fact that I had tried to do something to save the Earth. I just had problems finding people who would listen.

I knew that I was just making excuses for myself, and those excuses would not be accepted here. As I walked deeper into the chamber, I could sense that time was standing still and the voices of the cave intensified even more. Some of the voices actually seemed to accuse, some seemed to mock, and others just cried out in pain. The main chamber was solid rock, refusing to reveal its innermost chambers and tunnels. It was a superficial veneer of rock that met those who entered the cave without a spiritual calling. Yet I knew that this was as it had to be when viewed through the flesh, for the inner rock walls kept the secrets from all flesh. I walked deeper inside, slowing my pace to allow my eyes to become accustomed to the dark. The intensity of its depths became so powerful that I had to sit down for a moment to regain my composure. I closed my eyes to expedite the adjustment to the dark, and to go inside of myself for answers. I could feel the chamber surge.

Almost immediately, I heard someone crying and looked up with a start. As I looked deeper into the chamber, toward the direction of the crying, I could see that the main tunnel of man's existence began to emerge. The solid rock wall had opened and the voices of the past came echoing through. In the entrance, sitting on a rock, was an old man. His head was held low and he sobbed as he looked down into the tunnel. I walked toward him to try and comfort him, but as I approached he pointed deep into the tunnel and said, "It is gone." As I drew closer he looked up at me and in a shocked horror, I backed away. It was the old man of my forty-day Vision Quest, my grandson. Tears flowing from his eyes, he pointed deep into the tunnel in an almost demanding gesture.

Without hesitation I began to walk toward the main tunnel, then suddenly hit a rock wall. I fell to the ground, my head bleeding from bumping into the wall. The old man was gone, the tunnel was gone, and I was sitting in the cave's main chamber. The spiritual tunnels and passages had been removed and I did not know why. I was horrified, because I thought that the old one was saying that all future was gone, the cave was gone. Suddenly Grandfather's vision of the white snakes in the sky filled my mind. That, I thought, could be the only reason that all future was gone, and I ran from the inner chamber terrified at the thought. All I could imagine was that the whole world would soon be gone. Not only the world of flesh but also the world of spirit, as Grandfather's vision foretold. I ran from the entrance of the cave and into the night.

I was shocked at first to see the night skies, for I had only been in the cave for what had seemed like a few minutes. I then remembered that was the way that the cave was when dealing with the time of the flesh. One could walk into the inner chamber for what he assumed to be just a few minutes, only to walk back into the flesh and find that he had been gone for several days. That had happened to me before when I visited the cave for the first time. At this point I did not know if it was the night of the same day I had arrived at the cave, or if several days had slipped by. It was too dark to age my tracks leading into the cave. If the tracks were just in dirt I could have aged them by touching them, but the tracks were on solid rock, thus I would have to wait until dawn.

The age of the tracks didn't matter anyway, for I was far too concerned about what the old man had said and the disappearance of the tunnels and chambers. All manner of frightening thoughts began to run through my mind, to a point where my thinking became almost out of control. The ebb and flow of fear and anguish at times became unbearable. I began to also think that the old man did not mean that the inner chambers of the future were lost to the final winter, but only to me. Somehow I might no longer be worthy of unlocking the secrets of the cave. I had not fully lived my vision and possibly the cave was taking away its wisdom from me as a way of punishing me. Just the thought of that sent a chill through my spine, for that would have meant that the entire world of spirit would have turned its back on me.

In a way, I became a little angry, thinking that the spirit world had been taken from me. After all, I had done all that I could do. I couldn't make people listen to me or learn the skills of the Earth. Everyone I had attempted to teach was too wrapped up in the things outside of the wilderness and were not willing to put in the time or effort to learn. I wasn't about to go around preaching from a soapbox in the halls of society. There were enough people from all types of philosophies trying this approach and I knew that would not work. The only thing that I might have been guilty of was staying away from people as much as I possibly could. I had tried to reach anyone that would listen, and I had tried hard. I had no idea of what I could have done differently, or how to reach more people. The whole idea just seemed to aggravate the hell out of me. Considering all the years I had sacrificed and all of the pain I had gone through, it seemed that the spirit world would at least have helped me along.

Even though I knew that I had to go back into the cave, I was not yet ready. If the cave did not reveal its inner secrets to me and remained in the flesh, then that would mean that my fears were justified. I would surely know that I had failed my vision and that the spirit world would be denied unto me. Right now I did not want to find out one way or the other. I had to sort through all manner of self-doubt before I again faced the cave. I had to find out what I was doing wrong or what I was overlooking in the quest to follow my vision. I also had to decide if it was really me or if this truly marked the destruction of flesh and spirit as the vision of the white snakes foretold. All I knew now was that I was very tired, I lacked answers, and nothing seemed to give me any help. I also knew now that I was carrying a lot of guilt and anger and I would have to let it go before I could do anything else.

At this point I didn't know who I was angry at. I didn't know if I was angry at myself or angry at the worlds of spirit for giving me so little help. It seemed that no matter what quest I had ever been on in my life, the spirit world would make things more difficult more often than not. I was really getting tired of it, tired of everything, and so very tired of carrying the burden of the possibility of the Earth's destruction on my shoulders. I was especially tired of not knowing fully what to do about it, nor how to live the vision I carried. Possibly, I thought, after all of these years, I had not proven myself worthy of the vision, otherwise a way to live it would have been provided in some way. There were just too many unanswered questions in my life and I really needed someone to talk to.

As I lay at the mouth of the cave, I began to feel so alone. I hadn't felt alone in many months. The need to talk to someone became almost overwhelming, yet it was not Grandfather that I wanted to talk to. I felt a need to share my life with someone. So many times I would experience something wondrous but could share it with no one for, as always, I would be alone. So too did I yearn for someone to touch, to hold, and I longed for that kind of intimacy. I could feel now a need and a yearning that I had never felt before. I was so confused, so alone, and so lonely. I had to get some sleep before I could examine another thought or question. I especially wanted to sleep before I attempted to enter the cave again. If I was going to face it I wanted to be fully rested on all levels.

I awoke to a dawn that rolled with thunder. In the distance I could see bolts of lightning hitting the distant ridge and I knew that it would not be long before the storm reached me. I would not enter the cave for safety, for I still could not bring myself to face the outcome. I sat for a long time watching the storms approach. First the wind increased to a gusting frenzy of dust and debris that danced and whirled all around me. The voice of the cave changed to a frenzy of screaming voices that intensified with each gust of wind. Then came the lightning and deafening booms of thunder. Lightning kept hitting the valley below me, then finally struck the pinnacle of rock which was high over my head. As I ran to the cave, bits of debris from the stricken pinnacle clattered to the earth. I had been driven inside the cave and no longer had a choice.

I stood in the mouth of the cave for a long time, trying not to go in too deep. The entrance of the cave was like a megaphone, magnifying the crashing lightning to a point where it was no longer bearable. As I retreated from the entrance a bolt of lightning struck the entrance hard, nearly blowing my eardrums from my head. I ran to the back of the cave and into the darkness. I had no other choice, and fear of the cave was no longer a factor. All I could do was to cower at the back wall of the cave, watching the arched entrance flash with each bolt of lightning. I had to keep my hands over my ears, such was the force of the deafening crashes. As the flashes and thundering intensified, I lay on the ground next to the base of the wall and cowered like some child being punished. I could feel my trembling and I lost control of my body. It was as if the Creator and the cave were persecuting me for the sin of hesitation.

Suddenly there was a blinding flash and a bolt of lightning ricocheted off all the cave walls, exploded off the floor in a cloud of dust and disappeared out the entrance again. The floor of the cave shook with a violent surge and then came the rumbling from above. Rocks came crashing down from above, filling in the entrance of the cave with the violence of an earthquake. Dust billowed again and filled the inner chamber. All light was gone and I pressed my body hard against the inner wall. I just knew that I was going to die, if not immediately from the collapsing roof, then from being trapped in the cave. I could feel the rumble of the boulders rolling down the outside of the cave. Fragments of rock and smaller stone rained down within the chamber, some coming dangerously close to crushing me. The cave was being wiped off the face of the Earth and me along with it. I resolved myself to the fact that this would be a far better grave than anything I had ever imagined and all fear was suddenly gone.

As quickly as it had all begun, all sound stopped. Except for a lone stone rolling across the blocked entrance, the cave was cast into silence. Once in a while I could feel the deep rumble of thunder from the outside, but nothing else to mark time and place in the eternal darkness and silence I now faced. I groped my way to where the entrance of the cave once was, but was met with a wall of rock and rubble. It reached nearly to the center of the inner chamber and I estimated it to be at least forty feet thick. The horrible realization of being trapped was only dominated by the fact that I would die a slow and agonizing death. There was no way I could dig my way out even in a month. Many of the boulders were so large that ten men my size could not have moved them. The cave and the Creator had imprisoned me and I knew that I was sentenced to death.

I went through the gamut of emotions, ranging from rage to just giving up. I was angry because all of the years I had spent training were now worthless. I was now not able to live my vision, and all of my life had been now wasted. The only comfort I could find within myself was that I would not have had it any other way. I wanted nothing society had to offer, none of the things that my friends were chasing after. If I died right now, I would have lived life exactly as I wanted to have lived it and I would not change a thing. However, my anger bordered on violence, for now I had no choice other than to die. I could not live my vision, nor would I ever see the wilderness again. This would be my final legacy and I would never have a chance to make things better for the children to come. I felt slighted, but if this is what the Creator wanted to do with my life I would not argue. I would accept death like a warrior.

Suddenly the ground surged and I was cast off my feet, hitting the ground hard as I fell. I do not know if the surge was from a strike of lightning, a real earthquake or a spiritual tremor, but my fears became almost uncontrollable. Several more tremors followed until finally everything fell silent again. When I did finally regain composure I felt as if I had been holding my breath for the entire time. The air was thick with rock dust and there was no light whatsoever. At once I felt so very claustrophobic, as if I could not breathe. The darkness seemed to entomb me and my mind flailed about, desperately trying to escape the blackness. It was a form of sensory deprivation that tended to magnify all of my terror. I knew that my death would come either from suffocation, dying of thirst, or from hypothermia due to the cold heart of the cave. Any death would be slow and painful.

I do not know how long I had lain on the floor of the cave. Here in the darkness, time and place became a myth. There was nothing to mark time and nothing to mark place other than the dark. I began to crawl to the wall of the cave so that I could feel my way to where the rocks had fallen. Distance too was now obscured and it seemed as if I had crawled a very long time, yet I had not reached the wall. I thought that I might have been traveling in a circle, for the longer I crawled the less progress I felt I was making. Certainly the inner chamber of the cave was quite small, but I still could not find the wall. Everything began to get very confusing and I had to lie back down to compose myself. My eyes strained in the blackness, hoping for some glow of light to mark my place. But the blackness only seemed to thicken.

It became difficult to decide at this point whether my eyes were open or closed. So too did my mind surge with all manner of thought and images to a point where I could not tell where reality began and dream left off. In fact, I did not know whether I was asleep or awake at times. I tried again and again to find the wall of the cave but with no success. At once I got the feeling that I was still in the small chamber, but at the same time in a vast cathedral. I began to wonder whether I was dreaming all of this or if it was reality, but if it was a dream, I could not wake myself up. The fear now had all but dissipated and I was more curious than concerned that I was going to die.

Something more was going on than I was conscious of and now I wanted to find out.

I began to crawl again toward the walls of the cave, this time with a determination to keep going until I found it. I stopped reaching out with my hand as I crawled and just kept crawling as fast as I could. I did not care if I hit my head in the process. At least I was going to find it one way or another. I just felt so desperate now. I needed to find something that was real and tangible other than the floor and the perpetual darkness. I knew that if I found the wall of the cave I would have a place to orient myself and use that point of orientation to explore all the walls of the cave and possibly find a way out. At least if I was going to eventually die I would have fought for my life and not just lain down and given in to death.

I crawled for the better part of what I thought was an hour, but I had not found any walls. It was then, as I lay down again to rest, that I realized that the cave must have opened to me as it had years before. As my mind cleared and I began to understand what was happening to me, I began to search the darkness for a source of light, a light that might mark the beginning of a tunnel. As I searched the darkness, I could sense a light breeze blowing across my bare back. I knew from all the countless caves that I had explored that it might lead to an outside tunnel, so I began to follow the breeze. The breeze was so light that I had to stop frequently to feel it moving across my flesh, for when I moved, the breeze disappeared. The further I crawled, the stronger the breeze became, until I could hear it moving along the tunnel like some deep mountain breath.

Finally I began to see a faint light up ahead, cutting into the darkness. At first I thought that it just might be a trick that my eyes were playing on me, but as I moved closer, the light grew stronger. Though it was only faint, gray, and veil-like, it was still real. As I moved to the light I could feel a tremendous sense of relief filling me and tears began to fill my eyes. It wasn't so much that I thought that I was going to die, but had more to do with the fact that I would have another chance to live my vision. The light grew more intense as I moved, but it illuminated nothing of the cave. It was just a glow that was growing larger as I crawled toward it, yet it remained featureless. I had no idea as to the source of the light but it remained my only hope.

As I neared the light, I again spotted the form of the old man, bent and crying by the light. As I drew near to him I could hear his sobs and again he pointed to the light and said, "It is gone." In shock and horror, I asked him in a hoarse voice what he meant. What was gone? His feeble voice barely echoed off the cave walls as he said, "The possible future of hope is gone, or will soon be gone, for no one has tried to save it. If nothing is done, if your vision remains unlived, then the only future of man will be the dying of the children and grandchildren, as you have once seen. You have put off for too long the living of your vision. You have found far too many excuses, and now it may be too late." As his words dissipated, the old man disappeared and I moved into the light.

Within a few moments I found myself in the chamber of the world as it was now: the same chamber that I had been in many years before. There before me was the huge tunnel of the probable future. The probable future of man's ultimate destruction. I began to search the walls for all the possible futures, searching desperately for that possible future of hope. I moved to where I had seen that small tunnel of possible hope years before, but it no longer existed. Instead, in the place where it had once stood there was nothing but a small dark hole, which barely glowed at all. It looked as if it were flickering, the same way a dying flame would appear. I gazed into it, feeling the pang of desperation deep inside, but the tiny tunnel would not reveal itself. Just a few fleeting images flickered across my eyes, but soon were gone.

I sat back from the tunnel, feeling a tremendous sense of loss. That future of hope that I once saw was dying, or possibly even dead. I had let it die, because I had turned my back on my vision for so long. No, I hadn't tried to live it with all of my energy. Certainly I did not know how or what to do to live that vision, but I was out of excuses. All I knew now was that somehow I was responsible for the lost future of hope. My anguish became overwhelming, for in my complacency and denial I was as guilty as the most vile polluters that were destroying the Earth. I cried out to the cave, almost in anger, asking why I had not been warned earlier that the future of hope was dying. But my voice echoed off deaf walls and I felt so alone.

It was then that the winds of the cave began to stir and I could hear the sound of footfalls. I looked around, but I was still alone in the emptiness of the dead future. Suddenly a voice filled the inner chamber, and I knew it was Grandfather. He said, "You were more concerned for not living your vision than when you were concerned about losing your life. Your life, as you have found, without your vision is actually death. So then, Grandson, the final winter of man's world fast approaches. Go now and live your vision and the way will be revealed to you. As you have seen, the possible future of hope is dying. It is now up to you. Go home and find the raccoon that will lead you to the woman who will lead you to your vision. The final winter is at hand."

Grandfather's voice disappeared and all that was left were the echoes of the final winter. I found myself awakening from a deep sleep outside of the cave once again. The entrance was untouched, but my knees, from all the crawling of my dream, were badly bruised and bloody. I had no idea of what Grandfather meant when he said to find the raccoon, or who this woman was. All I knew was that I had to fight to keep the prophecy of the final winter from becoming reality. I left without hesitation and headed back to civilization. I had faith now that the Creator would provide the way and there was no doubt that I would live my vision, or not live at all.
